"Early on in *Letter from a Place I've Never Been*, a speaker worries, 'What if I'm broken and can't be mended, / or worse, the world is broken around me / and I the only whole thing in it?' Here is the Jewish notion of *tikkun olam*, that it's our task to repair what is wounded. Indeed, in this impressive collection showcasing more than thirty years of work, Hilda Raz makes an argument for poetry as a way of healing our brokenness. These are poems that remake the world of 'melt and fracture'—using language that growls from the page—so that it belongs to everyone, all the 'odd and splendid' parts of ourselves worthy of examination, of praise."
—Jehanne Dubrow, author of *Dots & Dashes* and *The Arranged Marriage*

"I love the immersive experience this book offers. Readers track Raz's imaginative language across the decades, as she mourns and meditates, catalogs and investigates. Resisting the cultural and technological policing of women's bodies, the poet evokes illness, recovery, sorrow, and delight. These narrators—gritty, world-loving, tenacious—bind the personal and political in unforgettable family and diasporic narratives. Unprecedented when first published, Raz's poems about mothering her transgender child have become foundational texts. 'Some of what I couldn't stand to lose I lost,' a narrator states, echoing Elizabeth Bishop, one influence here. Friendship and the natural world console: 'If the good life is coming / to us in our lifetime, / surely it is here / in this orchard in April at twilight.' Like her jeweler son's transformation of wire and gemstone into bracelet and earrings, Raz's transformations—of body, circumstance, homeplace, passion—work a resilient, wondrous alchemy."
—Robin Becker, author of *The Black Bear Inside Me*

"To read Hilda Raz's *Letter from a Place I've Never Been* is to open a precious gift, to sit down to a feast celebrating a life in poetry. If you've read Raz's earlier work, the poems will be old friends, made new by seeing them in this expansive context. If you have not, you have a journey ahead worth any price, let alone the price of a book. Raz's poems deal with grief, longing, and loss in all their complicated forms but interwoven with transformations that take your breath away. Her poems are in turns lyrical and challenging, but always precise, each word exactly the right word. And at the end of *Letter from a Place I've Never Been*, there are the new poems waiting to be discovered and savored, poems which, to quote a title in the book, serve as 'Letters from a Lost Language,' that haunting, that beautiful."
—Jesse Lee Kercheval, author of *America that island off the coast of France*

Praise for *All Odd and Splendid*

"[*All Odd and Splendid*] is about how life looks and feels when fundamental categories of being have come unmoored. . . . Raz uses the trauma of transsexual transition as Shakespeare uses the humiliation and madness of Lear: as an existential vantage from which to examine the transmogrifications . . . that wrench the very frameworks of our lives."
—Joy Ladin, *The Forward*

"This is Raz's strongest book to date: a gentle quotidian view of the world that then twists toward the sardonic/tragic; or else a steady drumbeat of hard life, out of which happiness and beauty flower."
—Janet Burroway, author of *Writing Fiction*

"Hilda Raz's *All Odd and Splendid* is unique, accomplished, and turns the 'genderings' of the world upside down, as they need be turned upsidedown. The poems are psychologically innovative and deft. There are tones of a masterpiece in this work."
—John Kinsella, author of *The New Aracadia*

Praise for *Divine Honors*

"In *Divine Honors*, we're in for a head-on collision with grief, the inescapable fact of cancer. Raz conveys joy and hope and love of others and of the natural world turned into poetry, after that horrible discovery and ordeal. The best of the poems are breathtaking—the sensuous imagery, the sounds she repeats for the pleasure of reading, and the surprising juxtaposition of images. I love this book of poems—grief and longing turned into poetry."
—Walter McDonald

"Transgressive and transcendent, Hilda Raz's new poems are intimately involved with the physical, corporeal world, and constantly making the leap of faith necessary to its re-embodiment in words. These poems push the boundaries of what language can do to enunciate perception. Their beauty, their clarity, their mystery equally compel."
—Marilyn Hacker

"*Divine Honors* is a rare book, one that does honor to its subject and transcends it at the same time. An unflinching account of the cost and the effects of breast cancer, *Divine Honors* illuminates much more about a women's life that has, mysteriously, remained shadowy in so many other accounts of women's lives. Few books change your way of viewing the world. This one does."
—Susan Fromberg Schaffer

Praise for List & Story

"In Hilda Raz's dazzling List & Story, a pencil waits for us in every room, a bride and bridesmaid hold a trashcan between them, and April is recast as 'a beautiful automaton' that lights peach blossoms on fire. These kaleidoscopic poems whipsaw between love and grief to create raw, unflinching elegies. Raz's exquisite formal control is paired with associative leaps in these stunning explorations of identity, mortality, and the threshold between language and speechlessness. 'Still the world rots. / But is not lost. Enough. / Look out,' the speaker demands, so that we may see her beloved 'melting sugar in red water' for hummingbirds. Bristling with brutal truths and sudden tenderness, Raz reminds us that, despite our losses, language and love will return in this life and the next."
—Hadara Bar-Nadav, author of The New Nudity

"'Here then is my life in letters. A great weight,' writes Hilda Raz. This harvest—of art, of ripe heirloom tomatoes, of bobcats and lightning—nourishes us body and soul. This poet wants 'to know how women sound in their heads.' These poems offer that, plus the beauty of 'the glow we can't see by,' the great mysteries of time and love and the night sky. Here is a poetry in the company of nature and art, saying YES out loud. Here is a poetry that acknowledges death, its nearness, then invites it to the table, where we feast. Thank you, Hilda Raz, for a masterful, profound collection."
—Peggy Shumaker, author of Cairn: New and Selected Poems

"In her poem, 'Women and Poetry,' Hilda Raz with characteristic irony, candor, and wit, invokes Robert Frost, 'I am trying to love poetry as a stay against confusion,' and in that saying she revives a poetics that shapes and moves her splendid and assured collection, List & Story. Raz's poems combine a deep sensuality with a lively and unsettled intelligence, gleefully quarreling with women philosophers and poets even as she welcomes their bracing intellect. But in the end, her mastery lies in her attentiveness to the senses— that which is seen, smelt, and heard—and she gives us a lesson in the love of poetry and in the uses of color in verse. List & Story affirms Hilda Raz's importance to American poetry in truly remarkable ways."
—Kwame Dawes, author of Nebraska: Poems

"Here, Hilda Raz meditates on the complexity of memory and family, of love and womanhood, of politics, grief, and mortality. These poems are lovingly crafted and virtuosic in their attention to the smallest enriching details: the half-drawn bedroom shade that doesn't quite conceal 'snow interrupting the field,' the dress 'of iridescent icy peau de soie,' the slipper moon 'thin as the edge of a Mercury dime.' There is much grief here—the loss of family, of time lived—but always a kind of grace, as well, that sense of 'a survivor carrying stories / from one life to another, yours, readers.'"
—Kevin Prufer, author of *How He Loved Them: Poems*

Praise for *Trans: Poems*

"It was Hilda Raz's remarkable book *Trans* that shifted ways of reading poetry for me. If you want to read a poetry of honesty and often pain 'in working through things'—then Raz's poetry is exemplary in this."
—John Kinsella, author *Jam Tree Gully* and *Firebreaks*

"Whether she writes of Aaron or Sarah, funerals or fields, Raz's tone remains sincere and open: 'Nothing to explain, no shield,' she writes, 'of paper thin skin between history and the untender world.'"
—Publishers Weekly

"What subject could be harder for a mother to document than her daughter's sex-change operation? Some of the strongest poems in this collection by poet and anthologizer Raz focus on that transformation."
—Library Journal

Praise for *What Happens*

"Hilda Raz has an appetite for the pleasures of touch, sight, love; an openness to the wounds of life and the 'common face' of death; a capacity for language that captures the weather and the details of a place and time, a day, the changes of a lifetime. The poetry of *What Happens* mirrors 'our great and perfect / need,' along with myths, riddles, and 'everything possible blooming.'"
—Alicia Ostriker, author of *No Heaven*

"Hilda Raz's poetic diction is always immediate and direct, engaging the reader. She achieves special intensity in her depiction of the human body, its vulnerability, and its capacity for pleasure (see 'Friend in a Distant City' and 'Pain'). Here is a poet at the height of her formidable powers to move and inspire."
—Robert Pack, author of Still Here, Still Now

"Underneath 'ordinary stars and a late moon,' extraordinary things happen to the people in Hilda Raz's poems. Love transforms, bodies transform, health transforms, and looked at freshly the things we thought we knew burst into strangeness. There is nothing like Raz's charged, smart, profound, moving poems, so rich in both intellect and heart, so open and wise, provoked by the question 'how can we live properly?"
—Floyd Skloot, author of The Wink of the Zenith

Letter from a Place I've Never Been

LETTER from a PLACE I'VE NEVER BEEN

New and Collected Poems, 1986–2020

Hilda Raz

Edited by Kwame Dawes

Introduction by John Kinsella

University of Nebraska Press

LINCOLN

Acknowledgments for the use of copyrighted
material appear on pages 433–37, which con-
stitute an extension of the copyright page.

Publication of this volume was assisted by a grant from
the Friends of the University of Nebraska Press.

Library of Congress Cataloging-in-Publication Data
Names: Raz, Hilda, author. | Dawes, Kwame Senu Neville,
1962– editor. | Kinsella, John, 1963– writer of introduction.
Title: Letter from a place I've never been: new and
collected poems, 1986–2020 / Hilda Raz; edited by
Kwame Dawes; introduction by John Kinsella.
Other titles: Letter from a place I have never been
Description: Lincoln: University of Nebraska Press, [2021]
Identifiers: LCCN 2020047076
ISBN 9781496226822 (paperback)
ISBN 9781496228048 (epub)
ISBN 9781496228055 (pdf)
Subjects: LCGFT: Poetry.
Classification: LCC PS3568.A97 L48 2021 |
DDC 811/.54—dc23
LC record available at https://lccn.loc.gov/2020047076

Set in Quadraat by Laura Buis.
Designed by N. Putens.

CONTENTS

The Bone Dish (1989)

EDITOR'S NOTE
Kwame Dawes

Hilda Raz has been writing and publishing poetry steadily for over thirty years. Her poems constantly remind us of her deep devotion to the form, her delight in language, and her reliance on poetry to chronicle the emotional and intellectual path of her life and her engagement with a constantly shifting world. Raz's poetry arrives at a time when American women writers begin to compel a different conception of the lyric in America by their complex relationship to a superficially male tradition and by their meticulous commitment to unveiling a long American poetic tradition that roots its meaning and power in the imagination of women over many centuries. It is not accidental that in the tradition of such poets, thinkers, and editors, like Marianne Moore, Hilda Raz's emergence as a poet, as an essential voice in American poetry, coincides with her assumption of the role of editor of *Prairie Schooner*, a literary journal, based in the Midwest, that has quietly and steadily come to be a critical presence in American letters. Under Raz, *Prairie Schooner* takes full advantage of the availability of some of America's most gifted poets, many of them women, who were not as successful in penetrating the defiantly male literary scene in this country. Raz would publish a stunning array of women poets we are now comfortable declaring as unquestionable voices in American poetry.

This collection commemorates the work of steady and persistent devotion to craft, fascination with form, and a willingness to face the shifting dynamics of American culture over the span of a life of engagement, thoughtfulness, and artistic taste and consideration. In this sense, these poems offer a rewarding, intimate accounting of American life, and especially of the life of someone living inside and yet, as an artist, outside of her society. In these poems, Raz traces her life as a woman, as a mother, as an intellectual, and wife, as artist, and as a citizen. She asks difficult questions and tries to answer them. She is also a poet of landscape, a poet of place. Her care for charting the evolving landscape of her world is striking.

As with all collected works, there are some peculiar complexities that present themselves here. One of the most important ones has to do with the fact of three seeming distinctive publications that have their own history. In 2009 the University of Nebraska Press published *What Happens*. The collection, according to Raz, was the pulling together of two of her earliest collections that had been published in the 1980s. In 1986 her collection *What Happens* was selected for publication by the then poetry editor of the Grove Press Poetry Series. Unfortunately, before the work would appear, the series was discontinued. Over the next two years, Raz would publish the poems in this collection in two books, one a full-length collection titled *What Is Good*, which was published by Thorntree Press of Chicago, and the second, a chapbook titled *The Bone Dish*, which was published by State Street Press in New York edited by Judith Kitchen in 1989. Both presses appear to be now defunct, and the books were out of print by the time U N P decided to bring the work back in its original form in 2009. I was faced with the question of whether to organize this collection in a way that reflected the publication history of the poems or whether to attempt to retain a semblance of chronology of composition. Given Raz's own introductory comments in the 2009 publication, where she "introduces" readers to her daughter "Sarah" and explains that the poems reflect a time when Sarah was in fact her daughter, it seemed to me better to treat this work as faithfully capturing at least one of the most affecting and significant journeys of self that Raz has charted through her poetry, and I decided to order the work as it would have appeared chronologically. Consequently, while the poems in *What Happens* are all represented in this volume, they appear in the sections that feature *Bone Dish* and *What Is Good*.

It also makes sense for me to comment briefly on the inclusion of two categories of poems in this volume, namely, the "Published and Uncollected Poems" and the "New Poems." These, together, constitute just under a book-length body of poems, many of which justified their presence here because of their importance to Raz's oeuvre and because they offer us some further insight into her occasional work and in work she may have written in collaborations with artists and with other projects, or work that she has had included in anthologies. Raz's acknowledgment list reminds us that throughout her life she has been an active and disciplined contributor to literary journals, and many of her most elegant poems, while not collected in volumes, are richly rewarding poems of their moment and, as it happens, of lasting and meaningful value. Given the extent to which the American populace only encounters the poetry of American poets in anthologies, it would seem that giving attention to this work is prudent and does justice to her work. These poems are organized chronologically, even though they are clustered in a single section, but reading these poems as a body gave me a delightful insight into Raz's development as a poet.

This volume appears a year after her most recent collection, *List & Story*, and so, since we are including work from that collection here, it could seem imprudent to be including "new" work. As it happens, Raz has some unpublished poems that we are fortunate enough to include in this volume. Since her departure from Nebraska a decade ago, Raz has begun to write poems that explore the quite different landscape of New Mexico and poems that open the path to her new stage in life, a life filled with the wit, curiosity, and wisdom that comes with experience and attentiveness.

In 1999 Blue Heron Press and the Women's Studio Workshop published a compact collection, *Truly Bone*, that featured a series of lively abstract etchings by artist Karen Kunc and short, largely imagistic poems by Hilda Raz. In these short poems, Raz writes of delicate sensuality, her signature whimsy, and her interest in studying the position of woman in society, in nature, and in relationships. The poems in that collection had all appeared in her 1997 volume, *Divine Honors*, and this is where they are placed in this volume.

Titling books can be a fraught exercise, but there remains a core principle that seems always to reward the quest for a title for poetry collection. The presumption is that, by the wonderful inevitability of the making of art, buried inside the actual work of art is the title to the work, or at least the path to the title of that work. Titles are what are now called "handles," and titles are also quite fairly, even if intimidatingly, called "the first line of the work." My tendency toward blunt pragmatism led me first to "The Poetry of Hilda Raz." But, as it happens, pragmatism is sacrificed in this. After all, as I was told, the work could have been mistaken for a work of literary criticism, and I conceded largely because I did see it imprudent to deny some gamely scholar of the title of a book of literary criticism that is decidedly necessary. Our title, then, is buried in the collection, and what a stunningly right title it is. "Letter from a Place I've Never Been" leads us to a most enigmatic poem in the collection that explores the idea of the poem as caught in that "still point" between time present, time past, and time future. Poetry is, indeed, a form that carries us to unknown places even when those places are known through memory. The relooking that poetry represents is thus an encounter with the unknown, and one that eventually proves to be necessary and exciting. Alaska, of course, is the place—at once mysterious, exotic, and defiantly ordinary in it harshness. It is not so much disappointment that characterizes the speaker's reaction to this idea of Alaska, but it is something else, the peculiar and satisfying beauty of discovery:

> I'm scared of the cold, of the dark, of the journey,
> the unfamiliar plants that perk into poems
> I've read and reviewed. Some kind of weed,
> not jewelweed from Robert Frost. Oh, why
> did I say I'd travel? The tundra is something
> strange like a sponge. And golden.

John Kinsella helps us to appreciate the achievement of Hilda Raz, her position as an essential American voice whose work rewards constant reading. His generosity of spirit and his sharp and expansive intelligence come together to introduce us to this work of great delights and insights.

INTRODUCTION
John Kinsella

I have long admired the immediacy and spontaneity that merges with a distancing tone of voice in the poetry of Hilda Raz—that ability she has to tell something of the everyday and make it tough, to move through the discursive to imagistic lyric all in one poem, and especially across books. It's that "I'm as hard as nails listening" aspect that sees through difficult times and confronting situations with acceptance but refusal to give in as well. Raz's is a poetry of real inner strength expressed through a boldness of diction, with often surprising twists and turns in the figurative to disturb any easy reception, often moving against its own grain.

There's an ongoing conversation with Adrienne Rich in Hilda Raz's work—the early Rich but more the middle or later Rich—but that's the incident of being an essential feminist in an often inimical patriarchal America. And she offers other strong ways through, too, with poems that talk and also compile experience and observation with tactile precision and purpose. By which I mean that we're welcomed into the buildings of the poems, though they are often wild cards that take us places aside from their familiar and sharing talk. There are some incredible pastoral inversions to be encountered, and the comforts of intimacy are always complex, with things not necessarily as they seem. Place is a dynamic of land and people, and their impacts on each other, and their conversations. Be it in Nebraska or New Mexico, we know where we are and why place needs to be talked about.

It's the affirmations that Raz's poems contain—as much as their sometimes bitter and always forceful (and frequently ironic) critiques of consumer capitalism that cares nothing for communities or the natural environment—that lifts us; this affirmation-critique dynamic of her books, and especially at work across this entire volume. I sometimes think of the activism of Denise Levertov, but poetically rather than in on-site presence (which is not to suggest Raz hasn't been on-site at protests), but really I am talking about a mode of articulation, the manner of address of protest. Levertov's voice was *so* public, Raz's so immediately to *hand* and often enacted within the teaching environment across decades—its own kind of public. We can all learn from these articulations of everywoman, every "woman of power," and a deeply sensitive respect for difference. Raz's intense awareness of the politics and vulnerabilities of the body, along with its strengths and wonders, is spoken through the mouths of her poems.

Antecedents for a poet are a complex array of people, texts, songs, traditions, rebellions, engagements, refusals, and so much more. We can add many other elements to this array—the point being that no single poem is made in a vacuum and that no matter how much individual poems are trying to connect with or distance themselves from poetries that come before, they are also in dialogue with and debate those pasts.

Hilda Raz is a poet who has both embraced and investigated her connections with many pasts but always with a degree of respect for difference and the politics and ethics of where and how one manages examinations of the past, of heritage and inheritance. Her poems are full of surprising twists and turns that so often go counter to the general meaning of the poem itself; so even when an event of memory, an incident or story, is being recounted or retold, it is with these provisos of why and how in place.

I have known Hilda Raz's poetry since the late '90s, but it was really her remarkable book *Trans* that shifted ways of reading poetry for me and prompted further considerations in myself about what I might or might not privilege myself to comment on in both poetry and general conversation—interpret outside my own physical experience. Raz's book doesn't give me answers and doesn't claim it should or can, but it is a dialogue of her own that will prompt many different responses from readers that will necessarily come out of their own experiences. Such dialogues are not ours alone but always part of other people's dialogues with their own lives. And the respect for the independence and agency of other's lives, even when they intersect, or even intimately or familiarly connect with our own, remains separate, autonomous, and does not have to justify itself.

Where does this leave the poet using poems as a way of interfacing with *world*, with their experience that necessarily draws other people's biographies into their own? I asked all these questions when I first read *Trans* and still offer no answers. What I can do is offer my respect for all journeys as being their own journeys, contingent in coexistence but not in ultimate need for mutuality.

Trans opens with a Rilke poem and moves on to questions of what is *self-examination* in the context of *another's* transition, no matter how close they are to the poet, how much their lives are implicated by heritage and familial ties. Because, of course, we are all intact and autonomous beings, and we all have the right not to be as others, not to be partitioned in any way at all—to live with an agency and rights to be who we are, and Raz believes this emphatically.

But being supportive is never enough; it's also a questioning of who we are when we're being supportive, and a poet intrudes with every attempt to work through change, confronting or expressing admiration as a poem might do, or both, and much else. But Raz is working through rights of involvement as a mother and wondering what they can be. Discourse around the oppression of trans rights is more active in 2020 than it was in 2001 (but not nearly enough, not yet—there is a long way to go in the rights issues around such necessities and choices). Addressing prejudices now is more broadly active than it was even twenty years ago, but lack of respect often aligns with acts of accommodation that can be as hurtful and offensive as denials.

Hilda Raz tries to find a poetic path in understanding (which is not a given, nor necessarily a right) and engaging with many forms of transformation but also recognizing that it's not as simple as an elision of journey as metaphor, as simple as "change" or "crossing over," and that there's also a "remaining the same" as much as a "going" and changing involved.

We can travel together. We don't have to.

We—none of us as the roles cast for us, the stories not working out as we expect, or second-guess. Raz so often uses the conversational storytelling mode but doesn't try to take over or occupy others' stories. Her complexities evolve out of where other's stories intersect with her own, and the nuance required in understanding those points—woman, mother, intellectual, activist, listener, poet. But her poems can be brazen—we see the working out process up close, and it's not always comfortable, and it is sometimes very confronting.

Raz notes early in the *Trans* collection:

What to make of our profiles: age, religious preference, marital history, hobbies, our experience with Hale-Bopp, did we see the comet at all, note its tail as . . . what?

She records a few poems further on, in empathy with her ten-year-old child:

How long will it last? she asks,
meaning grief, and I haven't the heart
to say a lifetime. Daughter.

—"Said to Sarah, Ten"

And it does, and it doesn't. "Sarah," as with any name, is a "giving" and is a reaching back and a projection forward, but it is never an entire story. Sarah was also Abraham's wife. Sarah is also not Abraham's wife. Names shift as signifiers. We are not our names, we are self-definitions in the context of social movements and associations. And we are victims of control, in the same way natural environments are controlled, and made toxic. It's difficult not to let analogies slip into associations they're not intended to merge with, but poetry does that, and we end up with the difficult space of frustration, fear, and doubt entangling with affirmation and differentiating of human rights and planetary life. There are transitions against oppressions (against gender profiling, and also as affirmations of the gender one knows one is or isn't, and not what one is told one is), but there are also transitions against every person's (and every group of people's) well-being: such as environmental destruction. But transition can—even in a general sense—be overwhelmingly positive and generative and joyous. The crossing over becomes in the poem as the mother works toward a shared understanding of their new-old personal dynamic.

Raz constantly tries to find a way through to how poetry can say what it means and not completely abdicate authorial intent to the figurative philosophically (though a surrealist might push to do this, as might dismantlers and contesters of language vying with the unconscious—but I don't think this is Hilda Raz's main concern or aim as a poet, though she can be as challenging to the shape and form of language as any poet can be), while existentially engaging with the metaphoric as a generative, healing force. She can offend (not toward individuals but against gross wrongs as she perceives them). We encounter the poisonous spray, the fires on the prairie—all are active in her positioning herself as commentator, which she is compelled to be, but doubting herself, often with devastating self-examination fused with meditation on art, the natural world, a core feminism that is too often misread as a kind of trope, which it is not.

So many Raz poems are confrontations with negations around us, of the negatives and hypocrisies of accommodation, of the ease with which others judge what we are going through, even vicariously. In fact, the relationship between the experienced and vicariousness might be a major thread of Raz's oeuvre because she refuses to allow the contradictions to be dismissed or ignored—she wants them to live and speak and assist us in our reconciliations with an often damaged and damaging existence.

The poem "Trans" is a mother's struggle over her "brilliant daughter" not being a "daughter." The mother's therapy, the interjecting voices of the outside world, all come into the anxiety of role and obligation, of the false binary of responsibility and place in the world. The poem, like so many of Raz's poems, works through the situation with various voicings in the story congruent with self-analysis, self-critique. If you want to read a poetry of honesty and often pain in working through things and even asking what right one has to work through them if not the person whose body is directly involved—in an effort to come to a just and genuine position of personal responsibility, of respect—then Raz's poetry is exemplary in this. From this stanza in "Trans" with its discussion in terms of signs:

It's the age, she said
not meaning puberty because he was long past,
thirty at his last birthday, but the times: everything
possible: hormones, surgery, way beyond unisex
jeans at the Mall, those cute flannel button-down shirts.

We move toward a strong self-awareness of what shouldn't be said as much as what can . . . crossing into a mutual empathy, into the essence of humanity:

I try to conjure his voice: "Mom
since sunup the sky's been dark but now we're talking
I see the sun come out perfect
for a walk and when we're through talking
I'm going out. Come with me?"
That voice: the same words and phrases, intonation
from me with his dad mixed in "like cake with too much

frosting," as my student said tonight in class. Be honest
here. Love is the word he said in closing. "I love you,
Mom." Transsexual—like life, not easy—in this century.
My kid. And me in the same boat with him, mine.

To me this seems a poem of integrity and respect—the transitions are flows
and movements that preexist as much as postexist, that are forced into being
dramatic and psychologically painful because of social expectation, because of
the same worldview that leads to the toxification of the planet.

Raz never occludes contradictions and doesn't have answers (and nor are
answers required—the question is, whose business is it?), but she is a witness
to her own processes, the truths around her, and the nature of affection, respect,
and love. It's intensely moving, but maybe because it's just as it should be.
Loss—*where is?* is transformed into *we are*, in essence. In searching for ourselves
in those we are connected with in the past, the now, the future, we can grow by
understanding difference as much as recognizable traits, and how much more
sameness there is than we are willing to acknowledge. Difference can be about
different kinds of sameness, too! The irony of control is expressed in poems
like "Women & Men," and this needs to be read against the activism of self-
examination (especially in terms of broader social, familiar, environmental,
and humanitarian concerns):

Women walk downtown holding their daughters'
hands, or can if they're inclined,
each generation adding a link to the chain.

And in her examination of gender as external construction, but also internal
affirmation of being, she never avoids the complexities ("Adam's rib" reconsid-
ered . . .), with the rhizomes and capillaries of pain and body, of embodiment and
body, of what health is when it brings body and the sense of self into argument,
stress, and sometimes trauma . . . the disrupted body ("Wonder Woman and
the Disrupted Body") and intactness, change, mutability:

Imagine Wonder Woman with one breast. Draw her costume.
Alter the top. Only one bracelet. Is it wider? The wooden boot.

And a few poems later, as a turning of empathy and the existence of analogy that is real and metaphorical, almost only able to configure as comfort in the space of a poem ("Aaron at Work/ Rain"):

> By the light box propped in the window,
> bare chested, scars rosy in artificial sun,
> he crouches over his workbench.

Raz utilizes alignment in seemingly incongruous ways to compel hope, but it's not easy, nor prescriptive.

"The dead" are never far away in Raz's examination of self, and that bothers her. The connective tissue of names: family, people, tradition, sacred texts, the blasts of modernity. And how do we read this here and now in nonbinary ways? This is a question inherent in Raz's self-examination of the effect of external events on herself and of how she feels about the effects of those events on others around her, and far from her too. Maybe we find intimations in an earlier poem ("G: But it's still not all right with you?" from *Divine Honors*, 1997):

> marriage, palm to palm, or
> no distinctions, races, genders, each to each:
> dear Darwin in his garden, counting earthworms.

and in "Doing the Puzzle/ Angry Voices" from *Trans*:

> Every book that documents birth
> puts onto gender a meaning.

Hilda Raz is a poet of very "diverse subject matter," but always with the concentrations of her deeply felt concerns, her sense of responsibility to the poem, to others, to the biosphere, to herself. She observes, sometimes witnesses, ponders contradictions and whether or not they should be resolved; she steps out of her comfort zones; she takes risks in body, mind and soul.

Another poet I see echoes of throughout the decades of this work is Maxine Kumin, and reaching the end of my read-through of this magnificent work of feminism, activism, humanism, environmentalism, acute storytelling observation, and respect for *not-being-herself*, which is not without its moments of humor and levity (though often wry, if not deeply ironic!), I come across the poem "Credo 23" and its epigraph: "I believe in . . . the grace of animals / in my keeping, the thrust to go on."—Maxine Kumin. Yes. And the poem that it accompanies or is accompanied by (*alone* and *in company* are variegating themes of Raz, I think) is a wonderful "later Raz" (or more recent Raz!) contemplation of contraries . . . of nature and the domestication of, of walking and questioning, of being and a kind of preventing the nothingness. Aside from being an excellent cat poem (always, Christopher Smart's "Jubilate Agno" comes to mind, whether it should or shouldn't!), it finishes with rabbits and change (good or bad, or good and bad), with the mutable, in her wonderfully controlled almost immutable stanza-shapes and line-making, holding the meditation in place:

High summer again; I am in its keeping.
Monsoon rains washed out our road.
The rabbits' number escalates, more
and more each morning as we walk.
Through my dark glasses the world
continues its flicker. Aware, I'm here.

Letter from a Place I've Never Been

What Is Good

(1988)

Franklyn Emmanuel Raz 1899–1957

Barton James Raz 1928–1968

Dolly Horwich Raz 1899–1969

For Carole Oles, friend and collaborator

I

She Speaks

I sit in this summer house
and, Adam, I think of you
and your preposterous naming
and talking, your making the world
new each day—how exhausting—
and the tall banyans you drew up
out of the ground to show me;
each day the tangerine rose-hips,
the azure of an ocean you called
blue, meaning one color, and which
to my eye was *variegated*,
a word you had no use for;
parrots and sparrows you
feathered in one direction
not accounting for the variable
air currents; the rugosa
and its blatant fruit, so
provocative, so showy.

Outside the cottage now
you are no longer here,
a pale basswood flourishes
in all this salty weather
and numerous foliages evolve
nameless in the fresh water
rain. Animals whose plush fur
matts away the damp howl
for attention, beg
to be let into any shelter
but this one, Adam,
a house of women
with no names, only
a companionable silence

that admits no visitors;
only later, perhaps, an orange
presence in a circle of stones
now like the sun, now the moon,
now flickering, now pausing,
now going soundlessly up.

Yom Kippur

Dear God of silence for women,
God, absent from bath and laundry room,
God, whose clotheslines on rainy days
never droop wet linen, look on this flesh,
this heavy head, and take pity
on those of us who neither rejoice
in the burn unit for another day's suffering,
nor insist on our worthiness in the halls
of power. What do we know,
who wrap our wet hair in towel turbans?

Bless a daughter in the distant academy
who stains her tissue samples with Toluidine Blue O,
watching under her microscope the group tissue turn magenta,
and bless the daughters who hunger not
for food, but only to subdue their bodies.
Forgive us the great sins of our fathers, and
of our flesh, and wanting knowledge,
for which we are punished by a ceasing of hunger;
and for the greater sins of the heart
that lead us away from familiar men.
Let us be free of them, except sons
and lovers and those who write well.

God, it's raining tonight on the day of the fast.
The dog next door is groveling in his yard.
Someone I love has a broken heart;
it can't mend, it won't be grafted on.

Those who are dead and melted in the boneyard
and those newly come there, or coming,
who rest on their chrome stretchers in the hall
scarcely breathing, or not at all, who
wait for the scalpel and the blood basin,
let those be filled with silence but for the dripping
the rustling of wrens hushed in dark.

Let me be worthy of keen hunger,
of ambition, and not afraid past bearing
of all that you offer and take away.
Let my eyes open in the morning
and my body raise me up
to my feet. And let my feet move
in particular service to all who revere you and worship
the world. And then let me leave it.

Father

is never home but she loves him—
adores him, really, and so does Mom:
his big, burly body, his flannel shirts,
woolens over interesting scars
with stories to tell. Oh, he is a raconteur
with racks of bottles in the fragrant breakfront.

He tells her not to talk so much.
His talk holds the world intact;
when it stops, the key piece
drops out the bottom and the whole
plastic globe fragments. Nothing's
the same ever again.

The size of him! The size of them all,
uncles, cousins, the brothers:
wide shoulders jutting through cigar smoke
in the breakfast nook. The deep black marks
of their synthetic heels never quite scrub out.

Under the huge dining table,
under the carpet where his big feet wait,
is the bell. When he pushes it with his shoe
an aunt, or mother, or a maid
brings out another dish
from the steaming kitchen.

But he paid for it, paid for it all,
sweaters, teak tables with brass inlay,
steaks, furs, wicks for the memorial
candles, silk stockings, full tin box
the color of sky, plants
and their white rings on the mahogany,

and the cars, deep greens, metallic,
and the cashmere lap-robes,
and the aunts and out-of-work uncles.

He was best loved, best beloved in the family,
    whose very shadow, even absent,
absorbed all color, sucked short
the seasons, colored gray
even the lavish lilacs of that northern city

she never visits. She sends money
to an old woman who tends the graves,
sends money when the penciled bills come in.

Shabbos

Sick with woman's blood and wanting
to mix flour and salt with egg and milk
I make instead this story of Mary,
a pale Jewish girl at the moment
her robe turns raiment. Still and waiting.
I am told by a Gentile to envision
that girl myself, newly touched
critic of women's poetry come
to writing in terror on tiptoe.

He says we're all come from bodies
of women, aren't we,
yourself a woman speaking in tongues,
(headachey)
your blurblings very like the cat's?
Your menses, the pauses and circumlocutions

of ordinary speaking, only a way of pushing
some door most of the way shut?

How am I Mary, whose womb shut long ago
against interruption just in time to get
this work done with my mind, slamming
shut her office door?

Day finished, I go to my kitchen for breadmaking
put on the apron of my service, fold the temple
pieces of my eyeglasses closed and hope
facing the frosted window
to hear open into place wings
lifting the golden braids by yeast,
the whisper of unfolding linen,
clipped eyelet edges,
the click of the spice palace opening its pierced sides
silver
odorous
gleaming.

Dishes

> Now is always still.
> —Antonio Machado

For years I have been doing the dishes.
Once, two months from giving birth,
I stood at the sink with my friend
(big with a child) who held lobsters,
one in each hand. They were shiny, black from the sea
and salty and would be sweet, later, in our mouths

and itchy to our bare forearms as we sat, one each side
of a crockery bowl, cracking shells, pulling meat
for the salad. But now they were struggling.
And I left off washing to reach out and take them,
laughing at their pegged claws and only a little afraid,
and watched her lift the deep lid from the steaming kettle.

Later, dinner. Music came across the lake
through the opened windows and air moved
on our wet skins, and we knew small burstings
of kernels torn from their cobs and deep ripples
behind our denim aprons as the babies who would so soon be
daughters rolled and elbowed. And then the dishes.

We sat together on high stools at the soapstone sink
and washed our hands in pale suds, and dried them.
The piles of plates grew and were transported
away and then the deep orange enamel pots, heavy
in our shining hands. And then it was dark.

We put up our dripping towels on the wood dowel racks
and, as balanced as we could be on the rock steps,
lumbered down the slope to the shore. We dropped
our flowered cotton clothes where we stood on the grass
and naked, walked into a cool water as dark as our futures
where we floated and sank and turned up, calling across
a widening surface of silver water, calling
and whispering and calling, *sister, sister*.

Accident

—for John

High summer heat.

Here clear storage bags
from a strange kitchen
hang upside down
from chrome hooks
high in the air over a bed
where someone I know
who resembles someone precious
is lying naked. It wears blue
hoses in its throat.

Air makes a sound it makes
nowhere else. What is lying
on the bed is breathing,
surely now absorbing
red threads at all
the body's openings.
I can't stay here very well.
I can't stay here long.

No flowers allowed.

They go in
they come out of the far room
where air is frigid.
They say *rigid*, they say *fluid*
they say something
I can't hear.
I'm not listening.

Light comes and goes.
I go into the room, I come out.
I say something again and again.
His toes are cold.

Going away coming back
trees unfurl
in an arch over some oval.
My hands and feet move together
and I move
into the arch
as the oval moves out.

He smiles
around tubes.
I smile.
He is sitting up in a cage.
He can't talk. He has a hose
in his throat.
His dials leap.
"Is this the worst from now on?"
he writes on a board.
Now he is sleeping more deeply
than I can say. Surgery.
Now he is rescued.

Is he breathing?
Yes, quietly. He is sleeping,
breathing alone.

Now he is beginning to walk.
He is more tall than my womb,
but very bending.
He leans on something chrome.

Now we are going home.
He is buckled into his seat
dressed
he is sitting beside me.
I am buckled too.
We are going home.

I have been scrubbing his room.
I can polish its wood
I can shine its windows;
it has food. He enters it.

He is very thin.
He is slow down the hall.
Behind him, I can't see
he is breathing
and moving.

Twenty-one years ago
I panted and bore down
into scarlet and dazzle
between my thighs
in order to release him
to the shiny air

that tick-turning cord
still pulsing.

You,
lift up from the bloody ditch
and watch
what's whole and dripping
come again into the world.

Piecing

No woman in my family sews
but Nana jumped down a well
to save my mother, the sickly one
they say fell in. And once,
homesick for her Russian village,
she took up babies and jewels, stitched
gold in a chamois sack between her breasts,
and set out from England, a runaway.
The oldest, not yet four,
remembered smothering underneath
a quilt while Nana slept, head down
on that duvet of her tiny daughters.
The border guards weren't fooled.
They did what any Prussian would
and sent for Papa. Of course, he came.
Next year they had a son.
Later that Russian village burned to the ground.

Gram, my father's mother, the beauty
of New York City in the nineties, said,
"For women, only good names matter."
Not a soft spot in the perfect body
she wore beneath her corsets
until grandchildren put her underground
at eighty. At twenty, she told her husband,
youngest son of the richest man in town,
her gates were locked, they'd stay that way.
She kept the children, sold the mansion
and bought a grocery store she worked enough
to push the kids through school,
tied off, sold out, and folded at forty,
still colorful, strait laced and blonde.
She didn't remarry, she said she didn't care for men

except her sons, Daddy—but fifteen years younger—
her favorite until he died before she did.
Her only daughter worked the books in a car wash
    to support her
and a frail husband, had no children
lost the name I took back and try to carry on.

My own mother, no handiworker, nevertheless left me
an unworn grosgrain ribbon dress she wove,
no doubt at great expense: two years' worth of pastime.
I refused to take it home. Her name is gone,
    her sisters dead.

Shall I stitch here Mother's damask sofas,
matching wing chairs, Morris wallpapers, hall brasses
she collected instead of horses (she was terrified of horses)?
Which words to applique her whole again
upon an English woolen from her favorite robe?
No silk can fill her paneled hall with light
or patch her shadow on that slate.

As Nana sixty years before
climbed over the stone lip of the well
to save her, so Mother, pricked
by a stiffening palsy into stasis,
woke one morning early in her rented bedroom,
turned without noise to wake her sister
caretaker in the other bed,
put on her silk wrapper, tied the cord,
shuffled to a high-backed chair with arms
—one of twelve she'd shipped from the big house—
and dragged it over the Turkish carpet to the balcony doors,
weighted to keep them level in the wind,
and pulled them open on the ocean view,
a curled iron railing, slick with rain.

She dragged the chair,
and stopped to rest,
then climbed, stood, and breathed the damp,
and jumped and fell.
"Blunt trauma," said the certificate
that came home with her body.

This morning rising early
broken ribs in a binder, ten pounds heavy,
I see in the mirror both the fine, full body
of my daughter, away at school,
and Mother there, intact inside her perfect skin.
I thank her. I begin to piece; I take up pen.

Saying Goodbye to the Property

On the first cold day in August
in a northern state,
the sun reflects on the gazebo
a lattice of light.

In the crevice of a rock in my path
forbidding farther progress
is a small pine in the shape of a feather.
It will not let go
though I pull on it, even to keep my balance.

Underfoot on the paths
I've wandered for years with the children
poison ivy flourishes.
They are grown into beauty
and the girls' breasts are like my own.

A quarrelsome age settles on us all
and on our parents
death shows a common face.
Not the red leaf
not the cry of the tern can hold me.

I will not come here again.

What Is Good

The banks of rivers
and rivers
and river dells
and patches of shade
in trees we swing from.
The grasses in winter,
their colors and swirls.
The birth
and the recovery
and the long swaths
we make walking in uncut grass.
The field to the horizon.
The horizon like a bowl.
Clay we scrape up
and carry home and wedge.
The potter's wheel
spinning. And its noise,
a ground in great music
we write. We write great music.

The shells we gather, the soft bodies
of their tenants swept to sea

or buried. The ice houses in poems
of the salt sea. The tingling of hand
and dipped arm. And the swell
and the dip of the salt.
The mounds of casings
left by armies
and the bones buried in shallow graves.
The celluloid film we expose to light
and our flickering images in dark.
The baleen of whales, their cartilage,
and the brackish residue strained out between.
Foam. An eddy.
Our soft bodies and their phosphorescence,
their smoke.

Kid slippers, each toe a hollow,
and the dance card. Teeth filled
with molten gold. Gold in a case.
The rising of sun
and its going down in books,
in strips of house windows,
and the hollow of the groin
fitted to another one.
The high shale falls
and their engorgement, their waters
a great weight. And the perfect egg.
The breath we take in
and exhaust. The dead,
honeycombed with rot. Their ashes.
Commemorative fires in brass trenches.
The ground. The ground.

Family

The famous poet is sitting, she
is sitting in a wicker lawn chair
drawn down by her arms to the head
of her dalmatian, unnamed on this book jacket.

One could ask someone, a friend
of the poet, not—as I am—a friend of the work.
I don't know her nor am I likely to, except
through the clear language covering
breast and genitals in her poems.
Everything stirs, always, in the final stanza
but what comes before is static, passion
is disguise under a cotton tunic flushed
towards pink at the armholes. Her poems
have no flowers in their arms, don't tell us
hold on tight, won't call us names
we won't claim no matter how we want to;
our faces and noses reject the restraint
of high forehead, middle-German flesh
packed in fresh skin, jut of heavy bone frame.

This woman cooks, she preserves, she leads horses by the reins
through the mushroom woods, makes rot into omelettes
redolent of basil, herbs grown not on the windowsill
but in their own plot behind the larger kitchen garden
where horse droppings are forked under
in service to what turns air to fire.

In the picture she sits, head lowered to the dog.
I love this woman and lower my head to her,
to rest on her text, rest my arms
(arms that flower into hands, on their center fingers
the pale mine-cut diamonds of my dead mother)
on the pink jacket of her new book.

  —For Maxine Kumin

Worry about Meaning

What if I'm broken and can't be mended,
or worse, the world is broken around me
and I the only whole thing in it?

The light at the window fractures to get in.
Trees in their winter doldrums, dun and silver,
static as desks, seem one thing, now another.
How to say the difference?

The doorbell, the alarms of the clock, the shatter
and stutter of tableware, what do they mean to us
eating and drinking with family who come from our bodies?
Our pets on the floor animate, lungs
rising and falling in lucid continuum
above their rounded bellies. Oh Lord, you've collapsed

time for us so the moment of conception,
its fluids and contortions,
exists at the moment the water breaks on tile,
splashes the shoes of the attending intern,
and the same child brought forth,

is off in a flurry of tatters and knits and leathers.
Why are the perfumes of the inner and outer body
filled with the smells of earth?
The prairie grasses, those healing sponges under our feet,
push up our shoe soles in patterns not particular, not saving.

On the tarmac, we hunch over weapons,
can't wait for the bloodflow to slow,
be staunched, for membranes to reach out
minute fibers of muscle,
silver under a dribble of fluids,
and ease, thin, scar over, meet.

Helios at Bread Loaf, the Album

In these pictures
the sun is so good to our faces
erasing the fissures, easing pressure
on sinuses, unstoppering ears!

In this photo
we gambol like goats in the mountains
and here we are resting on steps
drinking beer.
The sun does it all, fueling us, calling us
out of our casings, unmufflering us.
Our smiles attest to it.
Our legs are bared to it; hair falls
to our shoulders—so much heavy hair,
sun on it, sun priming us,
sun triggering us.

Explosion
behind the forehead unloads
words, works of the arts, parts
of a general legacy. Such
delicacy of feeling, layering
of attitudes, fiery connections
soldered intelligently together.
See how chapters emerge, poems,
tricks respected by critics of stamina.
We all carry papers.

See how we clasp hands
before the bush laden with berries,
three graces heady with wine, groggy,
transported to the dining room.
We smile, heavy-lidded, at the camera,
part of a gathering of images
for the book,
still unwritten.

With Stanley Kunitz at the Car Wash

Just as the boy with round pink glasses
takes my money and waves me into line,
a voice on the radio says what sorrow teaches.
I turn up the volume on the car speakers.

As the wide felt streamers jiggle past
the windscreen and over the top,
he talks about dying: like sex,
that informs the work of a boy in his twenties,
death comes into the work of an old poet.

And he is old, says the announcer
whose voice rises with the music
between commercials. Jets squirt
soapsuds around the wing vents
I daub up with a damp Turkish towel
someone shoved in the door before.

At talk of his father, a suicide,
something metal grinds at my expensive
aluminum: a flaw in the system
my car passes over, then back onto
the straight and narrow track again,

just as Stanley's voice rises
in joyous affirmation of fig trees
and shoe lifts, and we burst out of the dark
and go dripping but shining
back into the city's traffic.

The Man

I know a man
with a bird in his throat.
Sometimes
he opens his mouth
to sing.
It sings.
Sometimes he gags
and I watch.

Why I am interested
who can say,
liking only
the occasional song:
icycles
(as some kid wrote)
or *rope*
made into occasional robes.

When he drips,
an audience in Chicago
watches the puddle
forming at his feet;
he calls it, "The Middle West."
Sometimes the bird
splashes, chirps
Sandhills and *Platte*,
sometimes other names
of far mountains
and the climbers
who bring back
rhododendrons
for the wealthy.

Everything on TV he watches
and the bird
makes it into music.

Some men are born with a big mouth
and the hinge for opening up wide.
The dentist loves him
and certain young lovers
from among the academic classes.

In the meantime
the sounds from high trees
attract me: some
birds not caught
in a throat. How they sing.

Women Raised in the Fifties

Someone in my dream
says she likes my earring
over and over again
outside the window
the wren watches the cardinal
preen. Water in the birdbath
draws light to it.
My daughter praises the grace
and beauty of her stepmother's "face
and carriage." I look in the mirror.
From the far room, laughter.
Men through the door
beckon, say something to live for.

Shame, or the Computer Uses of Natural Language

—Sarah Stueber Bishop, *The Women's Review of Books*

Die
Option not listed
List options
Run   Lie   Confess

Run: I head for the purple hills
whose coarse vegetation packs
the eye with color: vermillion,
the season being fall, and green
in various shades, shapes, and textures.
Mud underfoot limns footsoles
on fallen trees, cool breezes
come down white into cones and rods:
a melding in this valley so low . . . No.

Lie: I have offended none, not the thief
whom I counseled in the distribution of goods;
not the woman crying silently in interstices
in the music, whose children eternally are
missing; not the woman counting her capital,
planning an order for the armorer;
not the scholar, whose excellent constructs
measure precisely the elegant dimensions
of the pasture, pegging down cerulean silk
at all corners; not the beggar to whom I offered
small pebbles blowing hard off the sand
at her belly. I have not done these things . . . No.

Confess: I have slender wrists.
Nothing excites me more than the mind
except it's the body. Where the weather is,

I am, or in the pew with Henry James
behind the hostile but bereaved family.
He won't speak to me, and for good reason.
Today I have offended
A friend who is childless
with talk of my children;
a friend who drank too much,
with chablis I took from a cup;
and a woman who saved me once
from the harsh absence grief demands,
come today with news and terror
I couldn't fight or succor,
whom I sent away with nothing
more than books and a cold supper.

The small birds balance on the mountain ash
again at dusk; nothing is altered.
The cat takes to the garden, rolls
on the hard earth. She is flesh to the ground.
Small yellow tomatoes suspended in air
from their upright vines. For centuries
the same five notes have come from the lark.
What can I do? Die?   *Option not listed*   List options.

Assignment

You say write
a poem about grief
but how can I
when snow outside
the window muffles
everything?

Falling onto
the cold of the kitchen
floor in the middle of the night
often, one terrible winter?
Is that how the poem begins?
Or riding to the cemetery
in the famous dark car
of my mother's brother,
the surgeon, who insists
on asking impossible
and rude questions about
the suicide of my brother?
They're all dead now,
what does it matter?

No, something about taking off
in an airplane on the way
to someplace healing, how the
runway splintered, all that silent
dashing around in the head bent
first over one bed, then another,
pushing aside the breathing tubes,
brushing the IVs, propping up
heads bending back blankets,
smoothing the sheets, pushing
hair back with the flat of my palm,
touching with lips the damp foreheads,
all that saying goodbye while the plane
jumped up, *thunk*, with no effort
and bounced, a lurch in the belly
back onto the ground, and took off.
And I said goodbye.

Three Ways of Looking at It

Having been given permission to write
hooks into the soft portions of cheeks
I write this down on a morning of trees
cracked, chimneys felled, decimation
the old way, by lot, limbs torn from trunks,
sockets exposed; stumps partially
uprooted, fracture everywhere
no glistening, no green haze:
hopeless December, month of death
like all the others.

Tension demands a second stanza
whose blossoms toss on branches
upward into the summer air
in the fists of lovers
whose gesture signifies triumph,
union. Even the sun is singed, fused
with the blazing sky.

And I am sitting in a neutral season,
autumn in the window, washed now and
again by shudders of wind,
now the throat catch, the faltering
lungs, now the heart beating
triumphantly if irregularly loud:
see me, see me sitting here,
still alive, see this ordinary
impermanent, failed winner?

Trying to Buy off Death

is no effort in the blue hours.
The feral cats feast in the garbage,
chicken bones that can kill them,
so good the cats don't die.
The whole fetid smell of the place.
Look, I say, look. I have a clean
business proposition for you.
Value in the vault. A real contract.
If I die, I say, you have none of my assets;
even my books are gone.
My small, aristocratic feet
up the flue.

With this thousand you can have
Mexico,
with this one, kid boots of
a charming softness.
And the last, the best,
pays off the death car, color of mourning.

See, now the sun is trying to rise.

Lacunae

Commercial questions we call them, questions
of disease, disuse, questions of nobody's
business. Disgusting. Everyone knows
the fabric they're cut from. Everyone warns us.

Cautious, I set out for the new city.
City of closed gates, she calls it,
Cool city. Wind rises in pines,
in cypress. Rounding the river bend,
the bright road passes the salt flats,
bright mica chips for surface, a sprightly
balance. I am traveling faster. See,
I am going the long distance.

Companion, will you leave me here
having taken me beyond fear, the flat
places, into mountains? We should both
be sorry to lose what we have lost:
night noises, susurrus.

Some doors are curtained. Ascending
the stairs requires bending. You have fallen
flat to greet me. Palm to palm we . . .
I will open. I will

Never forget this place, this price,
this proud house in the clearing. I will never
Yes. It is time to go for food.
See how the light brightens in the windows,
see how the wind rises again, air freshens,
sun, sun come to me here, come here I am

What Happened This Summer

> They put their heads on one side, and looked wise, which is quite as good
> as understanding a thing, and very much easier.
> —Oscar Wilde, "The Birthday of the Infanta"

A door slams.
"What is the message of the door?"
I ask in the dark. You don't know
and I don't know either but now
I tell you it meant goodbye.

From the shadows we made on the road,
longer than Giacometti women,
hooked shadows and no eclipse
of our bodies, light points. Above,
ordinary stars and a late moon.

"A few fireflies on the road,"
you said, "Look," and "look."

Divorce

You stand in the doorway saying
It's only a scab;
It's only a penny of blood.
Stop I say stop.

Then it's time for the suicide,
Daft, hitching his way down
the mountain. You don't ask
How was his nose broken.

His head is opened by the bullet,
the knife you let fly,
the flight on the lawn, punch
Counterpunch.

Listen I tell you
Stop. Anything can happen.

Detail

—with a line adjusted from Ezra Pound

This young woman is hurt
like the rest of us
but for the first time.
She is very thin.
When she is frightened
she goes to the phone book
and opens it at random.
Who do I know whose name
begins here?
She is living at these times
by the principle of the fine
nursery poems that have made her
famous. And she dials, she says,
numbers she hasn't tried in years.
Her voice so calm. She doesn't say
Please help me but says instead
My lover left me. What would you do?
This question they answer in detail, she says,
and detail is what she notices.
It seems to me as we talk
she has grown wise.

When she asks I tell her
the latest painful detail
of my life and she listens:
how the flowers, oh, the colors
of exotics by the ocean
make patterns, colors growing
in layers in circles behind
the wooden houses, and she hears
the names of these wonders
marigold, yarrow, Kansas gayweed,
zinnia, petunia, loosestrife,
wild rose and others,
portulaca and Russian thistle.

Now mind you *I* am not a poet
and not much for detail
except for the catalogue
which more easily represents
a proliferation of confusing detail
in my life: several children
from different fathers, old egg yolk
on dishes, a new person in my office,
the supreme courtroom of our state
whose walls of local wood
say, this is true,
"Eyes and ears are poor witnesses
when the soul is barbarous."
Really it is too much
to expect clarity of detail
when recounting the moment today
when a man stepped
unintentionally I am certain
into my very path
and I, forgetting the many years
of intervening detail,
marriage, assault, divorce,

his lawsuit against me,
patted in passing his huge belly
with my left hand. This new ring's
gold gathered around it the very light.

I'm certain he noticed.

1 September, 100 Degrees

End of summer:
higher heat
only absence
of light lowers.
Louring sky.
Moon fourteen days
from full,
dry ground;
fissures
marigolds droop into.
Nothing's waxen, creamy.

Across the prairie
hot air blows
down gulleys;
city alleys
hold the heat
their garbage cans
too fierce to touch
without a glove.
All beasts are fitful
come inside
except the mole

who dies on the patio
dripping babies.
We lift her
on a shovel
drop her in
just as the last one
falls away.

Journal Entry: The Tropics

Today was hot.
A morning of packing and cleaning
and sitting on the lanai high over the city.
Papaya for breakfast and Kona coffee.
The Manoa cloud kept close. No rain.

With Caroline I went to the fabulous
snorkeling beach whose creatures are on display
under the surface of the water.
She brought masks.
We climbed the black rocks instead,
thin women in black
swimsuits of the same fabric,
one fair, one so dark
I wear stars in my ears.
We sat by a man-sized oval piercing
in the rocks on either side of a cleft
in the rocks that whirled and filled
and overflowed in our laps
jets of sea water.
Such salt.
"I want to lick the undersides

of those rocks," she said,
that beautiful woman,
"close-pored," as the man
would say at whose side
I have spent some happy nights, now over.

People took our picture.
Some sand nearby was olive-green,
Olivine from the lava. Inside
the cracked, volcanic rock
were light strands called Pele's Hair.
We said we'd meet again.
We touched and parted.

At night after a meal
of raw fish, sashimi, I fly home
to this freezing.

A Meeting with My Ex-Husband

You are well,
could be said
to be taking it well:
solid scar tissue.
You have lost 24 pounds in 22 days
you say over lunch,
a circle of greens.
You have had some money,
have bought a new bike with the money,
some gold, Cartier watches, two
color TVs, an electronic alarm,
some Gucci things with the money,

a pair of imported somethings.
You are nowhere in trouble, you say,
flipping through
the new albums. You play
me some music about a Halston
dress, about a classy
child, about traveling far.
A pomander on the display
case is left over from Christmas.
All its winking is gone, ribbons,
sweet scents, no proof against
contagion.
      Oh Lord.
I sit and obediently watch
Old Hawk, most radiant of creatures.
What can I, who myself am fallen,
do with such a crashing?

When I can go
I do go out
into the air
and annihilating sun.
It burns and promises
to peel me down
from the quick
to the bone
and I go home.

Version

Let me be better than
yellow at the window,
wind blowing a hat to the ground,
yellow hat with spent veiling.

Let the birds sing at a distance,
vulgar birds with their holes
and feathers. Let the children
sit on a bench under the espaliered
bushes, their glossy frost shapes
caught between pyracantha thorns.

Where are the parents? Sitting on lawn
covered chaises in their creamy linens,
drinking champagne. It's the right color.
And the sun? Overhead in all seasons.
And the beasts? Frolicking in the grass,
snouts to mole furrows. And the rain?
Seeping into basements where mushrooms
grow in beige cases on the carpet.

Scavenger, get to work. You have strength
and will to do it.

Pain

On the windy patio
all the spring of that marriage
we talked.
At dusk, torrential rain
flooded the plains
to hex in summer.
By autumn it was over.

Another summer I wake in the quiet
to pain filling my chest with such a water
as I must drown; wake, pull up
and say its name out loud
into the humid air. Sweat pours
that later I sponge off,
in case my emptied body
offend its shroud: I must die of it.
I say your name.
But no, you rise and put your hand
exactly pain-sized, on the place
and rub it down.
Though what you touch is only skin,
some vessel deep within
lets go, a crack, and drains.
I whisper something,
touching back, and for a while
can breathe, and float, and stroke,
and live.

Small Shelter

The needful things have been done:
sugar in the cupboard, honey, sweet
bacon in the smokehouse; buckles
done up, pines felled by lightning
shored against the flood bank.
Nothing to do now but wait.

I go to a tin box, remove
your ring, bed it for some long
season. Oh love, we have risked
our lives for this and still
it is over, long shadows crossing
over us. Fold, hands, be still for the sake of memory,
for our sweet sake who have done
the needful things, who have been true
to our hands, to our hard shoring up.
No floods can take us now.

I braid up my hair, our tent,
that sweet shelter.
Now winter.

High Ground

I am on my knees planting my garden.
The tulips are ivory bulbs, safe now
in onionskin as I bury them.

They grow all winter, February, March
snow breaking. I chase away the dogs.

The first one crests
broken but red, so bright
in the sun its bending should be
brief and simple.
I watch it fade through the window.

Stake it,
you advise, stake it
my books say
so I do, string sudden on a wooden paddle.
The veins in the petals threaten to open wide
and spill.

But it stands
and soon I am watching it,
shining. Now the second
shows pale below the shoulder
of the first. Bare strong buds
at its stem flare wide at the bottom
where they gather.

My cats are black and tan and lie on the broken earth
sharing the sun that warms into summer
the old lilies.

IV

Some Other Women Now

Where did the words go?
Thrown out the window
with grief, that perfume
of rush and obedience;
a collapse with mother
gone down to the pavement below
and crushed. *Blunt trauma.*

"Worse," she said, "was the defection
of your father. One Christmas morning
I woke up and he was gone, his mistress,
about whom I knew nothing, installed
in an apartment across town. The tissue
wads still under the tree and you
not born yet, still nudging my rib,
that sore place, with your elbow. Fancy it."

Petticoats, their dark familiar shadows
on the floor after the dance. Rustles
and tangos of taffeta ruffles at the hem.
And crinolines around our shiny knees
over the Vaseline shine of our ballet slippers,
crimped leather at the toes underneath.
Oh, the dresses: velvet crushed at the armpits,
sleeves for a strapless black bodice
with the creamy brocade. The money they spent
on dancing clothes the year Papa was davening
in the old front bedroom!

Click. A trip to the maternity
ward in deep night. A full moon means nothing only
a son and daughter he claims and won't feed.
Mucus plugs dropped again and again I can't

make sense of all this   crippled   and what for?
The best I can do is continue.

            Iced over,
not calling for help (who'd listen) she complained
to the cleaning lady, herself in tears, the keloid scar
at the corner of one eye collapsed on itself. One side
a cheerful disposition, poison on the other side, rat trap
to scare away the scurry in the kitchen. Women alone
one after another in wind in streets   in air   moon fled
moon bottomed   bottomed out.   Path   lost

Poor.   Poor kiddos   old crumbs
    on the ground.
The witch watches in her forest, rests a broomstick
    on a turret
cloud. She knows. Her language roils in her throat
    like phlegm
collecting. When she speaks, the syllables spill
like waves on a leap to air. If we're lucky below
    we catch foam.

Plate xii

—A series of seventy original illustrations to Captain Sir R. F. Burton's "Arabian Nights," in oils, specially painted by Albert Letchford, London, H. S. Nichols Ltd., 1897.

O I confess I am small.
Smaller than a thread.
Smaller than a thread of pond ivy scum.
Than the bead of light on a thread of algae,
the split underside of a beetle,
its iridescent least leg scale.

Before your might
I am tears on your tile floor.
A bead of sun at the carpet edge,
the rose thread of the maker's sign
in fringe turned under by the layer's knee,
he in his big apron kneeling
on a day you don't enter
your lavish, your least reception room.
His leather knee patch.
I am nothing fresh.

You nod in passing,
set trembling bells
on your vest edge, their musical calling
freshening air you walk through
your hand swirling air in its least blessing.
I stand back in fear. I tremble at the edge
of the vast corridors you pass through.
I tremble in the hair-like cilia of the inner ear whorl
of your least subject who sinks to his knees
before you as you pass.
Before your wrath I am less than he.
I am less than he is.

I am less than your camel driver's fingernail.
Less than your draper, your linen draper
who pries open the long teak drawers
to raise out the heavy layers, the lengths of your linen,
who wraps your head in their waxy scents,
who catches in the folds of your crinkly beard
this fingernail and tweaks, your frown he covers
    and drapes over,
your fine deep alabaster forehead
covered and wrapped in creamy folds, your cool linen
    headdress.
I am less than the fray in the golden cord
he wraps your head with.
I am cut off and dropped away.

I fall to the tile floor.
Less than a metal thread, less than a single twist of flax,
less than the scour cloth in your sweet-jar,
less than the sour rag in the palm of your least cook,
that she-servant, I am less than the base metal clip
on your least concubine's braid,
the tie that binds her hair closed,
the tin button on her jerkin you undo,
the thread gives way, the clatter, less than her shudder,
less than the gleam on the oily knife hilt,
the blade entering,
less than her cry, less than yours.

Widow

I have had this lesson,
not to care for the bones.
The cat in my lap dies,
he is replaced, the man who
casts me out is cast out,
the love that leaves returns
as a "wall of water," she kept
saying, as if the words
were the flood and all she could see
she would repeat: "A wall of water."

Wipe me out. I have been replaced,
supplanted, ignored, cast out,
ground down, spat upon, rejected,
refused, neglected, soiled,
reviled, dismembered.
I have lost husband and children,
beasts and possessions, I am ashes,
an orphan; my dearest self took a gun
into himself and died in the fields.

My breasts are empty pockets.
Pain visits my body; tears
my eyes, my mouth is filled
with wind, I speak nonsense
incessantly, silence is fled
from me, wisdom hides her head.
A feverish energy holds, then drops me down.
My children flee from me. A succession
of bruises bloom on the long bones of my body.

Oh God of the waters, God of the fragile body,
imperfect and weak,
watch over me, care for me,
raise me up out of the plumes of the dust,
the rusty canyons.
Rinse and nourish me. In return I have
nothing but my great and perfect
need.

Lot's Wives

He frees himself by not caring
about the consequences.
If she turns, he loses her.
He looks toward the distant wife
drawing near, their child
in her fair arms. He is happy.

Never has he been so happy,
no never, not in the first days
of this double marriage.
The dark wife recedes as he moves
forward. He doesn't care.
Behind her their children, grown now
he tells anyone who'd listen, follow.
Their mother, he says, is freed by their leaving.

He doesn't care.
He says he has done his part
waking at dawn on one body, now another.
He asks in close conversation
if *you* know whose face at dawn
will lie on the near cushion.

The wife with the new child
wins him because she breeds.
The trees breed long seeds
over the lawn, must or all
is lost, all energy fail,
the daisy, the dog and cat
and brief birds in rain forests.

Here in a corner of the desert
the dark wife bleeds away
his seed into the sand by choice,
washing away with precious water
all change, all chance, all easy access.
His salty sweet taste falls out
of her body—not barren, only empty,
as she wants it to be.

Gossip

> The little things may be none of
> our business but we like them.
> —Bernice Slote

At lunch she tells the story of an old lover
and his ten-year-old son, all canoeing
on the Swift River. Two took off their shirts
in the heat of work and swagger, to leave her
on the front seat bailing water and tidying gear.
Was she singing? Surely yes, and tucking up
her escaping hair in its pink bandana.
Sweat hung from her earlobes and its salt
mustached her upper lip. She was angry.

All at once her shirt with its oblongs
of damp at front and back, like open castanets
but blue and still, came off, she took it off
deliberately, they didn't see her fingers
reaching for the final, embroidered buttonhole
or the shine of her left shoulder shrugging,
or smell sweat running from her drying armpits,
her breasts, like theirs in air, the sun warm
on her hair as she shook off the square cloth,
stood up, and no one anywhere in the boat
said anything.

She

> There is health in brown and too much talk in silver.
> —Fredrick M. Link

I met an old woman once
who blabbed her theories
not a one grounded in fact
or if so she didn't say,
and though she made clear
the details, what she called,
"layers of transparencies
that hide or comprise
history, the universe and art,"
the while she talked—
an afternoon through, and an evening—
her famous husband watched in the background
or hid his eyes in his glass.

When I dream or lie waking
my mind fills with snippings
I swear if you asked me
I couldn't speak them plain.
But next day in the garden
lines overlap with the squares
until the map of the bulbs
resembles my moving mind.

At lunch last week my old friend
leaned on his elbow and said
the reason we get along so fine
is that he talks forever on
about himself and I'm still,
never liking to say who I am.
I notice the clear cellophane of his face
clipped at the edges, his blue eyes.

When I was a child my daddy
left often on business.
I'd cry for hours, yes, thrash
on the floor wanting him home
to cure the quiet.

I dig in my garden
our garden my husband turns under
with mulch. All winter
we lie on our quilt circling
the catalogues, talking new husbandry,
fat bulbs packed with life
I imagine tucked up but waiting to spring
loose in the border soil
he trucked in.
He circles daylilies on paper,
maroon with gold centers.
I don't like them. No, I like them too.

For sixteen years I've saved up
for special occasions, felt my body
brush loose
silk of my holiday dress.
In my hands
the paintbrush feels alive with color.
Pencil lines
over the cream primer on the canvas
guide me right
so what comes out is floral, almost
an exact replica of how lilies
bloat in the wind then bend.
Their powdery pollen once stained
my linen skirt. My large hands
brushed the silvery light, brushing it off.

Oracle

Everything good happens.

Except this: she betrayed me;
Said what I said to a man of iron
powerful enough to ruin me with lightning.
No, not really.
Where I rest in the center, over the earth, is still steady.
I'm paid to twirl in the steam and speak riddles and I do,
often enough to please the togas. They need me.
But to my women I say truth plain, straight
as their hems brushing dust in our courtyard.

I'm given wine every hour and mostly I'm quiet
until the yard fills. That woman served grapes

between chantings when my throat failed and the ache
under my ribs spread. She could tell by my flailing.

She gave what I said away.
My vision melted and ran down her arms
from her mouth, blind colors all salt-scattered,
what fixes my swing over the earth gone suddenly lax.
She sweated for days. They wrapped her in linen towels
but no good. I'd chanted vowels alone, a sullen token
from the InnerGods. They're fallen,

As I am, torso wrenched to one side of my sling.
When I feel better, the hooves gone from my head,
the temple empty and my chin dried off by wind,
I'll come from this cave of hair and my dung
to sing her healthy. She's sick now. No woman of mine
could betray me. And the man? Tomorrow

I'll know. They feed me corn gruel as the steam thickens.
It helps my digestion. The Gods are waiting.

Pregnant Woman

Whose husband is gone, take your daughter by the hand,
lead her to the window where the widow is framed,
raking her leaves. That woman is bowed down by fall.
Say, "We're not as she is, daubing her lips, blowing
out of our noses the dry dust. We have taken control of weather."

Make the sun rise. Raise up wind, mother of changes,
who lives in your mouth. Let the bellows of your lungs rest
on this infant's head, a fulcrum on which to balance the force

of your wind, a colorless rush through your halls
to rinse carpets, raise dust in corners, shatter glass
from the breakfront. Let the corners of furniture splinter.
Take from your armpits electricity of desire,
comb it through your hair and the hair of your daughter.
Sparks from her blonde head ignite your dark one,
the night moves off, see, you are doing it, she is doing it.

Woman of power and movement, woman who knows life
moving in your body, life passing through you like water,
the kitchen faucet you turn on full, washing potatoes,
turning their brown bottoms up under splashing water,
water the cushion, water the soother, water
the cleanser, you are water
and wine, you are
electricity, the power
you push into the world
when the muscles of your body clench hard
and you pour new life.

Rub your belly with ashes, with pumice,
sweet oils of clove and anise to glisten
on the round of your belly, reflect
sunrise and sunset, keep that fire intact.
You the water and the myrrh, sulfur you are
and strong smelling, strong tasting, elemental preserver,
golden in your powerful spasms and flashings.

Visitant

You're such an old person
to stand on tiptoe in position
at my window.
But I'm not in my chair. I'm in the country
shearing sheep. A nursery character.

What do you want?
It's not lonely here, or in the city.

I've got power? Yes, of a sort,
like my mother's, small feet in their fur boots
high heels (she was short and vain) and tied
with blue ribbons. In snow she walked fast if she could,
her only sport. In summer simmered
on the front porch.
Three times a day she changed stockings,
real power in those days in a city,
pure silk in short supply.
What did she do with money? She hoarded
for her husband who spent it on "business."
What's that, do you suppose? Not sin.
Power? I don't think so.

Sometimes I have trouble swallowing. Don't laugh.
The politics, even that artist I've known twenty years
come round to say he's "fallen from power"
because his friend, our senator, decided to retire.
Sometimes it takes away my breath. You smile, yes,
and so do I, running on at the mouth so I can't bend over
this love's broad shaggy back to clip it.
Age is tidy, I've found. My mother's chief worry
was spots on the bosom, that lovely rose silk
with the tie at the throat gone spotted in front
and no help for it, no cleaner to take it out.

Someone will spin this wool into yarn.
She sits in her yard in the shadow of an elm
sipping bark tea when her fingers tire. I help her
    comb and card
what I bring. Come cold, she'll knit wool thread
into a warm throw I'm about ready to wrap up in,
a bunting to keep away the chill
nights when even the cat won't go out
not to hunt or sniff or call at the window.

I'm through with prowling,
everything gone dry
between my legs but a small burning.
Mother, don't cry.
I don't talk like this much.
Funny, you used to say you felt your mother hovering
ready to advise. Now you call me on your birthday.
Last year you reached your arm out of clouds
to give me a coat. It's over there
in the farmhouse closet, waiting.
Keep yourself warm, you're getting old, you said.

Cradle

I buy a watercolor of a woman
on a bed. She is naked.
I call her mother. Her nourishing breasts
shine in light from an invisible window.

A woman sits on a bed in light.
She is far away. She is more perfect
than formal matter.

Her hands are working clay.
Life into life, plunging hands
into a tub half filled with water.
Pink light falls steadily onto her shining shoulder,
this light in my mind.

When I leave I turn mother-woman to the wall.
No man there likes her,
her large breasts, her mysterious closed eyes.
She is heavy. She is an other.
I am only slightly other, lean and narrow
front to back, side to side.
When I say, "I feel," they smile.
Mother-woman is silent. She is a painting.

The men are lean, their body hair
a tender fur at crotch and armpit; front to back
their flesh close to long bones.
I cup my palm to the backs of their heads.
I touch the skin over their skulls.

A pale fur
hugs the long bones of their bodies,
narrow bones cradled close to my nourishing breasts.
A blond beard catches light.
What does it mean, this soft flesh above my ribs?

Mother-woman's breasts rest on the hard cradle of her ribs,
her softness under my skull.
Where are my children,
my large-breasted daughter, my solid son?
Where have they taken their bones
that grew in my center like clay, the slough of the very air?
They have walked them away, cradled in flesh.

The watercolor picture of Mother-woman
calls me. Child, she says,
flesh is its own calling.
Your flesh is a cradle.
You live there in the glow of your bones.
Be at ease. I am with you.

I Am Sick

"Please," I ask my wife
but she doesn't hear me, I'm lucky.
What I mean is
please make light the window.
Last night
she sewed on my button with wax thread.
"That should hold you," she says,
pulling it through, patting me on the chest
where it leaks and hurts.

In the dark my head feels loose,
emptied, like the coffee thermos
on the sink edge.
I'm all bone. "Not yet," she says
at the curb. Cars, noise, a stink
I don't know. And we cross.

I pick up mail from the box.
I want to. The squares are heavy
from far away, stuck with a taste
on my tongue like paste I try to chew off.
The box is black and flakes
under its sun, a red flag I push up.
"Don't," she says.

"Don't," she says when I hit the dog.
Once it bites me, a ladder of black stitches
on my palm she kisses.
Every day after dinner
behind her back at the sink
a bucket of fire empties.

Visions

Three women in a niche
their robes verdigris; a pale moss
the color of bronze plushes the brick.
From their mouths the water of fountains dribbles,
darkens the cobbles, runs down and pools their bare feet.
An iron fence divides us from silver,
the copper luck of coins.

I dream about a fluent woman
trapped in a flood of language,
a living flux her body interrupts.
But into her is sluiced and out
a particular speech so balanced
she is a floodgate and from her mouth
the tamed waters flow and chant.

My son in his hospital gown,
flayed ribs raising the thin cotton
into a tent of air he breathes,
wakes from long sleeping.

A silent woman drowsing in a chair
his thin foot in my hand,
I startle at lightning.

He opens his blazing eyes.

The conduits of his body charge again.
Long filaments
lift from his perfect head
and sway like anemones
in bands of light
thickening the edges of his room
beneath the pale ceiling. Others,
sheer filaments, connect with, touch,
slot into and braid

an entire tough weave I know
keeps us, generation to generation, safe.
Waves of air rock the chrome bed frame
free of its straps and tubes
and his voice, unhinged from long silence,
rises in vowels he chants in counterpoint
with those in the niche of the saved.

Three women in a wet niche
their robes verdigris; a plush moss
like bronze clings to the brick.
Their mouths open in anguish
and out dribbles the fountain waters,
runs to and pools the cobbles at their feet
scaly with copper, the silver luck thrown in.

V

Jan's Orchard, Nebraska

Anything anyone human
might want of an evening
we've carried from the hold
of the station wagon
parked at the foot of the hill.
We loll on the grass and drink.

A spring orchard in Stella,
even the blasted trees blooming,
pear, cherry, and apple,
and we're eating a picnic supper
and drinking wine in the middle
under an umbrella of blossoms.

The sun at the horizon
catches rose in our glasses.
We say nothing.
If the good life is coming
to us in our lifetime,
surely it is here
in this orchard in April at twilight,
everything possible blooming,
the air—impossible—warming
as the sun goes down.

Everything here is becoming
summer if we let it,
three people who try hard
to drink and keep this air down
on the ground among grass blades,
while it bubbles and rises
and floats us, finally,
our pale quilts and jackets,

our jokes and stories,
into the night sky,
shrinking and whirling us
higher and higher
until we're dust motes,
no, lightning points,
no star folds,
nothing around us cold,
nothing around us, no,
we are nothing
but sighing over the flowers.

Locus

8 AM
Bach variations on harpsichord.
Cat puts head
into huge cluster
of peach colored
unarranged peonies
in stoneware vase
less open at top
than center where it bulges.
Pale sun
over my shoulder
falls and glows
on teak tables.

Looking up
I see the shout
of a cardinal
sitting exactly on top

the new leader
of the forty-year-old
blue spruce,
who stays
long enough
for me to consider
calling out.

Just as
tree
beast
flowers
bird
become with light
a natural blessing,
a sudden absence
of any sound
resolves completely
the exhausted music.

Sex

The white dove in your house perches on my finger
when you touch her breast. The sounds she makes!
—now babies nursing, now women coming.

In your garden the floodlight you hold strokes
rows of feathery carrots; dahlias fill up
their cages, tomatoes sprout through upright tubes,
the fluted shoots of your peppers. Corn rows
your son planted poke up soil in a grassy mulch.

The stars are cold and shivery as we touch.
O, put your palm on my shimmering backbone
in its silky trough. It wants you to.

Alone

It is late at night.
I am drinking hot milk.
I dip my fingers in it
    and suck them:
Breasts giving a sweet, thin
    milk to you.

My hand is on you, under your hand.
Your hand is on me, under my hand.
Close, you say
and I hear you.
Close, I answer
and you hear me.
Later where we come together
tips and fills.

How the moon dilates and swells,
   love,
How generously she spills her light
through my window!

On the sill, willow branches
   tap and still, tap

I cup my palm to my face:
You there, with me.

How hungry I am, suddenly
   love,
How quickly I have forgotten
these words.

Late March

Where you have come before me in the field
between the cedar windbreak and the sky
stands straight, now swaying, a poleridge pine,

its needles stiff with wind-bristle and cardinals
that on the ground tuck into each other's beaks
plump seeds, some evidence of spring and snow-melt;
it meets the horizon at the level where you flex

your beautiful, wide knees to crouch and examine
the minute particulars of stem and needle-leaf.
You, whose voice rouses deeply the wind

to swinging, to fingering lips, cheeks, the curve
of head rounding to its airy palm,

touching and retouching your pale hair,
thick-blowing in sun and moving with wind breath

I take you in,
hold you,
breathe and exhale you.

Look

anywhere. Someone more
beautiful follows with eyes
the color of caramel, the color
of denim, cornflower, topsoil,
overtone of carmine, new leaf,
hair the color of bittersweet,
patent leather. Over your shoulder
should you choose to look
she lolls on the grass
sunning, her tongue on *loose*
her eyes closed, no wrinkles
shouting *age age* at the corners.
Bow to her. Whisper, "nice day"
whisper, "my own brown tree"
say "love me, love me,"
and see how her shoulder dips
to you, all the sudden
hollows filling with silver
wide eye flicking open
then shutting askew
on one color, your color:
a sliver of bone
a sluice of water, running.

Piecing the Universe Together with Dresses

"Do you have many dresses?"
"Yes," I say remembering
the red dress, the green dress,
the marrow-colored jersey tight
across the breast with your names
on the collar. You are coming.

Under flannel my thighs cross.
Under silk my biceps rev up
for moving. If I were smart
I'd begin to sew a shroud,
an oatmeal woolen robe,
a linen wrap for after the bath. Batches of birds
distract me from this.

Somewhere in a square state
workers are starting a building
of rooms with cavernous closets.
Sometime soon, we may go there.
We will undress. We will fill
those closets with dresses.
In the mild air, birds will be singing.
We will bathe in a fountain.
We will lie down together forever
the electric coils of our arms
randomly touching. With the sparks
we will light rooms.

Friend in a Distant City

Touch me.
The flesh is absurd
its veils and encumbrances.
The thin membrane
the cat's eye shelters-in
is perfect, while we,
with tears in our eyes from twigs,
want only to be petted,
our eyes closed with kisses
only the soul knows how to give.
They brush from the corners
those tatters of longing
with no color we name
pearly or *blush*.
We are imperfect,
ridiculous.

So on a morning
I woke to light fingering
plush curtains, felt
the floor touch
the warm sole of my left foot
now my right as I pushed
into action under a pale lawn
nightgown. Where you were,
in another city, you got up
naked, the same light streaming
over your dark shoulders, oiling
them into muscles the soul delights
in touching on its daily round
through the body. Oh Soul.
Come forward.

Advice

Let's not begin with the body.
Let's put it in a chair, there,
ready to process its clickings
and boomings, dogwood or *My Sin*,
its cheekbones under fingers,
pizza or caviar at all-night places
whose lots are every color marked
in puddles. It will leave us alone.

Let's proceed, instead, through the veil
to a place without color, whose pearly
knots have meaning *sans* referent,
borrowing it only later, and in a way
we don't need to market or do anything
about, without consequence or spinning.

I Can't. Yes, You Can.

Listen to the rain
draping her sheet corners
over the roof edge, tucking
into the least cracks of the house
not only tight damp but overflow,
a plethora of water
to drown, no, to float
what? dust into the mud collars
around the new hydrangea,
the coleus, the hosta
in their raised beds of railroad ties.

The cat? The cat twists her head
as you do, hearing in rain
more than breath, less
than the torrential music of the tropics
where you lay once in a bunk
tucked under his bunk, listening
to the houses sway and sigh
in their hammock of banyan.

Deep night again. Awake.
All the children gone.
The loud thunder muttering
under her lightning cloak,
tightening her collar,
Where are they, where *are* they?

In their marble perimeters
the mothers lie still. Water
silkens their earth. In their cradles
of bone they sleep, their silence
the ground for thunder, deep rumble
of voices they no longer hear.

Under her hill of belly
some woman flexes her toes,
shifts her weight to straighten her spine,
hears her breath: in, out, stop,
then sinks into the opening of her body,
thunder, the crack of lightning
beginning to show hair, an oval of hair.

Where am I? Dark and thunder
lightning and rain. The cat.
I breathe so deeply only I can hear.
The children's doors stand open.
Their rooms are bare.

The sheet of rain
covers my house,
tucks into corners
a film of skin, a patch.
I stay inside and watch for morning.

C3

On the human brain: It didn't really evolve for the purpose of trying to under-
stand the space-time continuum or look at things in a hundred thousand
dimensions. It was there to keep you out of the rain and help you figure out
where the berries are.

—The mathematician, Ronald Graham, on the human brain as quoted in the NYTBR

The galaxy discovered
tonight on the news
is a fitting celebration of a promotion
from what I've been doing to what I'm doing.
So this galaxy is touted as new,
a recent birth twelve million years ago.
We buy it.
One galaxy with star cluster to pin on our pocket.

Vanity and personal affection: pin point
clusters to distinguish us from the idiot
girl on the corner, handing over bunches
of paper flowers to the man in charge.
Folks left her there on the curb
holding tight to what seems fashionable now,
blooms on wire stems, slightly drooping
in fresh water fog, hardly snow.
Not pathetic.

Tonight on the telephone you called to check politics.
Cool and polite, you indicated just what you wanted
in code and I, being quick (which justifies my promotion),
picked it up and spoke back. Berries and rain.
Shelter. You heard me, all right.

Tonight I speak as a man who works wood with his hands,
yes, a woodcutter gathering raw materials for fire.
Or a man in the rain with sharp tools,
steel he mounts in a frame of teak.
He planes rough places to straight.
I work with my arms until they ache, my hands hurt,
the spoiled places under my nails blacken with fester,
berries of pus that spurt out the splinters
if I'm patient. I'm patient.

God came to me as a child. I was a child and spread myself
a film of rain to give birth on. Long ago the earth spoke flesh,
I heard, deciphered berries and shelter, and Oh God, I lay back
and then I gave birth.

Dotted swiss curtains move in sun,
breathe in and out wind I bathe my face in,
bathe my face in a still room, the warm air
unmoving until the furnace coughs on. A sough, a sigh.
Be still. Hear cicadas begin their wire song,
that heat in the air. Now see the cicatrix under leaf fall.
Overhead trees whisper their code. If I'm patient I hear
birds moving in code they care nothing about.
Be still. Speak nothing but silence.

Prospectus

Time to order
the disorder:
task:
an electrifying novel
in which the hero
is seen to have lived
fully clothed in lies,
to have loved
in solitary
and so is penalized.

A non-fiction account
of the trial in which
his old partner
takes to task
his rival for doing
what he did, but slower.

A couple of couples
drink sweet drinks
all summer, growing
thinner and tanned;
the world pivots
on the jut of their hip bones.

Told from the vantage
of the hip bones,
it might catch fire
and generate money.

The cheekbones of the lovers
rub in a most convincing way.
On film, their oiled skin,

the sheen, can stand for another
more explicit encounter.

Or a book of poems
whose sexual and political power
rivets each to the roiling teak deck.

A bestial encounter
in violets
behind the house,
the thread narrative.

The only immutable:
a surgeon's knife
opening swiftly
the chest of a son.
His heart leaps
into focus
at the very moment
the brother's brain
meets the bullet.
Blood in tubes
and basins.

Clear mask
as the small head
rises, falls
back into the hands
of strangers.
The audience is riven.

From terror
comes action.

In the garden
easy flowers,
the marigold and daisy,
flourish in the season
of tomato blight.

What is the reason?
History is a nightmare
from which we can
never awaken. Source:
another better novel.

To kneel and rock
in autumn
on cliffs
over the bay—
the *auteur* wants to be lowered
to the water on ropes,
wants to be learned and just,
unlike the others,

and swims away.

Life Outside the Self: The Uncertainty Principle

In air, scratched portholes
canted to the stiff balloon sides
on which drops flatten in patterns,
air holding water close in thin film
without color:
only a sort of proof
that the closer you are to data
the less they show anything.

I'm told all this is the consequence
of looking, and the very ground and field
of modern physics, a subject
that used to kill off its practitioners
if they, turned forty, hadn't detached
one brilliant fragment from the whole mosaic.

The Times says, now (a more modern age)
they work in concert, just another team,
each one a plonk in the music of the tin bucket
at a corner of the exploding sunflower field,
slowly filling with soft water as of now
an unspecified composition
without a frame (though closely studied here),
and every kind of color.

The Bone Dish

(1989)

—for John Franklin, Sarah, and Dale

That's Something

In Springfield, Nebraska
on the central flyway
in March, the geese
at sunset make such a ruckus
as you can hear for miles
either side of Highway 14
west or north on the gravel
marker roads, in the marshy
lowlands; you can park
and watch wave on wave
funnel and circle down
and down, peel off
from the main torrents
to land by what looks like
accident of blowing air
on farm pond or lake,
hog wallow, or bathtub,
or corn stubble or milo field—
to sleep.

All this, mind you,
against a black dish
of fiery sky that erases
detail and depth and leaves
these cutouts in the air,
scarcely geese at all
except where the final light
flashes pure white on their bellies
almost, not quite yet,
touching the water.

Sarah's Wing

On the teak table,
bare except for a spring primrose
brought home from the grocery,
is a wing. I've never seen it before.
It's copper-enamelled,
called cloisonné, turquoise and jet,
lapis lazuli, coral: the colors, she calls
from the kitchen, of Egypt; and it's etched
on the reverse, where the feather spines
would lie, if they were real, flat
against the frail skin. The wing.
The wing she made so small
I can hold it in my palm,
a perfect pretender:
her amulet.

She is my wing.

April Teaching, Outstate Nebraska

A week in Gere, seven hours down the interstate in fog.
Then double snow days—no school, who would believe it.
Women's coffee at the house of the Supt. (he's gone).
His wife is fiery but banked; his children are blond.
What he is there's a word for, but I don't know it.
When I leave, he hands me a check, strokes my throat,
asks near my ear if his handsome face isn't enough payment.

All week, all night I am restless under an electric blanket.
The snow melts by my window. The grandfather clock,

made by an uncle, chimes against the bed wall
where my head is, telling each hour, each half,
the divisions a loud ruler measuring
something I'd rather not note

not here, not now as the snow thaws
shiny in the street gutters, pouring above leaf rot
silver runnels into low places that jar
my car as I skid away from the new school for little kids
to the high school where what waits
is hardly friendly, that old spring enemy
stirring everywhere in them, in me, in the deep running
recesses of these heavy bodies we wear
and hesitantly touch to the sunlight again.

At the end of the hour, incoming seniors grunt and rush
to throw open the windows, they say the room stinks
like a gym where we've been working out;
they teeter on the frames, lean and breathe in the air.

Diction

"God is in the details,"
I tell the kids
in the public school
at Milligan, Nebraska.
They wonder what I mean.
I tell them to look
out the window
at the spring fields
the mud coming up
just to the knee

of the small pig
in the far pasture.
They tell me
it's not a knee
but a hock
and I hadn't ought
to say things I know
nothing about. I say
the light on the mud
is pure chalcedony.
They say the mud
killed two cows
over the weekend.
I tell them the pig
is alive and the spring
trees are standing in a green haze.
They tell me school is out
in a week and they have to plant.
The grain elevator at the end
of Main Street stretches out
her blue arms. The kids say chutes.

Native

—for Paul Olson

You tell about the soldier,
"who gave button polish to a savage
who knew little about cures
for his sick infant.
And the child died," you report
in the tone of the scout

writing down in his book
the events of the day.

Someone gave you the book.
It is old and the scout
according to the ways of the world
has stopped writing.
He is cleansed of the world
and floats near the child
on the crest of the air.

Only the painted father is left
stalking the grasslands
watching our footfalls
sharpening his weapons
on the stones of our fields.

Words

Deft and *dexterous*, its sister,
are some so defined.
Meanwhile the air glisters,
no, that is water in the distance,
a warm bowl beckoning.

We are alive, hurrah,
unlike some precious others
and others, still anonymous,
whose life's work is done.
How to enjoy the moment, then,
the salve of breath unnoticed
and grief, waving its handkerchief
from behind a holly bush?

Or the ones gone
whose warm skin
nightly becomes
an embrace so habitual
as to be painful? We push them away,
those we most want:

orphans, women stranded at the front,
figures holding aloft other figures,
alive, human, in ruins, rubble
of human waste at their feet.

We grieve so quietly
how can we live properly?

Birthday

You made a small gray dish of clay,
glazed it something purplish
and filled it, years later,
with minute bones, perfectly intact
you delivered with your scalpel thumbnail
from an owl pellet: scapula, mandible,
four perfect teeth the size of seeds,
and pieces of a backbone ladder,
all pure matte white, "from a mouse,"
you said, pushing up your glasses.
We sat looking, forehead to forehead.
The air was steamy. The shaggy residue
went, swept to the floor by an elbow,

but the rest is here where I sit by the window
on my birthday, looking out, missing you
daughter, preserver, maker, eyes.
I stroke the bone dish and write this down.

November Night Driving

You can't find the brights
so when the deer flush from the ditch
we catch only the fists of their tails
as they turn, swerve away
from the front end where I sit stunned
twenty feet from their hard haunches.

All day I have been following
snow geese so high in masses
against flat sky
only pattern can be
the eye's subject.
Tonight the thud and rush of deer
pulled onto pavement
by legs so thin they are poles
pushing boats
through dark waters.

Now I see them
particular, clear,
a near miss, buff and flesh.

Town/ County

Beyond the city is the prairie.
Breathers there have found their places
in the tall, common grasses
on the land, intact in webby roots.

What crises of decisions come
in the empty air of the city,
don't matter. Meadowlarks and finches
hurl their voices across the ditches
in the silence of the summer wind
and speeding by, we hear them.

Or the wind wraps itself around our houses.
Some people complain of the leaves' noises,
their voices, but we notice little,
only our animals sitting in the windows
asking to come in, asking to be let out:
they hear the wind.

Or so I speculate over a cup of mango tea
brought, God knows how, from the tropics.
The brown kettle steams on a Japanese stove.
Padouk coasters protect the teak surfaces.
A Siamese cat sits on our knees
and outside, the prairie stiffens for winter.

Bear

The bear inside lies down.
The fire gutters.
Winter comes on
fields deer browse in,
hunters' guns a hollow muffle
we hear from ditches we scour
for grasses, dead husks
without seeds to transport.
Geese overhead, wing tips silver
against blue flats, steel sun
glittering off icy branches, a ricochet
of splitting color lancing lids.
Eye pupils contract, black pinpoints without choice
light will enter, will enter.

The Sandhills, Early Winter

The girl in the back row sits perfectly still,
doesn't answer my unspoken question
about her pajama top, why she wears it
as a blouse today in school, fifth period
when I teach her class, or why her eye
is bruised shut, her glasses broken
in the same lens, her skin cut.

Or why her paper is tattooed with hearts
and arrows, broken in places under the ink,
for yesterday's lesson,
but today's is blank and she's slumped

when I bend over her to brush the page
with my palm and ask questions
the other kids hear, about sounds and smells,
the texture of wind on gravel, on hard ice.

But as I move on, she bends to write
what I'd rather not read
in my gym corner office behind the stage
and later I wave in the face of the principal.
I read her lines out loud and when I'm finished,
he says a sentence coupling nouns and verbs
in a way I've never heard before
and ends by saying, "No,
No, we've tried, we can't do anything."

That night I buy her a bus ticket
out of there, drive fifty miles to the Greyhound
station and click her seatbelt shut before the motor starts

and again, a plane ticket for where it's warm
and the close sun heals
and take her home to my daughter's room

I drive to her trailer house in the country and when
her uncles and father come to the door,
her brothers behind them, I smile and say
I'm the visiting teacher and we've got a problem

and on Friday, as always, I'm out of there.

Conversation

My daughter calls long distance
about a Binturong, to say
it smells like popcorn; imagine
(she went on Sunday to the zoo)
this animal! And she wants
a pomegranate and some kiwi fruit
(the last were rotten) and that sausage,
and the Loeb Library's *Natural History*
(Pliny) in twelve small volumes
for her Wednesday birthday,
through the mail; and did I know
women's hands were small once
smaller than ours, and men short
but twice as wide as her father is?

She's looking for an overcoat to wear
and gloves for her wall—old ones—
and her heat bill was a hundred dollars,
is that too much? She waits. I wait too.
The phone weather blows the bars,
this freezing distance, farther apart.

Photograph of a Child Sleeping

> God is Good. It is a Beautiful Night.
> —Wallace Stevens

Blond head,
my lips lowered to brush it.

Brown bird,
your notes rise
and fall in the world
washed now by a skim of snow.
Sing sound in patterns
without meaning
so I hear.

We open the earth with spades
and enter it with our bodies,
or bulbs of tulip and crocus
that decay with years
or daffodils that bloom longer,

or amber, washed onto shores
with beetles preserved forever

not alive, not breathing, but intact,
surrounded, green and iridescent.

Where is sound rising
to meet spray,
sap hardened to a fist
only flame changes?
Where in the snow-scrim
is the bird you promised?

Bend close, fair head
to my milky breast
where you are nourished.

What Happens

In Alma, Nebraska, at midnight
into a spring storm the young doctor
goes out. He says he is going
to deliver the widow's baby.
I am sitting in the parlor
with my new friend, our landlady,
who is painting my nails
what she calls *a good color*.
She paints her own and tells
the story of the widow.
Outside the window the rosy snow
comes down on the crocus.

My Daughter Home from College
Tells Me about the Gods

Ra, whose chariot they ride
over us by day
under by night, is
in the Unworld. They are Pharaohs
or their indispensable retainers
named in advance on the tomb walls

thus guaranteed a place
in the sun boat.

She kneads dough
while she talks
then rolls and folds
the long loaves.

Horus, who is both one
God and another . . .

The bread rises under a linen cloth.

She says human longing for mystery
leads to a commonality of belief
in immortality;

and who is to know, she asks,
patting the loaves onto a cornmeal tray,
whether the unburned woman
isn't really impervious to fire.
Isn't it belief in the fire that makes us burn?

Ambition

suits up in ruffles,
doubles at the waist;
one foot circles behind
in a fluent gesture; dips
the chin down and smiles
at the camera, eyes fringed.

God makes the mails
through which come invitations,
letters of introduction,
peach parchment with messages,
come over, sit right down,
check here, seal up,
send out, pass through
the brass gates to heaven.

Oh how we want to believe
in the power of stars
in deepest night; even seasons
of familiar breezes, flora—
the pesky varieties of insecta
in the copper screens of the back porch.

So we remember in print
long afternoons on cretonne chaises,
reading aloud to cousins from one volume
after another familiar adventures: mice
in ceramic suits, darning-flies flickering
in deep recesses of the Chippendale
wardrobe that lets on alleys, paved
with golden cobblestones that buy . . .

whatever it is ambition wants, that deceiver,
leaking scents at the public occasions
where we star, standing straight
as a parent dictates, looking ahead
into lights, eyes watering for the sake
of all our adventures, all our brain-cells
strutting together, telling old news.

September: Getting Married Again

In the night of the long day
On which we have driven five hours
To find your father,
Who has prodded and measured us,
And we, afraid,
Have said *this one* to the gold bar

In miniature, for the rings,
And he has promised to make them;
At midnight, on that night,
Cold and afraid, wakeful,
I come to the kitchen.

In the midst of a welter of china
My children have dirtied in the course
Of their bodies' nurture—
In my absence, yellows and reds
Crusting the sides of dishes—
Is the cardboard box
Your mother has filled
For our pleasure:

A butternut squash in the shape
Of our body; onions
So rich a purple they are royal;
Their papery brothers;
The orbs of fall tomatoes,
Scarlet, rimmed with gold
And capped by a green star;

And dull green apples
Round beyond compass measure,
Pure white at their center,
A perfect fullness of flesh
That taken hold of and opened,
Will make our eyes water.

My Dream, Your Dream

In half-light salt
crusted in my eye
corners but I haven't
been weeping, only
traveling in a country
where you come careening
around a corner on your bicycle, wind a wall
you've smashed into,
far side of your face
gone flat on the bone.
I reach to wake you up
to me but you say *no*
and turn into a half-light
of your own, hair a crest
on the pillow and you're
heading into blue rain
rising fast over the windy
crescent of some western hill.

Inside the Geese

an alarm clock is ticking.
I can hear it so I stop my car
by their muddy field.

They are resting, now listening
to the noise my car makes, its engine idling.
They are poised on their mainspring,
wings ready to spin out with tension.
They don't care where I'm going.
But now, the waves they are
begin to rise slowly
line on line rushing to air
moving as if they are air
that cools the ticking metal of my car.
They rise, I press my foot
into the accelerator to drive
down this road to a new school,
watching in my mirror
the geese settle into sky.
My time is up. They take
themselves from the heavy earth
I move across,
heart ticking again and again and again.

Divine Honors

(1997)

May I see what I have tried not to see.
—Cynthia MacDonald

. . . divine honours will be paid to shallow depressions in
the ground, domestic pets, ruined windmills, or malignant
tumours.
—W. H. Auden

Prologue

Repair

In my house, men tear out the floor:
hammering, then wood splits—
hour on hour. You almost need
safety glasses for this work, the blond says
and truly, as I go for the phone,
the kitchen is now rubble. Delight
a paste bubble in my throat. If anger is tangible
here it is, a danger to these men
who let fly plaster, the smell of something old
letting go. They unmake what I made
with my life, or where I made it.

Narrative without People

The soaked books lip open in piles.
The shelves stoop, slough paint.
The doors, their locks sprung, hinge air
open to weather, gulp rain.
Something here enters the trees.

If we believe in ghosts, white pearl
shadows the batten and boards. Rust
runs on the shelves. The sounds on air
wail, a nail in the thumb. Stickers
underfoot poke holes.

In rafters, wings or the suggestion of wings
rend air, whoosh of rubbish, burnt rubber

hooks for skeleton elbows. Ash,
dry sift through moist fingers
in a room where everything's mold.

Let's consider the consequences

only,
the damage,
the number of bricks cracked
in the passageway, doors swollen
by water-rot, frames to pare down,
mildew to scour, how much
to seal up, or seal out.
       Let's count, yes, quantify
so we can sort the pile of damp clothing, the
discarded underwear with stains, the breakfast napkins
to hang out, hang on line the number of bodily fluids, mixed,
the shrinking lengths of divisions, weights of bias . . .

Now you have a notebook, pages filled with digits, the sweet
wise voice of the wire turning, connecting, recommending measure,
   a count,
the quantifying of the salt and the sugar,
        "Well, now
you have the damage report, the bottom line, the sum.
Consider the lilies of the field, how they sway in wind
without reference to your pages, how little they care
for laughter or the dour voice, the smile tucked under the chin,
the complaint, the whine, how—if nothing else—you have
your dear cornea, lungs that puff and inflate their wings, lucky

muscle of the calf, the knee, if we could cut an oval and put
the celluloid disc in place how we would see movement, the universe
shifting and settling down in its elliptical orbit, add the catch
    in the stars
breath makes."

So you are advised to burn the notebook, its pages,
the maps and wire measure of damage and move on, move along
until what happens is only a measure of forgetting, detaching
distress, your upset, your dyspepsia from the air of the orchard.
Move ahead and not refer, never refer to
anything other than the sweet taste in your mouth of breath,
the steady blood beat, the road hot and loud under your feet,
    infinite.

Isaac Stern's Performance

Here plants—gold and dry—rustle up
green at soil's edge.
Music roils in the room
where I wait, my chest holding even
at the scar's edge.

Whatever chances I took
paid off and now I have only
the rest of my life to consider.
Once it was a globe, an ocean
to cross, at least a desert—
now a rivulet, or a blowhole.

"I remember it was like a story,"
Rampal said on the radio.
"He told you the Beethoven concerto."
I am telling you cancer.

I am telling you like moisture
at soil's edge after winter, or
the bulb of the amaryllis you brought,
raising stem after stem from cork dirt,
one hybrid flower after another unfurling
for hours, each copper petal opening its throat so
slowly, each shudder of tone—mahogany, coral, blood—
an ache, orgasm, agony, life.

I

I Hear the Name of the Moon and Am Afraid

Squeals, groans, chirps and whistles like red birds
pinched in the crotches of yews
and their pollen song, beaks.

Or window on rain, fire
thorn tossed down by the instrument of his hand
aloft, thumb letting go of the nape,
apex a great height, noise like a body breaking
on ground.

Hiss, splatter pattern of wave,
wire at the nadir holding the blood fan closed,
blood fan open as red as a cardinal, an orange,
the moon with her blushing face, liquid earphone
static through hot bindings where I toss and listen
to the breakup, earth forcing flesh into new shapes
whir and chitter of arm rising, arm falling, this arm, her name.

Weathering/ boundaries/ what is good

Your sweet silence, your hands, skin, your mouth.
On the telephone, sleepy, the son of my body.
The sun on my body. His alarm clock ringing. His birthday.
She, matter-of-fact, cool, saying she knows, promising
to discover what she doesn't know, at the library. Daughter
of my body, Persephone and I Demeter. You with your $125 worth
of spring bulbs divided three ways, three friends, three graces.
We plant them together, warm earth in the garden where your
mother watches, who has cancer too. I make stew—you bring
veggies I cook with meat—and rice custard. You build onto our

patio garden. The patio is rich and crunchy with acorns. Cat and I stand on the driveway—warm—to find Orion. Now
you are naked and sleeping as I write. Dear God, keep us all safe. My breast is healing well. I am supple of body. My spirit what? Still at home in my body.

Cancer is one of the few internal diseases that can be cured. I am a person who has cancer
now.

You show me fronds of prairie grasses, beige/ lavender in sun in your garden—sun, sun all day—in high 70s—on your garden. On ours.

Waiting for oncologist with you, v. scared. I'm still me, same me no matter what he says. Biopsy report shocks me. You say, "So you know more than the doctor?"—you with me all afternoon, read report with me. Necrotic tissue. Adjacent cells abnormal. We go shopping, for a walk. His nurse says, "Recovery is partially dependent . . ." on my attitude. I buy an expensive purse in the shape of a pouch, what's missing in my body, that last year's thievery. She speaks about her dream of ribbons and banners, floating upward into light, and her ecstatic sense of losing individual boundaries, losing them and merging into the natural universe. I am fascinated and afraid.

To Explain

The future is what does not happen
—Colette

The euphorbia shot a pale rilled tube
toward the light, so all week
I have been grieving, pouring deep gutturals
into the stone edgings of the back garden,
down on my knees, seeming to dig the impatiens.

Nobody heard me but the shade and rain in air.
I must have seemed from a distance
doubled over a dumbbell (what you call weights)
so deeply did I hold my knees to rock
minutes at a time, then stop.

Then once on Sunday as the sky cleared for an hour
I wondered how to say
why I couldn't say
words had gone
in their ashy fans,
and only the wrap of my body
around loss, stayed.

Mu

. . . the old root giving rise to mystery was *mu*, with cognates MYSTICAL and MUTE. MYSTERY came from the Greek *muein* with the meaning of closing the lips, closing the eyes.

—Lewis Thomas

Misery a block in the head
a block I hum mmmm through, the way mother
mmmm helps me move to. Umber attaches to shadows
in hedge-ribbons. Feet mmmmmmmm, hit-sounds like murder
stitched to lips, the miles, hummm, eyes shut shuttered, cement walk
studded with dark I'm afraid mmmmmo
and now I am come alone at midnight onto the pineneedles of the park.

I am come to say goodbye in the dark but my mouth won't open.
What opens is my eye to the open edge of the metal tunnel under
the curve of the spiral slide I'm afraid to rise to. I'm standing at the
base to cry out at midnight Whose children will come down? Who
bashes into my arms so we open our mou ths to this cadence no no
no no mmm mommy up again to ride the big slide they and I falling
into the dark air. Open is the mouth of the metal tunnel.
Tomorrow, mmmmu, the knife.

Coming Down with Something

Black plaques, the windows
give back my face framed
by its noose of hair
and snow, one on one side
the glass, the other out
in the cold with bushes.

Sleep shoved away
by prickers of pain
flickers with streetlights
now off now on
as the cold limbs shiver.

What's gaunt and thin
deep in the body thickens
with phlegm—someone's
hungry some woman
with child and flies touching
at breast and forehead.

I take tea from my kitchen,
a clear mix of water and leaves,
mild, pale, the color of saffron
or urine, like blood like petals

like the robe she wears
over her gray body
impacted with jewels in gauze
smuggled past her husband,
to come here for surgery.

Maybe an aspirin would help.
Certainly, something's swollen under our eyelids.

Fish-Belly-Mound

Press in hard to hurt
nine times, twice or more
with your thumb,
the other hand on
that puffed up place.
Thumb rigid and forefinger
a rictus. Tight fist,
fingers merged. Now
peace will flood you,
an overwash from some
ocean of light.

We lay head to toe, neighbors
on tables for treatment, both ill,
both having lost too much to mention.

The side of my body, numb forever,
my clothes hid, still drifted on.
He smiled through a red beard
as our attendants strapped on electrodes.
And the while his naked foot jerked
and kicked and we talked, I pressed
and pressed and now have come home
to shadows where I flail and sink
in light these words swim through,
my fingers a net he tried to weave.

"Two Are Better Than One . . . For If They Fall, the One Will Lift Up His Fellow; But Woe to Him That Is Alone When He Falleth, For He Hath Not Another to Help Him Up."

. . . opened my chest
. . . opened my belly.
You stayed close
your food bowl empty
your feet unclean. The steppes in your head
filled with wind, static, a glow of sand and grit.
Or were you only sleeping those days
you sat by my bed, our hands touching,
the concave round of your skull
a focus mirror, your eyes radiant?

Several times when I slept
you lifted the phone and whispered:
Later, sick, I knew whom you spoke to.
God! Your handmaiden, her fruit cheek
rosy with health, not bloat.
The camellia she brought me
floated in round water its petals
germane—the only flower in that
floral room I could see, night or day,
follow with my bare shoulders, shiny,
intact above the bandage wrapped like skin
in moonlight, in midnight shadow.

In the mornings, in window sun I dozed
and woke repeatedly, myself camellia
on the skin of the hospital bed.
You never left me.
Now I call you scar.

Getting Well

> If I get well . . . I can take a walk in the snow and eat a red apple.
> —Anne Truitt, Turn

You gave me four fair hairs
from your head, locked in the pages
you left Monday morning in my mailbox,
a sign of the passion of your reading.

You would have me know how to write
an essay, commissioned, on the stuff of my life
on this model, Truitt's, or any other
we might find together, the pleasure

of our reading in concert as colleagues
hiding our camaraderie in health,
your sure recovery from the disease
I'm sure will take me off.

So I touch the binding, unsure
of what to say. Work
can keep us alive to the world?
Writing down some truth will help?

What I know today has something
to do with your hair, caught
in a book's pages. Fair
you stand up in the world

to walk. Fair, you sit down
in the sun to read, your head
bent down to eat an apple. Here,
you draw in the breath of the air
and breathe it out so we can write.

—for Sue Rosowski

For Barbara, Who Brings a Green
Stone in the Shape of a Triangle

From ocean
this porous shape
indisputably green
color I tell you
of healing, the color
I have chosen around me
like a vapor, this towel
on my shoulders, its green
drape an air over my scar,
then a shirt I pull over my head
and let fall for the green
lint-shed filaments of healing, moss
some ancestor might bind up with spit
and press onto my breast, no, the space
where my breast has been.
                    Yesterday
for the space of an hour, a woman
came here with her child, raised
up shirt, her breast was flesh.
The child pulled where her nipple
is, and touched his mouth
to her and filled himself.
She talked as he drank.
I listened to nipple,
a hiss of milk.
Miracle.

In your photos of green ocean
and boats, a line of women in green air,
their arms muscular, pulls against green water.
Their breasts are bare.
One, yours, shows a faint scar
my skin wears.

                        In the past year
I have given up four of the five organs
the body holds to call itself woman.
                                    Green
healer, today my body carries
in its clever hand the triangle
sea gave up to you
and you gave me.
                        I press it to my chest,
empty of nipple, of milk, of nurture,
and feel you there: friend, lover
of women, teacher. You speak to me
each green vowel of the life language.

Day-Old Bargain

Bargain tarts, raspberry, goose
he said, don't write about that
surgery, women who have hacked off write
all parts and natures of women
who lose food in the bottom parts
of refrigerators, onions, scallions,
sour tomatoes, tiny cocktail weenies
lost in the airless dark write
When you give over your breast
to cancer, for God's sake don't
write about it.

Write about silliness, holding hands
in sandboxes, small girls playing fudge-
and-find-me-alley-tag at dusk, Rochester,
state of pubescent, New Yorka roonie.

. . . day I leaned to drive aimed car
at horizon and floored it. Got there.
God in color, no cable, firsthand.
Going and coming back I thought I'd live.

Not much for visions, still at sink soaking
pinkies in sweetalmond suds, I heard Mom.
Come on home, she said. Scared the witless bejeebies
out of me. Next day I opted for surgery.
Cut that mana off and saved my life.
Big daddy surgeon said right on the mark, sweet honey.
It was done.

He's got a girlfriend works at his office, don't you know
she thinks he's licorice stick swinger. I caught them
hugging in the mimeo room. Ain't nothing to it, he said,
rolling his cup of a palm over the scar. Mmmmmm-mmmmm,
this hillock is a sweet raisin, roll over baby, pour me out.
Okeydokey.

What came next in the woods, wooly dark trees
don't give a fudge if what's hugging them hard
dents in two places. I hang on for dear life.
Filled pockets with seedpods, got bulbs
I shoehorned into clay pots for life's sake.
Nevertheless the disc shone hard, or didn't.

Breast/ fever

My new breast is two months old,
gel used in bicycle saddles
for riders on long-distance runs,
stays cold under my skin
when the old breast is warm;
catalogue price, $276. My serial number,
#B-1754, means some sisters under the skin.
My new breast
my new breast is sterile,
will never have cancer.

Once every sixty years
according to the Chinese calendar
comes the year of the golden horse.
Over me your skin is warm,
sweetgel, ribbontongue, goldhorse.
You suck the blank to goosebumps.

HowmIgonnaget there when you're gone
back to your youngthing, sweetcurl?
He moans over your back
twitching your buttons raw. My scar
means nothing to him, a mapletwirl
a whirligig, your center and maypole.

Death waits in the book, the woods,
the TV, the helicopter blades merging
over the house, your hair a fine curl
mist over your haunches, smooth hook near.
You'll curl red over him when I'm under
the ash, gone, all mind or nothing.
Who the hell loves a tree?

Don't tell me on the phone your voice
a fine ringing replica of mine that you've
got sickies, fever, ticks from the job
you won't worry about don't I either
you nut, you bitch dog mother I bred you
out of leaves and mash my blood on the floor
my liver colored placenta curled in a cold bowl.
Who do you think you are with my sick breasts
on your chest. Oh God let me live to touch her
working out the next generation of women.

An art that heals and protects its subject is a geography of scars.
—Wendell Berry

Sarah's Response

Research is what she promises to do for me,
right now, immediately, she knows whom to call,
where to go, or she'll find out, I'm not to worry,
what there is to know we'll know. And soon?
I beg, far worse than any child terrified
of disappearing, held down only by the thread,
her voice, pulled through the wire at 20,000 megawinds.

She calls when she finds out the bad news and the good
to promise a package: tradition mandates gifts
to make it better. A kiss is what I want, her hand
in mine. But this is what she sends: a box.

The huge carton is heavy, cardboard walls they
let me batter until I get to what's inside
intact within a web of tape and swaying,
entire six foot stalk of brusselsprout,
a hundred knobs or more, each perfect head
enfolded pattern. I know her message instantly.

In the world that gave us life, or takes it from me,
beauty so precise and orderly if seen by microscope,
or cell biopsy, or tissue through the light
is what divided cell from cell and made her mine,
and him and her, and you, dear reader, whose gel-filled eye
reads out this message written two years later by my pulsing hand
to honor her, harmonious daughter far away
whose play is radiance. Let her live.

Sarah among Animals

—Priam's Green Birdwing

Night. The elephant in his pen
waits patiently for Sarah.
His vast ears inflate like sails
as his head, the size of a ship,
veers toward her compound.
His great foot lifts.

Among her butterflies,
a golden handkerchief bordered
with jet draped on her fist,
Sarah listens. She wants to go.
In her veins the thin blood flows.
Were she able to enter the field of light
her arms would flood with veins, and lift.
She lifts her shoulders, shrugs off his charge.
Night. The arc sails on.

Sarah's Head/ 16 March, Four Months after Surgery

First the jaw goes, teeth and all
hinges, intricate slivers of bone.
Then silence. Then the brain pan
opens its lid, falls over
with the velocity of a hard-pitch
baseball, spit everywhere. Then nose
in comic relief pops off, a sound
like old bubblegum. What's left?
Light on trees, on sidewalks. Magnolia.

Into the null that clay head cries,
huge skull forced back against
scream's lift, pulled from the void
by Sarah's hands. It rests between glass shelves
on a bronze collar, jagged edges cut to hide
the scar from neck wrenched
out of gray earth: no torso, only sob
out of the gape of this head's loud mouth, and mine.

I conjure comfort with a table set with pottery bowls,
each open like my cupped hands for her newborn head,
tomatoes resting there,
chives the color of amaryllis skin before the bud
breaks open, round bread.
And soup from cabbage and potatoes,
most homely food to nourish me
and a friend, mother of daughters both.
A spring feast. All I can do.

Sarah Fledging

Soft feather heart
blue jay and thrasher
and eagle's down she has gathered,
each nail smoothing each barbed shaft
oiled so her fingers shine.

Meadowlark and finch, cardinal,
the junco, right-upside-up nuthatch,
feather skim on teak where she dips
from a bowl to chamois
against afternoon chill,

pulls her needle through
blood spots dried mahogany.

Flutter heart of feather bowl
as she shakes loose another
amber and dove wet pebble
from the patch by her elbow,
reaches, gathers each shaft for a linen loop,
and waxes and ties off.

Whirl, circle, and wave of feather
jackdaw, hawk, the golden swift
scooping mosquitoes from the backyard lathehouse,
her hands reach to steady the softening cloak—it quivers,
air from the floor vent—she turns.
And now she reaches for the lamp and rises.

Sarah's Waltz

—for Randall Snyder

Now she is gone she is dancing, here
in the kitchen, the oven cold,
bare table a platform
as she pounds her feet—one two three—
soles rosy with henna,
the old teak's oils rising to meet her
to warm her as she twirls, linseed floating her
as she bows, and dips, and bends to us,
and now she raises her arms.

Years ago I grew her
as easily
as the clay pot holds
the primrose.

In her hands as she turns, light
catches and flashes
on crystalline bells
she has fashioned,
carries and tosses,
and catches and releases
into this silence their chime.

Wherever you are, Composer,
hidden behind the arras,
woven into the wheat hanging,
icy drop swaying on its filament
fracturing the moon
as she pivots and whirls
and scatters her clamor,
please capture for us Sarah's heartbeat.
Sound it now.

Balance

Circular ear ornament inlaid with a mosaic of turquoise, mother-of-pearl, lapis lazuli, red Spondylus shell, and green stone, surrounded by a shell ring and border of gold beads.
—Chimu culture, northern coast of Peru

Postcard from your drawer, daughter,
when the need comes and I
pull on the handle to open, take,
and send away some message: come!

The last gift of earrings I gave
came from India, silver lace fobs
hung from a scrolled wire, tiny malachite tongues
at the tips: Happy birthday!

The last gift of earrings I got
came from Indonesia, silver half globes
with a golden nipple on each domed center, ear breasts
we joked, touching and touching: Live!

The lobes of my ears are fleshy and large, flushed
with health and sturdy for ornament. To pierce each
I employed the services of a surgeon, bribed
my best friend with a martini to come along.
In the waiting room she held my hand.
On the surgical table I stayed still while the nurse
measured and marked with charcoal the equidistant point
on each lobe where the needle would go in.

Tattoo the blank breast with a nipple,
alternative advice but I hold out
for an ornament. In the long silver winter
I recovered from surgery I pinned each day

to my shirt some concoction of old buttons
from her grandmother's legacy. She glued together
what I seemed to need, pin for nipple I wore, day in day out.

Now I fancy some commissioned shape of lapis lazuli
Yeats might like, or I fancy exactly in the proper shape
of a woman who nursed babies two years of her lengthening life:
some mother-of-pearl drops for milk, some blue veined marble
for the hardness of full breasts, some silky pin back, something new
and fabricated by hands, by my daughter's human hands.

Order

This time, Sarah fabricates a pin
I'll wear each day on my pocket.
Over the phone when I say why
she laughs and laughs, my far daughter
with her "humongous breasts from Hell,"
at this folly, that I in my sadness
chose to have two ornaments,
one flesh, and one she'll cut.

Two months later she comes home
to fix a tiny silver moon
with dark brass nipple on my chest.
She pins it fast to heal my loss:
a breast she made, as I made her.

Axe-earrings, abalone shell

in leaf-humus by the river, buried
at the base of the arc, a light she watched
fall, sun-fall on silver fastenings, thrown
from her earlobes, flesh
scarred, healed, for the holding
of ornaments. What I wanted. A gift.

Leaf humus smell around her, rising
like water, red from sun, red falling
from body, scarred, sealed,
healed, an ornament now.

Path over bridge, scar over mound
healing now, puckering, leaf mold
over earrings, gift snatched from lobe,
thrown, thrown an arc, light
flaring from silver hooks, thrown
away into river humus, leaf rot.

At my elbow, holding, a woman.
At my breast, that news, skin
smell of the new born, borne out
into this world of melt and fracture,
here at my side, holding, woman.

Birth

Hours taking hours
to pass, no gray
to the sky, no moon,

only a light triangle
blurring to signify
you've taken

What? Nothing.

In this dream the mushroom
picker's light shines
on a white swelling.
Everywhere is pale
or pure
darkness. She is
picking me
she is picking me out.

I choose you.
I am not blindfolded
or surprised. Palms
touching palms are buffed
pale in the mushroom light
before dawn.

Here we are rocking,
each forehead a fulcrum,
my arms crowning your head
a great weight holding us
down. Now we are crosslegged
in the scorching light.

The touching of your ribs against my thighs
has nothing to do with me.
I tell everyone here this truth.

Was there not a way of naming things that would not invent names, but mean names without naming them?
—Gertrude Stein

Opening/ Working/ Walking

If you were to go to one of these factories . . . you'd see dozens of girls
standing there pushing levers. That's how difficult it is.
—William Dorward, The New Yorker

That's how difficult it was,
snow geese dropping into their images.
And the earth, still opened, steaming,
a gash where she disappeared.
What could I do but stare down
and wail? My tatters at wrist
and throat flapped and the crackle
of wheat under my feet was all I heard
for weeks. No wonder I returned to the factory.

I am her mother!
In this city I sing—the enemy is everywhere—
walk in a ring each noon, rifle cradled under my shawls.
The others? I tell you we are mourning. They say nothing.
What they're making is silence of these off hours,
sun hot and familiar smoothing our dark veils.
Some days the dust of earth punctures,
surrenders its mud with teeth, a thigh-bone.

Now the body remembers its openings
without banners, the slogans we chant mornings
to the clank of levers, a din we carry home.
Coals, then out into market again.
We circle the pavement trailing our cloths
of silence, our lace a small singing—the enemy is everywhere.
What crowded place have we come to, women, to be grieving and armed?

Hey You

You don't have to be a farmer to love soybeans.
You don't have to be a rocket scientist to talk
on the radio. Beginning Thursday, anyone
can address mayhem in far places, assassins
with animal names, gangs of them hurting us.

Trouble is, life isn't worth more than breath
in a troubled chest, the rattle, the rictus
without cloud, a check mark of dark against sunset
but not quite night. Darling, where your freckles
meet your empty eye sockets, sparklets erupt.
Nothing language about it.

You should have heard that knock-down chicklet
rock out her grief. Honey, no mom can soothe
her sore throat: ululation and a life so wracked
a bamboo thicket looks like a Serta Sleeper.

                                        God!
Whatever mountain you've taken up,
come read us a story. We need to sleep
when our paint brushes wear down to nubs,
our reds and yellows evaporate on the pale margins
or drip past the wash.

                                We burst from your forehead
obediently primed, pumped up to meet.
Merging is what we do best after all, our boundaries
so blurred what's her worry is our worry: a good job
is what we've done, heads rolling off our shoulders
into the mass grave, our torsos blurring as they tumble.

Hey, you there. You listening?

Grieving, she hits the red fox

—for Vera Spohr Cohen

crossways. In fog. High beams
backed up. His head turned to her.
She knows his eyes flare.
He is gone under her wheels.
She could turn.

He is gone from her long before, ash,
to the floor of earth just buried,
body heavy with shadows.

The car speeds in its tunnel of light.
She could turn.
                    Spirit lover!

Not even the black mirror
draws your eyes from the gravel.

Mapping/ Bleating

I think chemistry has much to gain from reviving the personal, the emotional,
the stylistic core of the struggle to discover and create the molecular world.
—Roald Hoffmann, "Under the Surface of the Chemical Article"

The graphic depiction of molecules . . . Hoffmann argues, is so central to the
science of chemistry that its conventions and ambiguities deserve reflection.
A chemist faces the same difficulty as a landscape painter: how to represent
three-dimensional shapes in two dimensions.
—Emily Grosholz, "Roald Hoffmann's Praise of Synthetic Beauty"

My fingers, mine, my fingers
instructed as ice molecules
in trees, now on this airplane wing out the window,
to address the subject of
no, not war (planes and missiles
we pop as objects on the nightly news,
the morning news we set our short wave
scanner to)
but death, a subject
breathing
used to seem to catch up to
and expand as atoms of air, pure ether.

My fingers move at random, push
the words out on this paper. Fog
smothers the wing tip. I can't see lights.
Am dizzy.

Where are we going? You are moving radon
gas over the sensor box. He buckles the web.
She tucks the head of a newborn (thumbs
a half moon around each apricot ear) under her rib. I am
aloft, yes, tucked in. I am going to smell,
no, say right, apprehend death, its
molecules in cells cut out,
excised; only a prim removal
of some feeder flesh, her breast. Mine's
gone so I'm immune. My friend gives me this gift
of witness. Once there, I'll hold her daughter's ear. Going,
my chest is laved in apricot lotion under the linen of my shift.

What next? A band of clay braided at the lip
of the gift cup wrapped in my underwear,
milk spotted with chocolate floaters, or brandy

in steam, tea steeped until mash of pattern
predicts the final outcome: death. When we land on earth
first thing is, I'll unpack this stoneware cup, brew comfort.
Still, to be honest, down small or up here,
the light plaids, curtains golden on cotton, and I'm bleating.

Trope

Edith Wharton "did her best writing in her fifties and sixties . . . Her appetite
for life seemed to grow and sharpen as her time ran out . . . she described
herself as 'an incorrigible life-lover and life-wonderer and adventurer.'"
—*Vogue*

She hates us, our race, our hair
each day we breathe in air.
She loves the pits under our feet
and listens to my arias on each escape,
her green eyes avid, her rough laugh
pulled up from her navel. The closer we draw failure
on our paper table mats,
the faster she erases. At the moment
of catastrophe—the lumps, the rejection form,
the denied promotion, the deaths of sons—

she is at the door, her arms open,
her leather bag filled with books
and perfumes, fresh flowers. Endlessly
over bad dinners, she outlines and synthesizes
strategies, asks questions, listens to amours,
then divides the check scrupulously, right down the middle.

She keeps us close, who are not her equals,
for comfort, in case she's wronged, or sick,
and her greed for what we have
is filled with radiance and a miraculous energy.

Our triumphs she dismisses out loud as politics
—she is right, undoubtedly—but our hurts
are the real thing. She knows the tone
of the true howl, the keening, the bruise
at the throat, the last gasp, and she wants to be there
when the ambulance wails, the police beat down the door
and someone gives up all that oxygen.

Where I write, J'accuse, she adds illuminations.
She clips articles with your name in them.
And though she is brilliant and speaks well, she holds scatter
and babble close, a friendly shield. When your breast is taken
she divides her bulbs and brings you half, pushes onto her knees
and drags you down. At the oncologist's office, there she is
reading over your shoulder. On the day you die, you know
she'll go for your eyes while digging in her bag for coins for Charon.

Sow Sister

The sow sister in barnyard mud
shifts her crinolines
to one side and lifts her thigh.
Sun beats on her knuckle bones,
"Sow-sister, sow-sister, mind me."

Not that she doesn't hear
but staggers to the far grass

staggers and sleeps, her hair
drying fast, stiffening.

Sow-sister, psst, wake up!
Past patience I am boiling you
to nonsense, your hocks and breasts
bone-bold. Your oils melting.
You must thrive, burlap sadness folded
into packet-statues, your cousin beaver's pelt
stiffened with glue mercury into hats, shining.

Ah, no? Well, so I will tell you a story.
Lie down in my wild mud, slippery and warm.
Now you will hear whuffling far off in a bottle
and the heavens will open with malt. Cooked,
in your mouth you'll come to know sift
of slivered almonds in vanilla sugar, this story.

Bernini's Ribbon

—an aerial sculpture by S. Roth-Kent

Someone else's voice in this lobby,
clear but unfamiliar, "I was an executive secretary
before I went to med school,"
and again a familiar male voice saying,
"You don't get it, do you?"—the female tag
at the end of the sentence, "do you?"—
as in The Exorcist when a small girl opens
her mouth and out comes the voice
of the devil like musk, a shock.
Getting personal with someone new,

unfamily, unknown, someone to help, to help
you.
     So in the course of the day's spiral
from garble comes story: she was healing
at last, the edges of crust dissolving in warm
water, surface only one foreground of many
textures, only one shiny surface leading the eye
out and away until color takes over the job,
lifts with purples and golds and sulphur, galls
the eye up to the proscenium arch, the ceiling
higher beyond, and Bernini's Ribbon
through high air a dropped clue
to follow: voices, the maze.

Petting the Scar

—for Alicia Ostriker

You know what? I don't want a brave death,
faithful children mopping up after my body,
sweet thing, nubbly fissures and skin so soft
it's silklike. Let my daughter wail at the side
of her lover's bed, her heart in its tough covering
beating powdery as a butterfly's wing.
My son, oh no, let him turn up his torso
to the Greek sun, his heartscar sexy, raised
on his dark skin.

So what are we to do tonight, finished with passion,
roaming our rooms, our thumbs hooked
under the spines of books, notebooks by each chair,

forbidden smokes flushed and fats scoured away?
You tell me to reach under my shirt and pet the scar.

Did you hear about the lozenge of blood on the binding
of our friend's new book, who is trying hard in a far country?
I forgot to tell you. "If I can bear to touch it," she said.
"Yet," surely you'd add.

Under my robe—I must put down my pen to do it—
my palm finds chill: this is not a metaphor
but an image, true, a fact: I swear it.
No pouty lip the color of eyelids. A cold blank.

But the scar!
Riverroad, meandering root, stretched coil, wire chord, embroidery
in its hoop, mine, my body.

Oh, love!

Teaching, Hurt

Bradshaw, Nebraska, near York, forty-eight miles
the spring of the heart
loud under its breast
wild heart at its single lesson,
spring of sterile apples, trees a pyramid of white
spectacle overflowing buttermilk at twilight,
spring of buttermilk, the body's affairs,
heart broken under its absent breast the beat so loud
she fancies they can hear it thud
in a room loud with her perfume's diversion.

Spring teaching again, gone to the highway by six,
alone, fields ripening in some color
she can't name. Bradshaw, Bradshaw,
rhymes with bedsore, rhymes with bad law,
lockjaw, she can't find a place
to work without disturbing someone.
At lunch the teacher names her boys
twins, and an older. "It could be worse," she laughs
out loud, delighted, and someone whispers yes,
the first child has cancer in his brain.

Into this mess, new life:
week-old Peking ducks, and mallards, gray brown
and plain, some with green heads
you can't tell yet which is which, girl from boy;
a Hamburg chick, sole survivor of the trip from Omaha,
flat comb, wide tail feathers, an exotic;
and Partridge Cochin, feathers down to their golden feet,
colored like pheasants; twelve babies in a Wheat Chex box
small as first graders who make the circle work
holding chicks onto their newspapers. The water dish
overflows onto the floor of the lunchroom where the kids
make nests of their legs to sit watching
and she hunches over them, hungry to see
what they see, to see them.

Riddle

I'm the one who pumps all day
all night to let you live.
All I get in return is broken.

This one from Scott, grade nine,
on the day the kids say
they like me, write hard
as I roam their aisles in Crete
the spring after the year
I had cancer, two years after
my body emptied.

This from life, the body blow
the medicine ball lets swing
from the rafters in the gym
and you in the way, the thump
and thud as your blood rushes
to cover up, the kids in attendance
as the bruise begins to color.

Outside hail pummeling the car,
my minotaur thudding
against ribs bruised but holding,
the flesh cage, against his rampages.
And I drive like hell in the din.

Today I am eating again. Donuts in the lounge
soothe my throat, enter my empty belly.
Coffee. A plaque in italic on oak
a creed about acceptance. I'm trying.
In my ninth grade year, the elastic band
in my underpants stretched out—all seven pair,

each day of the week an accident. I was thin.
Who could love me again in a world so dangerous I was food?

Now, each breath a gift, the soar in air
of hawks on the highway searching for road kill:
some sure sign I'm present. This world is dangerous.
I hurt in the teachers' lounge where TV dribbles
and the choral teacher warbles his vibrato
in answer to the second grade aide, a soprano.
Their voices braid in time to cover my hiccup.

IV

A fetish is a story masquerading as an object.

—Robert J. Stolles, MD

Chigger Socks

She told how
on her wedding eve
playing badminton at dusk
with friends on the lawn,
she in shorts and high socks,
her last chance, she thought,
to be a girl, though she was thirty
and carried divorce decrees
among her important papers;
so she leapt into air after feathers
and grew shiny and damp at forehead and heel
and threw herself, finally, into alfalfa grass
by the net to rest at the horizon,
and drink wine, and wrestle with the dogs.

When her mother knocked next morning
and entered the dark room,
she was sitting on tile, feet cold
and aflame with bites, swollen to the knee
twice what you'd think skin can hold of flesh.
By noon, after basins of ice, elastic bindings,
she could stand in her mother's arms and was wed,
lace stretch stockings hiding almost all.

Waking this morning to light breathing
I remember the queen and her iron shoes
dancing her fiery feet off. You're gone.
You entered another shoe to tend another
child or two, forgetting ours, who grew head
to heel under my leather tongue and grew up
and went off. One wears your face exactly,
and I have grown old, my feet pins-and-needles now, cold.

Daylight Savings: Sandy Creek, Nebraska

Between shelves where I work in the dark
the librarian comes to visit. I'm a farmer,
he says, bankrupt. Like many others,
I say, polite, the visiting teacher. He turns pages
of the new book he has come to show me
with a hand minus a thumb.

One book about travel he likes especially.
The cover shows a high-wheeler parked by a fence.
I ride them, he says proudly.
Another book about Nazi resistance in France
shows a child with a spade. Farming, he says.

I don't know how to do this job yet, he whispers,
wondering about his book choices. What do I think?
I think he's doing fine. Books about women,
books about history, books about politics.
Nicaragua with a picture of trees on the front.

On Tuesday nights after school he's learning
EMT, Emergency Medical Training. They don't have doctors
out here. No better way to give time. He's got kids too,
he says, locking up the room for lunch. In the hall
he opens a folder with pictures: broken chests, sutures,
flailed lungs. Over spaghetti I ask if he's ever afraid.
Never, he says. I castrated bulls, dehorned them,
the blood flying, vaccinated for black leg. Some get the vet
for that but I didn't. I never did. I've seen it all.

In the afternoon I teach freshmen and juniors.
One, handsome with a neck hickey, surly and quiet,
writes well about death. In the state hospital for a month
last year, says the teacher. What can I do for him?

Outside spring raises the smell of urine from the fields.
I walk through, breathing what cures.
I watch the sun go down late. Next day at eight-thirty class break
the librarian calls out, "Sure hard to get up these dark mornings."
"Sure is," I say.

Cobb's Hill Pond

The snow at the edge
froze it was so cold
the January he was eleven,
big brother in hockey skates.
Bent over my double runners
his knuckles whitened
at the buckles of my ankle bindings.
Our steam of breath
touched the scarred bench
where I sat, indifferent,
as if the warmth of his body
could never cool down
no matter how thick the ice grew.

I'm seven-and-a-half Sunday.
Papa puts my peach snowsuit
over my head, zips up.
We're going fishing. Big freeze
makes magnolia blossoms mush
but sky's clear. I tote fly
fishing rods for Papa.
We'll go where target rings in the water
are primary colors to break the pond.
Must be the red one calls him in.

You wouldn't say why
you were humming;
you cast
feathers onto water.
Something shiny must've waited
under the pond's surface.
You hitched up your boots,
stumbled off the bank
humming
deeper and farther
until your hips in their rubber trousers
soaked cold—you were shivering.
Then you fell over,
log with only half a side showing,
and lay still.
I ran—stone without slingshot—
around and around
the flower tree
on the bank
until some snap went off
and I flew home for help:
too late, too late:
messenger, bad pebble.

I never saw them again.

Fuss

Vowels, the O of his voice
shaking comics loose from the Sunday paper
his hands on their crinkling
and later the gun in its opened sack
shaken loose, lifted
to the O of his mouth.

We walked through grass to the reservoir
high circle we moved to enter
a girl in patent leather shoes
a man in boots, that stiff uniform
swishing khaki twill.

His voice on the telephone, lift
and catalogue   the possibilities.
What he bought   What he gave to the poor
His resignations
He lay on the metal floor of the car
rich with his blood   rich with his swill
and the round wind fussed for me
Sister   it whispered.

He turned to the door
chalk   his bones whitened
and began to dry
He put the gun
into his mouth and shattered
so he and his bones left me
for good, for ash.

He turned his face to the wall   to plaster of wall
to amalgam of fire and earth   to clay. And he
and his voice left me for air,
for naught the O of his mouth.

Zen: the one I love most holds my tongue

                              done nothing to deserve this
                              am something to deserve this
sleep.
          If he is right, the world
is a broad river of emptiness,
currents of everything tangible braided
until the banks expand: dark sea
shining within, dark shine flowing.

If he is wrong, each leaf is a needle
of light my skin encloses. Folds over,
petal by petal, until the coal ignites.
Sleep. Emptiness. How to reach shore?

If he is right, I am the shore, skin
no barrier to sea, skin sea
the salt molecules twirling,
pain a current, electric swirl in a boiling
we hold. Whether we ask it or not
we are all carried off.

The one I love most carries my tongue in a pot.
Without me it says nothing to our common silence.
Is sea. Hisses out.

Camarada

Oh you with broken back,
you curled on the bedspread, the curb,
clenched with the knob
of quilt between your thighs,
you hugging your country song—
nowhere to go and no way to get there—
to your chest, that cave with its nubbins
of bat rocks, your friendship,
your camaraderie, your hollow under the house,
you deer.

Safe away from your skin, the hollows
of your rough cheeks, poked holes,
your silk hair I wrap around me,
a gift, a present for someone else
who loves you too. Presumptuous,
a stiff word your tongue bumps into,
presumptuous to suppose she'd turn to you.

Safe in my white room above the nursery,
above the garden, the smokestacks
belching their bones, safe in my history,
the home you never had. How do you get
a chair? you ask me. Dummkopf. The shadow
I am on my walls wants you too.

You open nothing. You clamp your music
onto your ears and wind dies down,
rain in its bowl of cinders, the possum
slitches its body through grass—you don't hear.
You have only the cave of your ear to escape to,
a dark place you light with music, a place
so small I can't find you, a place safe but austere.

I am your keeper, your jailer, your truant,
the villain who keeps you from coming out
to play. Our words are babel to each other,
our touch a magic wrapper. Dear loved one,
give me freedom to come and go as I will.
I'll stay home, the fireplace ashes, my fur shoe.

From Your Mouth to God's Ear

Off the cliff, into air, the mother shout
blackberry-jam thick, stirred down
into a soothing lick on the needle-pricked
thumb, from God's mouth to your ear:
Stay put! The clouds won't, that's for sure:
the rabbit, no voice and frozen on the lawn,
won't for long. And you'll have nothing to say
again, as usual. For sure.
Wasn't that old story about a man spinning
straw into gold a lie? Oh? He did it for a girl.

"We don't deserve what we get, but
we get what we deserve."

—Phil Condon

Rain pours
into the heart
of the hosta.

Each one
of fifty blooms
opens a throat to the wet,
can scent a room
each flower smaller
than your fingernail.

In the garden for herbs
basil and parsley, tarragon,
you stoop, take our scissors
to a fair chin,
bring in one blossom
leaking.

G: But it's still not all right with you?

K: But it's still not all right with me.

—AWP *Chronicle*

A blend of peppermint/ spearmint
for a sick tummy: tummy mint
a poultice for embroidery on ignorance.

Mine's a muslin bag; yours chamois for vision,
poked with herbs: feverfew, forget-me-not,
sweet nettle, powdered thistle, rue
for dreams: marriage, palm to palm, or
no distinctions, races, genders, each to each:
dear Darwin in his garden, counting earthworms.

They'll feed on us, our knowledge mingled
under a thatch of gravegrass. Dear me,
you stuff your pack as I embroider,
prick my thumb on floss flowers, pure silk,
the one substance eugenics could not touch
in its indifference. My tummy hurts.
No poem can salve me, or beach grass
in sun. I deliver you to hear
a lecture. I trick myself with tea.
We go our separate ways again. We try and try.
Yet what rhymes casts up her barbs.

Mutation Blues

Got blues so harsh they take my breath
Got blues so strong I'm on my head
with your fussing and praising and denying and saying
sweet honeybun you're the mystery of my life.

Each day I wake up praying you're gonna stay.
Each day I raise my nose up to the sunny sky
sighing God above you gave me what I wanted
Sweet God above I begged you for a chance.

My breath comes up goes down my cinnamon throat
breath clangs hard in my head and in my ears.
Sweet honey stick I gave away my heart to
what's natural is what I give to keep you here.

Close to me you watch my eyeballs swell.
Far from me you turn your head away.
I wear a rag and screwturn on my skullcap
but you never notice me at all until I'm gone.

Oh lord above please tell me what to make up out of
Oh lordy above I don't know what I know.
I'm a honeybun that's used her days for nothing
and now I'm going home I don't know where I've been.

Insomnia Again

My friend, who is nearing eighty, calls to praise me,
a recent honor, and says "Posh" and "Fah" to my worries.
"Conflict," she says, "is the source of life.
Without it we wither."

Is that what keeps us keen? Is that what keeps us up
in the night worrying? We have no stomach
for it. I don't say so but reflect, at 2 AM,
on someone in the Bible, in the fiery furnace,
lean and glistening of muscle. Did he thrash, did he hurl
himself against the hot, locked door? In these versions
of our torments, we do well to remember the finish line:
He got out. The Lord (praised be his name) sent him a friend
with an uzi. Or, the keeper loved him. In their sweat

was lubrication enough he slithered out a hole in the wall.
He was reborn, a ribbon in air.

My other friend has a friend reborn in water,
who walked into the Charles River and drowned.
She was a poet; she wrote of the flood
in the voice of Nemach, Noah's wife,
in the few years of her recent life.
My friend is sad and thinks of leaving teaching.
I'm drinking Ovaltine, myself, in deepening night.
My children's father's mother recommended it
for tension before a truck ground her into earth,
and lactic acid, I've read, is kind to endorphins.
We will be calmed.

Now, so early in the morning custom turns our heads
to the window, we see birds, juncos framed by
clay pots filled with fern and air-climbing hydrangea.

Baskets of tuberous begonias with flushed double cheeks
and single heads. Fuzz of the soft kind, baby leaves.
Fire, water, earth, air: they're what we've got.
The world will rock us. We all go off to bed.

Service

I

Do they hate each other, I wonder,
she who will live on and he who is dying?
I fill their bird feeder with safflower.
Each dip of the orange pitcher scatters seed from its lip
to the earth, in ecstasy. An arc.
A small rain falls down. Bruised light
a nacre over everything.
My breast hurts, shoulder hurts—hurt body—
as I lift my arm to pour, in ecstasy. Alive!
Ready soon to paint their high door.

II

Perhaps I'm ready to paint the high door.
The phone shrills, 4 AM, and I wake
from cicada's trill to cicadas: nothing more.
Far thunder. The rustle the cat makes
reshaping her nest on the floor.
A far train moving cargo.
From the front room, light over the door
where he works all night. Under a microscope once
I watched hooks gouged in paper
by the pen's point, moving,
ink filling in after. A rasp.
And it's morning. Rain.

III

Car/ scars

The car with its pocks and scrapes
offends when God knows what's under his trouser band.
Do they mind skin's markings when what's under works on?
I'm having the door painted.

IV

The water fit to drink? he asks.
I put up the canning kettle to boil.
She goes to the grocery for distilled water,
maybe listens to the radio *en route*. Floods.
Thirst, that blessing. I drink and drink from the faucet.
What's under the skin works on in spite of pocks, cut.

V

En route to the barn, their horses hang their heads over thistles,
for sugar. Girth: barrel-bodies, vats hops-colored, caramel, the
safflower bare-skin scars no trouble to hide.
Are their mouths the width of my hips? Breast? Is their water fit to
drink? They mean no harm to the world, you say.
Their muzzles are cut-velvet. Apples.

VI

Fury/ night again

Velvet muzzles. They mean no harm
who fit you out. Rain needs the stage now,
chestnuts broadcasting their available stink.
Tuck in your chin, here, sheepskin cup and your tongue cut
on metal, your tongue on sheepskin . . . you'll do no harm
to the world. Thirst. No water, fit or no.

VII

Overheard.

Under her skin, poison, but she died well
three years after the doctor said. "I've stopped wondering,"
she said at last, tucking her chin under her tea cup.
No nickering. No sugar, no thistles, no apples, no sass,
a pin through her neck. At the fence every day
you'd never have known her, ribs broken from retching.

Once she was fed earth's bounty.
I'm ready now to paint your high door.

VIII

My nightshift covers earth's bounty
erased. A shroud would be worse.
No fit water to drink. Blessed thirst.
He writes all night, drags pen
over paper. Light a nacre over everything.
Night. Thistles. Apples. In my palm
velvet muzzle, water. In my breast, a cut mouth.
In my mouth, tongue's cup. High door freshly painted, my arm
lifting in ecstasy, seed pitcher an arc flung high over rain's
ring on the horizon, broken.

V

Hot

That knuckle of bone
under the cat's paw
flies in the sky.

We breathe what sears.
Salt from our faces
cures battered leather.
We drink.

Under the sky's udder
loam fields crack and dry.
We suck tomatoes
grazing the vines
for fluid.

Insects thrive
in laundry bushes
we throw our indigo cloth on
beaten of its smell
to tint the river.
Welts rise.

What's behind the dome of sky
leans down, pushing blue to us
whether we want it or not.
Air inhales cotton's water.

Cracked shoulders
raise our arms like swimmers
to shake lengths of crumpled yardage
over our bodies.
We fall to the fields
that open and close.

Dying

Someone is dying; someone wants to die,
standing by a braid of onions,
purple, dry streamer, string. They pour tea.

Someone's body is crowding,
someone else's is hollow.
Now both bend over teacups.
The window at their shoulders shows
grapes, an arbor, and Look!
All heads rise, bright eyes, the leaves tremble.

Terror: A Riddle

—after Walt Whitman

Like air you seep into my body cavities
and take up residence, open charge accounts,
root, stalk, and flower a perfume of rush
and drum, violet as sunset, a bruise
over stitches. I walk, you walk.
Then I run—if I'm lucky.
Unlucky I lie in bed or worse,
too weak to rub the ice itch. God!

Want nothing, says her voice so I do.
Then you go away. You're through.

Nuts

to success. The third day lucky
on the job and nothing's changed: I work all day,
I worked all day. Nuts to beauty.
Bikini, music, then the childbed. Inside out
through the door of a birdcage: Margaret Atwood.
Now in the mirror, a sea turtle with goiter.

Nuts to the mirror.
Forty below windchill, she rides her bike
to work, is hit by a truck. Who's freezing
on the radiator is bound to freeze.
Nuts to visitors. They slip on ice like thunder,
clap closed their wimples, rise, then sue.

What's nibbling your liver, kid?
Birdsong. Nuts to praise,
the poet's contract, nuts to quicksilver
in glass, nuts to the fever it measures,
the belly's gripe, nuts to love that only
smells like a vine, to bougainvillea on the tongue,
to ice cream, to blood warm on the palm, nuts
to surgery, the pain it stops, the pain it is.

Lincoln, Nebraska

Here
gray sky and birch trees
an aerie's view
where I work to find
that safe place
safe from silence
from cancer, from isolation,
from the blue flame under the pot
that signals too little oxygen
the breath lost, the skin blue now
and death in Wyuka, underground
border at O Street, called Zero
in another place less pristine,
another poem. Meanwhile spring
in the crocus, yellow triangle
at the edge of Love Library as we turn
to enter for the board meeting.

Letter of Transmittal

Herein find one woman, used, in fair shape,
given to excess, too fond of what's personal
to star in meetings, intuitive
rather than learned as we say,
whose favorite pastime is the job
you've offered (which in our service
she defined), whose greatest accomplishment
is drawing breath.

On the office phone we heard
she heard this counsel, part of her job,
to pet the scar, croon to her body,
the surviving parts, sway and cherish
like a lover all that falls easily
into the upturned palm. Representative
of the job she's done.

Her last assignment is her signature, here
at the bottom of this letter. Take her.
We have voted, given voice to her eulogy.
Where she goes now is her own affair.
Our names are below. Take her.
Everything we have been able to do
for her is done. What's left is truly bone.
If you wish it, take her home.

Now

Some problems of self-loathing, worry:
the thumbnail blotched in a bank box
door grows out, three-quarter moon marrow spot
filled out with white bruise travels down
my thumb at regular speed, so when I glance
down it's what I see left of center, not
the odd breast, the malformed scruff
at head, the old thought leaking pain
on the pages from my brain, which ought
to be gainfully occupied with rain
as an emblem of loss and gain, and is not.

Who Does She Think She Is

Risen from the cart,
the sick bed, the steel trolley?
Witch of the world, her roars
hide in waterfalls so small
no human on earth has seen them.

Small, I wander the paths
of the world, dust, a miracle
nose to scoop air, breathing.
Between my skin and spine a thin layer
of cells, a silence.

Who do I think I am,
a solitude, a poor bridge, small beer?
Enough that my eyes focus
on that emerald tree, that spruce,
blue in its huge dying.

Risen again, once more
the heat of my skin
pours radiance, praise,
salt and hops into air, my skin a bracelet
of psalms, my navel invisible, a veil.

Earlier

Life offers up no miracles, unfortunately, and needs assistance.
—Weldon Kees, "A Distance from the Sea"

Three years since cancer and I seem to live
a smaller person than I was before—
Then: racked by darkness and desire, fear:
whatever needs I could not meet.

For years the baby crying in his crib
and she I bore in blood and ecstasy
seemed hooks to tear me limb from limb
with suffering, theirs far worse than mine,

and at my hands. Who gave them over to my care
must be unfit, a sadist human life can hardly understand
and I, forever loosening skirt or bodice, or my mind,
could only bend to scoop the baby from her bed

or raise my ass or wit to yet comply
with needs I had myself, or didn't, or dimly knew
but learned to satisfy, then damp, and so to die.

Vowels

Holes on the page
the eye picks up,
the ear opens to,
the I finds irresistible.

Wide mouth bass
drift on weeds
by the dam's breach.
A lake
in upper New York state,
a pond near Syracuse,
both yield their fish
to the lone fisherman
in autumn, his monofilament line
hissing and dipping over water.
"Watch the bowl the line makes
before fish strike," he calls,
seating bait on his hook.

Or, heather in fields
a purple glazed mist
the bagpiper walks through,
breaking stride
only for the boulder, his pipes
blowing for all Hell to hear.
Get out of there!

He touches her breast with his ear
as she cradles him now, against
an oval to break his heart
so she moans, or he does
touching her there.

He made of the sound a conduit path,
a drumbeat to his heart, a traveling
and when it arrived he exploded and burned,
and fell ashes into the bass of it,
the flower.

So they begot music
and were saved.
And the ewe was in the thicket
well used, and the fish ground
in the mortar, and horseradish
and another year
turned.

Epilogue

Gloxinia/ Flicker/ Oxalis

Fists toast-rose, the color of your palm
push up through leaves plate sized
no more sturdy than the crockery you broke
throwing out everything soiled. Junk
the dirty pots, the cups with tea . . .

These leaves broken by careless handling
functional enough for buds
thrust out on some time scale
other than ours, furious to be free
of shade, their record of growth
a trajectory like Louganis
leaving the board, lift, tuck,
his body like a bud
knees tucked into his arms against the fall
held to make a fist
punched through air . . .

Out this window on the copper bowl's lip
where you've made a pool
a bird folds down
not dainty like the chickadee, or the hummingbird
fed with oranges skewered on a bolt
but big enough, hunky like a robin, and bold . . .

The sour wood sorrel, oxalis,
explores the brick
creases the wood mulch
raises umbels like milkweed
flowers rising from the core
in profusion
many colored, like the coat

air wears when soaked with the hose
you hold gently
the spray arc
rising to fall tight in a stream
until you open the nozzle
at the bird bath
and the flicker there
opens her wings in holy light
and the hot body leaps
to mist enfolding all the garden there is
and enters . . .

Recovery

The fingers of the rain are tapping again.
I send out my heart's drum.
Blood stripe on the feathered tulip dissolves into wet.
All night a low thrumming.

Up, up the two-toned hosta
green from sopped earth.
Along your bruised ribs, cream bells.

My Award/ The Jews of Lukow

It comes at a good time, I say
across the table next morning
blessed by Muzak floating down
over toast. We talk of children
our life continuing on the planet

where a new study shows the complicity
of tens of thousands of citizens,
good burghers come to watch, staying to slaughter
not coerced as we'd thought
but diligent volunteers—
as Bosnians killing Muslims, Khmer Rouge
the Cambodians, Hutus Tutsies in Rwanda
Turks Armenians through our long human history.

So last night I rose and walked to the stage,
ascended and turned to the lights, to the microphone
as to a lover's mouth, and everyone
standing, clapping . . .

Not mind you that I deserve it
not for anything I put my mind to
only my body's luck until now:
this morning the first rolled leaves
of the straight line of crocus
through arid soil on the driveway strip
at six the sky lighter
better than the deep absence
cold proclaimed all winter
in case I'd forget.

Oh, glad to be here.

And I suppose they in the auditorium last night,
the ones standing, were glad too
so many of us in the ground—
Rose Meile whose mother checked the furnace's clang
while Rose stayed in the kitchen mopping the floor.
Then she was motherless, burned but not up
the explosion a goad to the child
then the woman who helped us all
even with the kind of cancer that took her in.

A walk in the country
myriad of what's wild, that gorgeous catalogue

revived and then the cultivars in our garden
showy, flashy the oranges and fluorescents
and the natural Stars there with hybrid vigor.

All winter looking up
following the flocks of geese
on their round from Saint Elizabeth's to Home Lake
and back, appearances of the wild:
broad V, exchanged leaders and the muscular flap
in concert. All illusion, the flocks tame
as Romulus and Remus's mom with two human sons to rear.

In recent dreams you say no
to ice cream and won't stay
by the table where my child
is radically changed
nor buy the wire basket
of tomatoes at the farm stand
you speed by like a demon, a ribbon . . .

The man entering
with a cell phone to his ear
takes the next booth.
He has the right to command
our attention from the page.
It's business. Or only a break
from loneliness we all want
deprived of conversation
yearning for the best seller
explaining THE calculus, gorgeous,
or company on the rack.
He orders bacon and a bear claw
pastry held together with butter
such cheap thrills.

Last night at camp
or a conference in a hotel
with crowds
I put forward my best foot
for an encounter with a man so young
he's the rival of my kids,
with a follower younger than he is.
He flirts, I resist
preoccupied as usual with wardrobe.
Next, a cataclysm of nature
some riot, a maniac with a gun.
When I return to the desk
exhausted after hours of eyebeams
you're gone, with her
with my homework, which you lose,
and I'm in the wrong school again.

But look, you two in a corner
over coffee. In my room
the message on the machine

the real thing, you're lost, missing
in action, believed to be dead,
and my grief drizzles me awake to dawn . . .

The miracle of the mind prescient
please God no, only busy at its planting
and excavating Russian, German, English
selves electric and busy remapping
and presenting alternative histories.

So yes, now, finally
I've been given the perfect award for being human.
Poem, as always, we salute you.

Ecstasies

The wing tip lifting
my body opening
lilacs entering your wide mouth.
They scent the entire water.
Storm. Storm clouds and rain slant on the windows.
How fast the parallel plane travels
small in our sky.
Whose toy?

You open wide
as I bend to check you out
touch blood with my fingers.
Twilight office, empty
where I squat surrounding you,
embryo, celebrate with salt.

And I swear now, the bike
steadied as it flew out of his hands!

The fresh places you probed for gravel
so gentle as the gauze wiped grit
no panic, the young aunt steady
at my knee.

Alone on my pillows, clean after surgery.

The sun on our shoulders
adults whisper behind newspapers.
Surf bubbles we catch in pails. Heavy sand.
The salt tongue cups up from the wrist.

Between rails between ties our skate blades
hit perfectly, propel us on our way
to the rink. Horses steam on the ice.

Someone opens his eyes.

In the cold bar, I drink tea.

The door opens out
and in walks my brother.

On the phone, the lost
revive in your vocal cords
and you know nothing
more than the hour of arrival.

Sometimes as Einstein says time folds
an envelope in the pocket
and my robe opens
to fire on a rounding belly.

Where I am now,
every ecstasy dissolves
back into the pool,
the lap of waves,
the filled basin.

Trans

(2001)

for Aaron Link

Trans-, prefix. The Latin preposition trans, across, to or on the farther side of, beyond, over, . . . beyond the boundary or frontier . . . to look through, to transcend, to transcribe . . . to hand over, to lead across . . . a crossing.

In English . . . the chief uses are as follows:
1. With the sense across, through, over, to or on the other side, beyond . . . from one person, state, or thing to another.
2. In verbs, as in *transboard*, *transearth*, *transfashion*, *transship*, *trans-shape*, *transtime*.
3. In adjectives with the sense across, crossing or on the other side of
4. With the sense beyond, surpassing, transcending.

Oxford English Dictionary

What Survives

Who says that all must vanish?
Who knows, perhaps the flight
of the bird you wound remains,
and perhaps flowers survive
caresses in us, in their ground.

It isn't the gesture that lasts,
but it dresses you again in gold
armor—from breast to knees—
and the battle was so pure
an Angel wears it after you.

Rainer Maria Rilke, translated by
J. B. Leichman

I

With the sense across,
through, over, to or on
the other side, beyond
. . . from one person,
state, or thing to
another

Avoidance

Today I'd like to write about epistemology or quarks, the habits of the leech—so useful in medical treatment, a horror in the pond—the growth and development of the precious embryo, attended, monitored until the radiance and blood of birth, the crash of hardwood cultivated for lumber, delight as the oak falls through undergrowth, the whine of the saw, the layers peeling off into fans, falling through their own fragrance to muslin pallets, dust in the chilly air raising a grit halo—or the burble coffee falls from into the cup as you pour a refill—all paid for, earned, the morning deserved, the back seat of the car piled with book bags, their bright canvas a rainbow of good work done, evening hours invested, the lucky deposit on cabins in the Maine woods, moose, ponds, gravel paths and in the near distance the salt, the crash of an ocean contained by its verge of rock.

So you consider the weight of the child in his mother's arms, the reds and yellows of the photos, the leisurely flow of language, no compression, nothing packed or forced, no attempt to move in, no microcosm/ macrocosm, no abstractions tied into the concrete, no natural paths sealed over to retain or meander, no wretched friends to accompany on their final walks.

Consider the tick, then, veinless, says the biologist in the deep voice of the woman he was, useful as a figure for survival, researchers crush them in vises under tons of pressure, in sealed hermetic chambers devoid of air, pumped free of all essentials—and the tick scurries out, alive, cheerful, the size of a grape.

We all shudder, down to the last woman at this table of learning, old friends all, colleagues.

What to make of our profiles: age, religious preference, marital history, hobbies, our experience with Hale-Bopp, did we see the comet at all, note its tail as . . . what?

What Do You Want?

Only when I write do I feel well. Then I forget all of life's vexations, all its
sufferings, then I am wrapped in thought and am happy.
—Kierkegaard's journal, 1847

Well, to be honest, a lace blanket, holes
fabricated as patter, light through tapping out
hello and a window wide enough to hold it all up.
A filigree shirt opaque at navel and breast.
A rosewood trivet of openwork made
on the lathe to support a column, to support us.
Oh, silly configurations, a pile of light.

The smell of cold air, your skin as you crawl in
the pull of the tooth leaving its socket
your cheek in my palm
our knees firm in their tough ligaments
click of rotating ankle, toes sucking mud
boots and woolen socks hard from the wash.
Your birth.

The end of it.

Drought: Teaching, Benedict, Nebraska

Merce says, it don't do to get too attached to any of 'em,
her grandson for example, he's four—you might lose them.

In 1972 she come home from town, some fool party
or other, to find her husband lying on the floor

under the kitchen table. You can't hide from me,
she said, I can see your feet. But he didn't move.

Nothing worse than that except the tornado
come right after, her sisters driving out of town
after dropping her off on the porch, their car stuck,
must have been a swirl in the middle of that wind,
the vacuum, that kept them stock-still though the tires rolled,
she could see it, until they drove loose inches only farther south,
and got away. Meantime she called Mama two houses down.

When the neighbor seen Ma running in the road, she come too.
Then the kids from the farm, and Judy from York, her girl
just back from the hospital with tonsils, wrapped up in a quilt
(like the doctor said). We all went into the storm cellar
and Juddy, my oldest, insisted on pushing up the door
just as the funnel passed so his boys could see it go
—David still on the kitchen floor, they wouldn't let me touch him
before the doctor—and all of us there for half an hour
till it passed, the sheriff's men stationed one at each corner
of the section to watch for the ambulance.

Later on the porch with the family around, all afternoon I leaned
over the railing and heaved and gagged—just nerves, was all it was.
I hope I don't have to go through that again,
but that's what a life's for, I guess, they say the Lord
don't put more on a soul than she can bear.

Merce fills my cup with good Swede coffee, starts the breakfast dishes.
She's eighty and I'm just up from an operation, come from Lincoln
to teach my first poetry writing class this spring.
The gray sky promises rain and believe me, we need it.
Drink up, she says. And I do.

Tough

says Mom, that's tough. My list
of near escapes, excuses for late
homework, curfews, periods.
Really, Mom, I say, I can't.
Tough luck. Tough turkey.
I do it, wash the car, run
to the store, shine my shoes,
finish my math, finish my
Latin—ad astra per aspera—
brush my teeth. Tough it out,
the bad back, the alterations,
the droops and tucks, the altercations,
war, the political party, mayhem, tough
titty, tough luck, tough chance. Too bad.

The tough steak breaks down
in a marinade of vinegar and spices
the muscles give way, acid a broth
of change, flavor. Ah, but under teeth
delicious resistance.

Melts in the mouth
says Aunt Anne
grinning at us,
three nieces in lawn dresses
eating crème puffs in a hot New York deli.

Names My Mother Knew

Hinda for Hilda: her mother
and me, and also the cousin
with freckles, and the red-haired
pixie we visited by boat
the summer her mother, *Vivian*,
was pregnant with *Peter*.

Skeezix, her name for my embryonic
brother, awash and safe in her
tough interior; then *Jimmy*,
the toddler; *James*, the professor,
and graveside, his full measure,
Barton James, ash, buried
again, perfectly safe.

Aaron, her daddy, our Papa;
and *Frank*, from childhood
her beloved; her sisters
Anne, Jane, Phyllis, and the *Dolly*
she was; *David*, her brother.

The nicknames she called us:
Shepsalie, little sheep, for me
and the habit before sleep
of the catalogue of the loved ones
called to God's attention.

Rosetta, who helped her clean
Harvard Street; *George*, who set the screens,
washed windows, scared us with his false teeth.
Dr. *Wollans*, who diagnosed mumps;
Dr. *Kerchel*, who straightened teeth;
Mr. *Thumb* who lived in my mouth.

She whispered his name before
she pulled him out.

Mr. *Eastman*'s house; *Palmyra*,
the ice cream place; *Canadaigua*
for hot dogs and hamburgs, onion rings.
Genesseo Hospital where we were born.
Nana she was to her grandchildren.
Devorah, her Hebrew name.

Parkinson's patient 723 in the medical study.
West End Lane, her Hampstead address; the *Flandre*,
a ship she sailed on: lost
with the rest: her favorite novels
all foxed, gone.

Houses

Something about rage
about women merged with houses
their flesh loosening over emerging bones.
Something about never, no never
able to refuse, to choose this life
or that, always bent over the sweet flesh
of our small ones, making shade for fragile skin
how much our palms love to smooth hair back
kiss the nape under the braid, the damp forehead
under the baseball cap, brush palms over flushed cheeks,
the little winged backs, tuck curls under the elastic brim.

She asks each morning to be remembered to God
in her 100th year, at the same time

wondering why in her chest the ta-dum,
ta-dum goes on. Each night she councils
her heart to stop at dawn, to rest,
but it doesn't, she wonders why, laughing.

Let us be content each day
with the circumstances of our life.

The geese at the reservoir fly at sunrise
without compunction, they have no use
for our presence, nor disuse. They choose
or are chosen by the light, and rise
over the dam to fly. Or does the ample
grass refuse them? The house of the earth
they had no part in making, no curtains
of dust to hang, no towels in the anterooms
they enter, and tuck their tails down to push
forth eggs they shadow from hot, unseasonal sun.

To rage against the cheek gone rough
the nap of the body hair, so soft once,
the risen flesh—

Curtains of lace I hang against light,
the palms against silk thread, the spider's web,
yes, even the Recluse my broom passes over . . .
House, my body, my boys.

Against concrete my soles press, complacent
in their rubber housing, the heat of yesterday's sun
radiant there. Yes, if the children—yours, or
any—were here to enter the household
take up their sneakers, bend their knees
to the sidewalk's warmth, tie up their own shoes . . .

My hands close on my own fingers. Today's sun
is hot, complacent in its house of sky.

Let us say no to the small child
who pulls at our earlobes, pats
the flesh of our inner arms, winds his fingers
like silk, his touch like silk
as he slithered from the house of our body.

Across from me she is writing
we are both writing and she is making
small sounds, she who is reticent, so tidy
and careful, so finely boned as we have been
walking and she listens and breathes
quietly. It is only now, yes, a catch
in her breathing that makes me look up, raise
my head to see her cheeks begin to shine
as she rubs her cheek. And she is still writing.

Can you tell me, please, what use
this weeping for what we both know is coming?

Said to Sarah, Ten

> And scribes wrote it all down.
> —Gilgamesh

There is no one to say why
this face on the scrap of newsprint,
The Times, is not the face of my brother.
No one to say why her cat wastes
in a nest on the sofa, shawl and heating pad.

It yawns and gapes and whines
and arches its back.

How long will it last? she asks,
meaning grief, and I haven't the heart
to say a lifetime. Daughter.

Epistemology, I said in the dark
to her father, my head on his arm,
is my favorite subject, how we know what we know.

It will take so long, she says at intermission.
We hold each other in our common arms.
Mother and daughter, we are bound by mucus
and blood, the spilling of waters, flesh,
and the uses of smooth muscle.
I don't have the answer. It wasn't wisdom
brought to her life. I did nothing.
Now we sit in the dark watching
the orderly art of the body. Dancing.
People sweat in service.

I tell her in the dark,
when we're gone, when they're gone
under the earth, when all our names are forgotten,
this will continue, this dancing.

Fast Car on Nebraska I-80: Visiting Teacher

Early sun on fields.
A pheasant flushes and skims
the north ditch on air.
Students, I say out loud, rehearsing
in the car, this morning
our subject is nouns,
how to pin them down.
Gold is the color of freedom,
I say, the fields Mennonites farm
to yield more than an acre can.

Later, the most compelling noun
is car, fast skimming away from a class
I've asked to describe death
in terms of silk tatters, the smoking gun, for example,
of a brother shooting over his sister's head.

The girl in the front row
who daubed her eyelids purple
wrote about the-one-who-is-gone,
meaning her sister. And wrote
about the-one-who-did-it,
meaning her brother who shot the gun,
whom she ought to hate—and doesn't.

She doesn't. She misses the black hair
of his head, his brown eyes, her sister's
pale skin, now gone dead-white.
I don't make her read out loud.

First things they said, this is a Mennonite community
and a boy killed his sister here two weeks ago.
But they forgot to mention the family, the other kids in school.

Early Monday, driving through wet air at seven
I'd noticed the horizon did a good job
on my heavy mind: what had seemed a knot
so snarled I couldn't get a nail in
began to unwind as I watched through the windscreen.

Here, the town is groomed, each stubble lawn smooth
in a yellow fallow. The houses are brick.
Each child in grades two through twelve
is clean and well-dressed. Some seniors
they tell me in class, drive Thunderbirds,
or go visit China in the summer. In the library
I have a glassed-in office usually reserved
for the Monday-Wednesday speech teacher.
I work undisturbed. Nowhere here
is violence I can see, only the peace of community.

Not here, or in the deep ditches where pheasant harbor
or the deer. Who couldn't be happy here?

Afternoon, with Cold

What's outside is summer.
What's inside is phlegm,
a foul effluvium rising
through lungs, gateway
air enters to dilute
miasmas, maybe environmental
illness—collective noun
for everything wrong,
the exterminator's spray,
chemical prods for growth,
hormones, the caustic

cleaners for tile, drains
all emptying into our
Ogallala aquifer—
some vision, magnifying
as my temperature rises
and all I have is a cold
in the head. Some
summer complaint.
That's all.

Sick

The third person I am
watches you bring tea to the iron table
rescued from the dump
put the knobby kettle steaming hard
by my arm.

I notice the porcelain cup
thin red stripe like blood
circling the rim of your mouth
you bend to me peppermint
what's wrong tell me are you
dumb now stupid tell me where
you hurt? My mouth is stretched
over a rubber ball of fat. Everything
loud blurs your face inessential
dissolve you're gone and you know what?
I know nothing about who you are
body solid in its misery stupid melting
at every boundary it touches the hot
iron kettle the whole world we share.

Back

Jump, says the therapist
hold to the bars. Lean
backward, lean forward. Now
in sets of ten, early morning
late evening in the front room
working through the pain.

Light from Papa's body
light powdered his shoulders
light moved through bowing,
bowing, rocking, light
a burr language not to get close to
his child again closed out
the mystery of phylacteries
bound over freckles, the golden
hair of arms, muscles
and the black boxes on straps
packed with prayers at pulses
between the portals of his eyes
on lying down and on rising up,
brow smoothed by prayer, davening
before he goes fishing, my hand in his hand,
before reading, his body my cradle,
before walking, my head at his elbow,
before sleeping, my blank forehead under curls
useless, tangled, my empty portals. Pain.

Friday

Anyone possible to offend
I have. Today, spring out the window,
the flesh on my bones not clay
but firm over tibia, fibula,
the vertebrae of the back,
the particular small bones
of the feet, one of which you fractured
this winter, and the myriad
bracelets and chokers there
for the flenser/ artist
who'd make jewelry of the dead.

Not today. "I'm putting out fires
with both hands," I explain
as I cancel lunch. I'm sorry,
I didn't do it right, you misunderstood,
forgive me, bless us all in our bumbles,
send me out to the brambles to dig
roots from the blackberry canes.
A regular whirling dervish of contrition
in the service of berries for us.

They're setting fire to the spring prairie,
you say, sitting down, drinking coffee.
Hello, you're welcome here in town
where sidewalks interrupt the weeds.
For the morning, so long as I don't speak,
you're enthralled. Have you heard the groovy one about . . .
And Mr. Downes turned his cauliflower ear to the crowd . . .
Certainly the fisherman caused a sensation when . . .
Before she died we escaped from the hospital and went to a movie . . .
How you know failure is when the birds on the roof . . .

What's next?
Make lists, hex the infamous,
perform rigorous examination of texts, scholarship.

I'm pooped. Friday's when the dead rise
on some scroll or parchment. Let us
consider the unrolling of ferns
in the supermarket trash amongst which
in the marsh of broken bottles
the blue muzzle of a tick hound
and the barrel of a magnum compete
for the color of slate. Dust
in the nose, pollen. Heat
between my shoulder blades

strokes wing buds as I bend over.
They're growing iridescent. But not yet? Not now?

"The world is not something to look at; it is something to be in."

—Mark Rudman, *Rider*

I want my head to stop hurting
my heart to quiet. The light comes back,
ouch, more stimuli, on fire, needles.
I think of you in your high attic of words
a sudden salve. Nothing to explain, no shield
of paperthin skin between history and the untender world.
Every rush stilled.

Imagine buckets overflowing,
dear one, your warm hands plunged in.
Imagine children, their history and form.
And yours, the ones in folders, the ones forming
as the water swirls. Let me be in the world with you.
Let's walk, footsteps no sound on the river bank.
Let the calm dark lead us along, every muddy step a poultice
for our journey, our inquiry.

II

In verbs, as in
transboard, transearth,
transfashion, tranship,
trans-shape, transtime

Secrets

Teach me, they say,
the women with childbirth
three months behind them,
one with a dead baby and tears
the other come an hour down the highway
to find her car towed, her shirt front wet
with milk, and no money in her pocket.

Teach me, says Ruth, whose secret
is identity, pale face but she a blooded
Sioux. And Amy, muscular dystrophy,
who says no, you can't, when she doesn't
show up
for class.

Teach me, says the toe
leaking blood under the nail,
Teach me, says the rigid carapace,
solid, sealed on all sides
so the pulse amplifies, stirs
as currents of fire in the toe.

Teach me, babbles the darning needle
or the drill in its pan of water
burning over, settling on the stove.

And my job, to scald, bore, hold steady
under the light, the singe, the push,
the steady pressure, eyes open, the flash,
the bubble of blood,
the maroon gush, the icy relief.

Teach me, says the hole in the nail,
tiny, a door, and around it, rust, mold,
acrid release of what's sealed,
a tender probe to open, to hurt.

Heart Transplant

Here's the crowded restaurant
where we celebrate his return
to the law, marriage, friends.
His powder-blue-paper mask
puffs out and in with his voice
as he gives witness: First

a four-minute flat line on the monitor.
Then he's behind a crowd
of doctors and nurses around the bed,
then scalding light,
then the tunnel,
and then, he's surprised,
the outline of a human head
large, faceless, before him.

On my office bookshelf two miles away
a souvenir of my child's art class
a small head, smooth, blank face, head, neck, shoulders,
a clay bust—plus a delicate pile of interchangeable masks
each one thumbnail size. The head.

I listen like a Benedictine,
all ears for his words,
shaking, scared at once

by his absence
his unchanged presence
ruddy skin, blue eyes calm
over the luffing and filling mask
exactly their color and the hot sky.

He invokes the donor
a farmer across town killed suddenly
and cites his new passion for exercise and prayer
an hour's daily meditation as he mounts the treadmill.
Of course his wife is glad to have him back.

I gather this story in, ears cupped, torso bent
to the table edge between us. He reveals
his pain as the paddles struck, "greater than any,"
a gift of detail with lunch, for writer's hunger.

All night I toss and negotiate the pillows
for space, a cool place in the hot bed for floating,
trembling, afraid of good fortune and its wake.
The silence fills with the cat's long purr
and the steady heartbeat of my love and you
who sleep on for a while, thrown back into life.

Not for you the toxic chemicals, the hormones,
nor the surgeon's cuts to keep you up in the world
where the hunter's moon lights all our driveways with cobalt.

Footnotes

—for Burke Casari

1. The matter of shoes. Transsexuals have problems with size.

2. Wardrobe is a matter of taste, not gender.

3. As in, "If they don't know I pass muster. If they know they want to see my cock." Interview with subject 10/19/XX.

4. The first question, "Does he have some kind of constructed penis?"

5. The problem of voice. His mother wondered if he had a cold for eighteen months: Esophageal cancer? This problem is representative.

6. A handwritten card dated two years before subject came out: "For Mom, who once said something about the difference between becoming an ornithologist and growing wings."

7. The mother's birthday was celebrated in increments, each one noted, every choice apparently made by considering other options. ". . . opening cards, breakfast out, cappuccino, choose two new books (Patricia Dunker's *Hallucinating Foucault* and Lisel Mueller's new and selected poems, *Alive Together*, the Pulitzer winner), a cherrywood picture frame, a new bud vase, ice cream cone dipped in chocolate, a salad for dinner, eight lobelia plants for the patio pots, four with white stars four purple-blue, phone calls to and from . . ." (cf. chapter 1, page 4).

8. "You will listen to me today and I will say everything I have to say, at once." Journal entry, quote from conversation.

9. Unpacking, phone messages, laundry, refusals, interest. But she had found an agent who liked the book.

10. Unopened Fosomax tabs with directions.

11. Her habit of walking out after dinner. His addiction to weight training for musculature. The sprained wrist.

12. Baci Perugina chocolate fortune: "One is alone with all the things he loves."

13. Bumpy weather traveling in a small plane.

Doing the Puzzle/ Angry Voices

Pieces of prairie—the colors without names—
a tree of juncos, gray bellies rising, some song.

Prayers for the dead must praise God,
no mention of sorrow, no mention of death,
as if at the moment of inconsolable loss we might forget to praise God.

The prairie we live on, what's underfoot plowed
to make a road we drive to the overpass—
eyes ache, what if I couldn't see the sun on Lespedesa, prickles,
but only a purple sheen on the black cardboard piece to reveal
    its place in the whole.

Praise in the midst of disorder, so if the eyes roll back
    in the china head, fall in,
and Marjorie is broken in my fifth year, praise Him.

Every book that documents birth
puts onto gender a meaning.
That piece of the junco tree is filled with sparrows.
The black is all color, no, the absence of color,
no engorgement at midnight, no purple.

On the puzzle board, what grows
is a picture of Adam and God

in collusion, all the beasts and no companion
to help. But still, if incorrectly,
each beast must be named.

In the office room I inhabit
a new lamp drapes light on
daily rituals of departure, a party I skip
to walk on new snow, granular, wool socks.

Here's narrow focus, patina, the coat of glass.
This piece: against a wedding feast, cranes at sunrise.
Every moment of night sleep, alert.

Praise at the keys   ivory, ebony.

We have to function twenty-four hours a day, seven days a week.
The responsibility of the body—catalogues coming through the mail,
    pages of photos, description, legends under color charts, alveoli, taste
    buds, hair follicles
so busy until the end, the rooftops—you, heart not only head.

Mother, each day of my life you raise your hand to touch me.
When he left me this time, my palm held the heat of his cheek.
Where does this piece belong? Who will tell me?

Prelude

We bring to our booth
pages packed full
of subject and verve
blood and tissue, the nutshells
of her history sharp under her elbow
as she leans hard, the full weight
of her language on this vision
or that one, and take in
the full length of our throats
swallowing, breathing air
we share with fifty others,
the smells of ripening toast
in the chrome slots, and we breathe out
tone, shading, the shouts necessary
for our Monday morning before light
streaks the sky, before the curtains close
against the glare for patrons in the next booth,
and the whole world opens . . .

For weeks, staticky news over the sink
as each night at the open refrigerator
I transport, unwrap, scrub, pare
and transform food for the family body.

Oh, Child-God who pushes
across the glass table top
the sharp clatter, the ruckus of our lives
blocks of Legos, steel gas tubes
torn across at the throat by some
torque from a machine too terrible
to posit now, at this table rinsed
by the kind and disinfectant cloth . . .

Trained by custom to serve
I set down the burden of dinner
wash my hands and begin to eat
the only possibility, finally,
turning away from the heat
reliable torque of hip socket
and ribs allowing the swivel
my body makes to sit down
or reach for the phone, gut
courage, to climb on the plane,

transfer, hoisting luggage
into the overhead bins, and arrive
at your side, child, in time
for your long surgery to come tomorrow
and I'll be there, your mother, where I belong
the old miracle of your birth belief enough
to see us through cut and clamp, the blood price
I signed to pay, and will, and will myself
onto the plane with books and cash, pastilles,
ribbons, cashmere socks, spare eyeglasses
and ribs, hip bones, reliable bone sockets, and
every recipe intact or documented, soft sacs bathed
reliable tongue tucked up into the silence broken
by only one word, love, one phrase, you can, one other,
I'm here, child, your absolute company
as you are changed—radically—from one thing to another.

Part Coquette, Part Monster

It's not clear precisely where she got that picture of a different arm, which in the montage becomes a giant phallus. But the impossible and very funny result was . . . part coquette, part monster, a parody of the cliche of woman as sex object, elevated from a clever joke into art by the elegant twist [she] gives to the ridiculous body.

—Michael Kimmelman on Hannah Hock, the German dadaist, *New York Times*

Mother and child, a montage of rage
and humor: Breast(s) the graceful center
of the installation: a rectangular panel
that twirls and quivers while the whole thing
     trembles
          continuously.
Cranes, a part of the high
backdrop, in the fields
like brown kites dropped, take off eventually
as solace; their wings unfold . . . silver hint
          of the Platte River at the right corner.

To pull yourself up by the teeth, clamp on the near bar, a standard tube of metal, a chrome bit. Lift up over the shivering landscape until you pop through, into vision, the blue void with clouds backlit O'Keefe entered and later, point fixed suddenly, a bone china cup, the real thing, held up between your fingers and the window. Oh, Lord, to surrender terror now abruptly, to lift free!

Trans

What do you care, she asked
at last, letting me get the good
from my hundred-dollar therapy time.
She's still your daughter. Whoops
she said going red all over the parts
I could see—face under permed hair
her neck chicken-wattled, even the top part
of her chest the V between her bowling shirt button
(marked JAKE on the pocket) showing blush.
I sobbed, quiet at first, swallowing salt
then louder wailing like some beached baby.

Son you mean, you old biddy, I croaked at last
crying a good ten bucks worth of earth time.
Who would have thought that little one
whose cheek turned away from my breast
would grow up HE. He started SHE,
a brilliant daughter.
                                It's the age, she said
not meaning puberty because he was long past,
thirty at his last birthday, but the times: everything
possible: hormones, surgery, way beyond unisex
jeans at the Mall, those cute flannel button-down shirts.

What will I do I whispered so deep into misery
I forgot she was listening and I was paying.
                                Afterwards on the bluffs at the heart
of the weirdest sunset since July 4th
I try to conjure his voice: "Mom
since sunup the sky's been dark but now we're talking
I see the sun come out perfect
for a walk and when we're through talking

I'm going out. Come with me?"
That voice: the same words and phrases, intonation
from me with his dad mixed in "like cake with too much
frosting," as my student said tonight in class. Be honest
here. Love is the word he said in closing. "I love you,
Mom." Transsexual—like life, not easy—in this century.
My kid. And me in the same boat with him, mine.

Trans formation/ Feathers/ Train Travel

Meadow sun
on your shoulders
erases shadow
from behind the lens

I open the shutter.

In the photo, your hand is
a wing, feathers erupting
from your fingers.
You squint and smile, my hunk, my beauty.

The gorgeous Hulk's green skin
split reliably open his clothes each week
when the doctor he was
got angry, on TV. We both
loved the moment, Lou Ferrigno
in rags, entering the scene,
you prone on the shag grass
of our carpet, the kid,
me the mom with a plate
of warm brownies we expect to eat.

Now, twenty years later, on a train,
scanning your picture, I recreate
your "marvelous transformation,
not a particularly pleasant process
for the subject," said Nabokov
to his students. I'm one,
and still your mom as I travel upstate
trying to review your change
as the train sings to the waterfowl
landing and rising in the wetlands
we observe as backdrop, my thoughts
mired in "the tickle and urge . . . to shed
that tight dry skin, or die."

Nothing here is metaphor.

At the station you'll appear
as the guy I caught on film,
his fist filled with feathers.

In last night's dream you were my daughter
still an infant in arms, wrapped in a sheet
over a diaper, the only one I had.
"Relax," I said as we ascended the ramp
steep with cars or foot traffic around an invisible bend.

You tucked your small baby body close. Wind howled.
"We're two strong women," you said,
baby mouth damp with my milk. Of course I looked around
for someone to tell, my prodigy, as we crossed
the bridge safely and came again to the library,
or a bus, or the New York subway where we'll ride,
mother and son, home to breakfast.

In my dream where everything's metaphor
you're new, my new girl, and I'm studying
at a library table. Hours pass, a blank space
called flow, or I'm blank. The new guy comes
to take the desk, he's blank, slow, his truck
collection, metal miniatures reduced to two
he clunks on the oak to show me. Rushing
to leave, I lose my purse, my keys, my coat.
And now we're two, infant daughter and mom
chatting up friends I don't recognize, one
with a collection of clinky jewelry she pulls
from a lightweight purse suitable for travel,
another an expert on natural childbirth.
Lucky you're nursing, but baby, it's cold
outside and you're wet. The busman takes us on
wherever we're going and although this stop
is unfamiliar, I see the highway beyond
and across it, my office. And on and on.

"Though wonderful to watch,
transformation from larva to pupa or from pupa
to butterfly is not a particularly pleasant process
for the subject involved . . . he must shed
that tight skin, or die. As you have guessed,
under that skin, the armor of a pupa—
and how uncomfortable to wear one's skin
over one's armor—is already forming."
"You have noticed," Nabokov goes on,
"that the caterpillar is a *he*, the pupa an *it*,

and the butterfly a *she*." The great man
is winding down. The train is slowing.
And stops. And now we're here.
Of course the iron gates open on you.

Stone

Aaron picks up goose feathers
until his fist is crammed
with a fan of feathers
and me with the camera between us,
distraction from our constant talking.
I need to frame and document him
from a distance: his straight shoulders,
barrel chest, narrow waist, hips, muscular legs,
dark eyes, tanned skin, intense frown and laughter.
So male. Walking behind him and his brother
at the airport, their identical gaits, arms swinging
loose from their wide shoulders, Aaron thin as
Sarah never was, wearing his stepfather's outgrown jeans.

Angry voices: his learned gait. Learned muscles, learned grace,
handsome man wearing the Lucas water-snake bracelet
bought from his workbench at Old Oraibi, one unbroken curve
of silver Sarah wouldn't have worn, not even to try.
No, Mom I don't wear jewelry, nor the Hopi belt buckle either,
the one Aaron wears now every day. Aaron is a handsome man,
say my women friends. Very male. His arms are covered with
a dark silky hair. His legs are hairy and straight. Sarah wouldn't
wear shorts, not ever. Aaron, yes. He eats carefully, is lean.
Men are? he asks. Women are? Tell me the story I don't know, says Aaron.
The story about women. Tell me the story I don't know says his mother.
The story of your transformation.
How a girl child is male.
When I used to look in the mirror it was blank, says Aaron of Sarah.
And then Aaron says Mom! I'm the same person.
You're the one who had the sex change.
I've always been as I am. You bet.
My eyes see someone familiar, someone I love.
But where is Sarah whose chin rested on my shoulder?

My eyes are red, they fill again and again each day
as I listen to the news from the telephone, the radio, conversation.
I think a friend is dying, each day her face collapses a little,
yesterday her lips, pouty around her perfect teeth.
And my cancer writer needs a biopsy now, her CAT scan
a little shadow where last time there was none.
She goes out for groceries in the city heat wearing
a short, red dress, she's strutting her stuff. On the phone
we talk about sex. In the mirror my face is tired.

Another friend remembers us as mothers
with young children at Woody Park Pool:
Sarah at two in her striped one-piece,
her brother four, blue cotton trunks,
me in a French navy polka-dot bikini,
wet braid heavy on my shoulder as we bend
to splash with the kids in the shallow pool,
all of us soaked and warmed by the late sunshine,
the heat of the plains in high summer.

Today is twenty years later, ninety-some degrees
where I write with a friend before work.
This breeze is delicious my aunts would say
to each other in the forties, fanning their deep
bosoms before the hundred-degree heat sets in.
Train sounds, the trucks. We drink chocolate
to begin the day. My friend is to arrange
a repeat mammogram, a little something on the film to check.

My favorite piece from Aaron's new show,
a gray stone drilled off-center, the hole lined with silver,
dropped from a silver chain. I'll buy it if I can.
My friend says, follow the pen.
My dress becomes wings filled with wind,
a crosswind on the dock this early morning,

pebbles tossed as the tide comes in
over rocks in Maine, the sheen light drapes
at the cliff foot, the prickly wild roses and blackberry
bushes on the path, the smell of salt.

The camera is unashamed to be examining
the body of my child. We are not shy.
I look at his scars, less red, one less colloid.
His belly, his genitals, the pattern of hair on his torso.
He is plain, like Quaker rooms, tidy now and still beautiful.
Sarah overflowed like me. But in my bikini,
slim, muscular, flat-bellied, small-breasted.

(Aaron is glad to be rid of breasts. I look
in the mirror and see nothing familiar,
scars and absence, say it, one breast.)

Oh, love! All these words I've written before.
My pen is empty of words.
The wind fills my silk shirt by the way of the sleeves,
stirs and opens my skirt.
The flow from the inner body, female, ample!

The mommy next to me on the dock lifts
her son into a small chair, unwraps his muffin,
pours juice. The wind picks up.

On this hot day I am chilly.
The doves at the white bird bath,
the crows at the copper
in our backyards, all will be thirsty.
They dip their beaks
into standing water and drink
in the hot early evening, dregs
fetid and scant, warm.

The child next to me lifts his cup,
sucks juice from the spout, fusses,
stretches his legs under the plastic table
which moves to accommodate him.
His mother steadies his cup.
The child chants his pre-language
accompaniment to the conversation of the aunts.
His name is Connor. *Connor, Connor!*
He runs to the edge of the concrete dock
carrying his stuffed puppy by the ears.
The longer I write, the smaller I grow
quiet in the rivulets of sound from the street.
If they toss me like the stone, I am content behind my camera
learning to point the lens, to look at the body of the world. *Click.*

No, cries Connor. No.

Why resist? In my dream I am unable to help, comprehend,
caught in weak flesh. My job is to pass on, distribute,
and as always, to witness.
Someone sees the cat with the flapping bluejay in her jaws,
says, *Leave her be. She's doing her job.*

Alive in the world, the chilled stone waits.

Before John and Maria's Wedding

In front of the throb
space opens in the skull,
space where the garden reassembles
without shrubs, golden yews flanking the gate,
pseudo-angels, the light at four, sword-like . . .

Instead, reassembling behind gauze
the thin time between now, over coffee, safe in company,
and flight—the airport, bus, and the blessing,
the exchange of rings, the lock sprung on the apartment
next door, your assault on the common wall
to make an extension, a tent, a shelter, a bond.

You, older son, will be married in the sight
of the company, blessed, and the common veil
of light will drape us all—great composer
and his wife, Elliott and Helen Carter, the assemblage
of blood—both sides—and the ancestors dead
on one side at the hands of the other, fled
from the scene—my mother who wouldn't leave
the car, not for anything, so her foot
wouldn't touch German soil your new wife springs from.

Time, thin fabric, the scrim Yawah plays behind,
bless our children, two in front
of this fleshly company, the other holding my hand.

The flesh will have to do now, this marriage
a healing you make for us, yourselves
who were never broken. Let our blessings
be sufficient here, the garden you move through
together, covered now by time and light.

In adjectives with the
sense across, crossing or
on the other side of

Historical Documents

—for John

Last night, dark windows, handwritten pages
in a binder on my lap
as I read again the story of your birth.
The papers turn easily as we labor, time moving
in a blur of day-after scribble, nothing
too bad, the dire predictions proved false
in coming years, and you here at last
in the same world we inhabit now waiting
for your child's birth. Son, you were the first time
I opened wide
for something wholly new.

My notes document vernix, the sheen of your scrunched face
fresh from my body, the length of your silence
in the delivery room. But

here, in the pages of my binder, my bald account
in simple language testifies to us both that birth
comes fast for the bearer, the child safely breathing,
the father, you, stunned by the dramatic head bursting
forth, safely standing by as the new child takes breath,
gives up its own first loud cry.

Fresh from the shower this morning, maybe the day
of her birth, I stand naked in my several scars, look,
and without thinking, reach for sky, stretch to hold
the supplicant's position, palms up to the sun,
stretched as far as I can
and breathe deeply in
a chant for Maria, who is your wife. Let her be safe
and wholly present, giving birth.

Mostly she is dazed now, talking on the telephone,
walking her miles, bathed in endorphins, vague
as she sort of remembers the camera's beep she turned off—
did she? how? The light in the bathroom is out
so she can't see what's happening, a mystery
she laughs, and your voice, son, going on about something,
my ears blocked, listening for your cry, the first cry
in this cold room where I delivered you to the world
we wait in for the birth of this child.

Where in myself is Victoria?
Where in myself is Hilda?
Where Samuel, where Dolly, Frank,
Aaron?
                    The germ of the self thins
out like bells as the cathedral recedes,
a visit only, a ride through country green
with promise or golden death, white
ice on the road as the brougham skids
sideways, the people under the heavy lap rugs
shift, fall against each other and laugh,
adjust their caps and furs, remove
a mitten to tuck up the fallen braid of hair,
shake the linen handkerchief, bend to wipe
the child's nose who sits in front
next to his daddy, a Sunday ride,
the peace of the car concentrated in the fierce
blade of thin sunshine bisecting the space
askew into two compartments, one for the aunts
and grandmothers in back, the other, the space
where you ride through the world, child,
now dark now light as the landscape flickers,
the peal of bells fades to a cry
we know is coming.

Volunteers

Out the window, a kid-robin on a branch
shows me her size, the same as mama's
but fuzzy, an outline and then,
turning, her all-over splotches.

At the back of the yard, a blighted pine
shows a beige fringe in the emerald sumac,
they're big feeders, you've got to tend them
so everything else stays healthy.
That pine's dying from something. A storm?

On the radio, a story about customers
come to the clinic for mary jane,
$40 a dozen for marijuana cookies
or $80 an oz. for the best stuff
and the police won't close it down
because they'd have to cart us off
in ambulances!—a snort of laughter—
this one with lesions on his arms,
thin, and open sores and bruises.
Poor guy buys cookies as an appetite
stimulator. What would become of him?
What will become of me?

Dark letters, welcome! What a deal!
I'm gonna grab a cup of joe, java, and a cookie
before the gas guys come to cart off the old grill
we cooked hamburgs—upstate NY talk—
and hotdogs on. Flaky rusty now.
Here I am, happy and healthy, tip-tapping along
one minute at the time. Eating.

Even though I don't believe this mess is worth saving,
writing is like digging in clay the sumac plays out of,
black letters, the sound of Mom's voice, the crisp edge
of Papa's celluloid dresser set: buttonhook, shoehorn,
brush, mirror, comb, and what's that odd receptacle with the hole
for hair combings? To make jewelry? Papa bald as an egg.

He holds me, listening to the radio
night after every night, each night a story.
I wouldn't lie down without a headphone later
after surgery, a novel or poems for the heart.
Mama, read to me. Papa, I'm fuzzy, read me a story. Like that.
Or on paper. Like this. Tip. Tap.

Some Questions about the Storm

What's the bird ratio overhead?
Zero: zero. Maybe it's El Niño?

The storm, was it bad?
Here the worst ever. Every tree hurt.

Do you love trees?
Only the gingko, the fir, the birch.

Yours? Do you name your trees?
Who owns the trees? Who's talking?

You presume a dialogue. Me and you.
Yes. Your fingers tap. I'm listening.

Will you answer? Why mention trees?
When the weather turned rain into ice, the leaves failed.

So what? Every year leaves fail. The cycle. Birth to death.
In the night the sound of cannon, and death everywhere.

What did you see?
Next morning, roots against the glass.

Who's talking now and in familiar language? Get real.
What's real is the broken crown. The truck shattered.

Was that storm worse than others?
Yes and no. The wind's torque twisted open the tree's tibia.

Fool. You're talking about vegetables. Do you love the patio
    tomato? The Christmas cactus?
Yes. And the magnolia on the roof, the felled crabapple, the topless
    spruce.

Lost Jewelry

My grandmother's diamond chip ring
set in filigree platinum, given to mark
my sixteenth birthday, a family gift
of transition. Carelessly removed
and returned to its box, dropped
into a suitcase I didn't lock
for a trip I took by air, on top.

My best friend's dead mother's watch
removed and dropped on the bedside table,
stolen by my boyfriend. Who else?

My first golden hoop—one of a pair
bought in Pharaoh's Jewelry Store, slipped
from my ear while swimming
in a friend's lake. NOT removed
for vanity when the bikini snapped shut,
sacrificed to that place of my greatest happiness.

My wedding ring—green golden filigree—
thrown from a moving car into perfect grass.

Lapis lazuli earrings torn from my lobes
by my own hands, dropped from a bridge
into icy water.

My grandmother's wedding ring
she flushed along with her spouse,
a family legacy that story,
now mine.

My second wedding ring, heavy
old 22k gold, irregularly beveled
by the jeweler's art, put off, unlucky,
to be cleansed by earth or flame
next generation, or sold. Now
hidden in velvet, eclipsed in darkness
in metal, behind locks, behind bars.

My birthday watch from Papa,
pink gold, tiny. "She's too young!"
cried Mom. I was. Gone.

The marcasite star on a silver chain.
I have it still. Fifty years. Don't I?

A double pearl ring from Daddy.
Which? The large or the small?
Same price. I'm fifteen. Shopping
together. The big one. The top
pearl cracks.

Mother-in-Law

In the nursing home you sit
in your wheelchair, fingers taped
together, hands in socks,
black cotton, marked with some guy's
name. Your head nods, you're a stranger
after twenty years, no teeth, no eye

glasses, no shoes. Our eyes
glitter on seeing you sitting
nodding among strangers
who are name-taped
to belongings, some guys
you don't know, one's socks

a mockery on your hands, socks!
Your son wipes his eyes
surreptitiously so I won't see, or the guys—
his brothers and nephew—sitting
nearby watching the TV duct-taped
to the wall against strangers

which is after all what we are, strangers
to you, your hands in socks
which at the wrists are taped
to your robe. I can't close my eyes
even though I'm sitting
away from the crowds with the only two guys

who are patients here. The other guys
are ours, my spouse and his kin, strangers
to their mom who is still sitting,
as she always will, in socks
not shoes, never gloves again, her eyes
blind without her glasses which are taped

so what, so what, taped
shut in her bureau. The guys
here in the home don't care if their eyes
weep in front of strangers.
They share their socks
and everything else on this floor, sitting

still on the floor, taped in, forever strangers.
They're all one of the guys in the chairs, sitting
still, their socks held forever in common. Sad eyes.

Women & Men

Women have babies, or can, or can decide not to
use the miraculous machinery.
Women walk downtown holding their daughters'
hands, or can if they're inclined,
each generation adding a link to the chain.
Women can work—or not—at the blessed
repetitive tasks of the body, cleansing
their flesh of the blood flow, a tender care
required—in whatever spirit—at regular intervals.
Women were girls, like boys, fast across
the meadow, diving into the pond
or carrying morning after morning the heavy buckets
of salt water caught up from the animal sea.
Blessed bone, ribs like his, flat brown belly,
small nipples, and the growing muscles of the shoulders
to lift . . .

Women, out for a walk, cross paths with men
holding red dogs on a leash, who strain and bark.
"Hi, Sweetie," calls a woman, smiling on the small
Irish setter, dropping down to dog height
at a distance. A man walks on, pulling the leash
taut against the straining dog. Smiles on the dog.
The woman walks on, slowly approaching the pair,
her palm turned outward toward the dog.
The man tugs, the dog skids on the twilight pavement
still hot from the day.
"He would jump on you," the man says.
"He'd love to jump on you."
The woman walks past, smiling.
"I'd be afraid," she says.
"I'd be very afraid."

Some Questions for the Evening Class

It is over already? Or have we just begun?
Janie writes an open door. Jason is revving up.

How did we start? Did light fill the window?
Did we begin in the dark? Pat has gone to Paris.

Holiday preparations begin. Opaque windows now.
We start to end. We leave each other stars.

What did you learn? Did you build a wooden dragon?
You said I'd stare at tundra. Denali walks in my eye.

How can I leave you all with your notebooks?
What will you write I can't read?

The year winds down warm still.
Remember the towed car? The coming surgery?
Stunned students? The cold wall?

Each one is writing now where we are. The rustling tree.
Still together here, free in this classroom. Will we remember
Chauna shaping a word axe? Mary Jane back from silence?

Insomnia III

He has a tumor in his brain
that much we know—and he's the father
of four children, the oldest fourteen.
Therefore this morning of sun so bright
we're asked to draw the shades,
let us praise the brain in its bone pan.

All night as I bow to the boom box
changing tapes, the electrical cord
between my ears carries a charge to respect,
adjust away from the fleshy thorax, over my head
to rest safely where it belongs, if it can be said to rest
anywhere naturally, on my skull.

              O disordered
self, to require distraction all night,
stories poured in the porch ear—
for example, news of the man who counts the angel
residue of birds broken on our picture windows—
in order to obliterate the polite rustle
the possum makes with her babes
through the laundry yard to home
under the shed. And to miss at five
exactly, this spring season,
first bird song with first light . . .

              O untrustworthy self
filled with appropriate terror of tumor
and broken wings, consider
flight, not the swollen plague tongue
in the sore mouth, but story.

Or the possum herself, laden, twentieth generation
of her family, in residence still in our yard,
how in spite of ghosts and grief
I know exactly—how?—her path
under the empty clothesline.

She

Organizing pneumonia is the diagnosis
for her lungs sick with emphysema. Rails
at her cortisone sentence for six weeks
hundreds of pills, a moon face, fatigue
under frantic energy, she is hard as nails
on the phone resisting all suggestions
attributing everything to the hospital
emergency room treatment for allergy
someone recommended—maybe I did.
I am hard as nails listening.

This blessed morning
of midwinter spring after a full night
of stories on tape, good ones, I am still
hard as nails wrapped in cellophane
ready to put one booted foot after another
on the blessed ground, soft air, soft color sky,
soft skin lotion hands in parka flannel pockets
her sick lungs in my chest, emphysema,
packed and crinkling under my own flushed wings.

Letter from a Place I've Never Been

Where cold was supposed to be, the sun is warm.
You've promised no wind. The grass is calm
under the snow. The map showed the interior,
which is where I am. The trip was long. I knew it would be.

From the top of the earth, I saw no mountain,
though you promised, if the air was clear,
the mountain would show. But ribbons
of light swirled the vault of the sky.
The sun set at four. The sun rose at nine.

Moose and sled dogs, exotic creatures,
I'd thought to discover around some corner
or other by the salmon processing plant, never.
I'd brought my sunscreen for a tromp
through the woods. No woods. No trees.
Flat rock that seemed to be granite.

Alaska is as far from where I am tonight
as Chicago is from Seattle, where the layover
is long. Or, to put it another way, the way
of a friend, the distance from LA to NY,
a trip I've taken.

I'm scared of the cold, of the dark, of the journey,
the unfamiliar plants that perk into poems
I've read and reviewed. Some kind of weed,
not jewelweed from Robert Frost. Oh, why
did I say I'd travel? The tundra is something
strange like a sponge. And golden.

Not Now

It's not my turn
It's been my turn not
now under the hot shower
everyone safe for the nonce
even the old cat no cancer
on her nose close to the brain
hoofing it into the spring evening
ice floe at the bottom of the driveway
even that one melting under the juniper hedge
the lilac flushing through its scale.

Summer

—for Aaron

This morning, up at six, waiting for
the flat white tablet embossed with a bone
to settle in my belly, I take up sharp scissors
and on clogs enter the raised beds to clip off
dead or dying flowers—various shades of deep purple
some with yellow throats, some lavender sports—
to gather a few full blossoms for the test tube
vase you bought me for my birthday.

The light flat against the old railroad ties
holding hard against earth, heavy clay overlaid
with wood chips . . .

Somewhere under the chenille robe, behind
the long zipper and the scars, is the young girl

packing for camp. White shorts and Ts
for the Sabbath, candlelight to welcome
a day of rest—reading on bunks, bare feet
rubbing the scratchy wool blankets.

What does that girl know about dying
or illness, AIDS, the cancer in the brain? How,
as she lifts the toad free of pond moss,
hot fingers carefully moving over the smooth skin,
to thumb a wedge against the cool suck, can
she touch her power to watch over the world, live
here touching tenderly with passion, teach
the scarred woman sitting in early light
deadheading the flowers, teach her to watch?

Surely I didn't intend to confront
anything more this season of planting
than the hired work I do—reading manuscript
texts for Longman, diddling through writing a book
with my transsexual son, in good company,
filling the patio pots. My tragedies already
suffered, transformed, and put between covers.

Better the inquiry into the nature of ticks
their habits, their prodigious swelling
without bursting, bodies thick with life,
scurrying, detached without host, to another.

Anna Maria Is Coming, or Maybe
Thomas Barton, or Max!

New life! Will he toe out like Dolly, like John? Will her eyes be fires?
Blue and green, like Papa's, the ocean at the shore?
Will she sing in the bath? Play piano in her diapers?
Will her heart leap at large machinery? Will he say, "Dribe, dribe,"
to his daddy, entering the tunnel? Will his hair be red? Will her hair curl?
Will her little face have the circumflex eyebrows of her mother?
    The pointed chin?
Her hair be fair, bright blonde? Will she frown at the light by the river?
Oh, let her head fill with Greek Owls, her mouth with honey wine.
Let his hands cup the keys, the air of the studio filling with sound,
    the crunch of cornflakes,
the sift of raw sugar on the tongue, the great chords.

And let the parents be fierce forever, Lord, as You are, exacting
price and penalty for Your gifts, so they grow strong and joyous,
blessed by the memory of the black car, open to air,
chosen by a child in token of the power they give over,
their lives in service to new life, the great melt of petals under snow,
    the green rising.

IV

With the sense beyond,
surpassing,
transcending

Hello

my best shoehorn, my malachite pillow, my tulip of chocolate, my shoelaced
rib, my waterfall below the kitchen, my dark pressure, my icy back of the neck
migraine specific, my castle in the birdbath, my supreme coffee grinder, my
ice cream refusal, my airplane crash, my bottle rocket exploding leaves in the
gutter, my no-you-don't thermos thrower, my gummy bear licorice eyelash, my
mountain of glass slippers melting into tropical punch, my stars, my neon, my
bonefire, my passion.

The Address on the Map

Rosemont Crescent
179 the address where my confirmation
class meets each Thursday. "As in Genesis,"
says Mrs. Levis, "the woman from the man's rib."
Mrs. Levis is Selma, she drives a convertible,
sling-backs and mules, not like Mom or her sisters,
in cotton housedresses, who don't drive.
She lists the false Messiahs, Zabatti Zevi, the others,
to explain smart men with grand but wrong ideas
like Mr. Levis, I think, who worked in the yard
Monday through Friday and did the cooking.
Mrs. Levis has ideas and glasses with rhinestones,
that book, The Fall of the Temple, and History,
and she invites George, the handyman who bikes
into our neighborhood to put up the screens, take down
the storm windows, whooshes out his false teeth
to scare us, into her kitchen for tea over ice
then sits down to talk, her pink mule hanging
from her painted big toe dripping feathers.

Wonder Woman's Rules of the Road

1. The wall? Walk around. Your legs work, don't they?

2. Wear armor at vulnerable sites. Perfume at pulse points? Better, silver bracelets.

3. Learn from heroes: tools extend range.

4. The best asset is a wise mother, better a goddess.

5. Absent a mom, girlfriends, comrades.

6. Bind loose hair with a fillet. Keep your face exposed.

7. Anger is power.
   Justice is power.
   Make laws when laws don't suffice (*Herland*)

8. Stand with legs apart: a triangle is more stable than a stick.

9. Avoid camouflage.

10. Don't tangle your legs in a cape.

11. Strong abs are to die for.

Wonder Woman's Bracelets

Do they cover scars, a suicide attempt? Self-mutilation? Cigarette burns, tiny cuts, gauze and Band-Aids? In the '60s, you bet. Those mad girls who wrote. Controlled hysteria. Let loose. Therapy. My jewelry box, top left drawer. A trio of silver cuffs (one a spare). The water serpent belongs now to him. (Him?) You.

In the '50s, they were armor. Underneath, perfume at pulses, why? The flutter to waft scent to the boys. I lift my wrists in chemistry class, breathe in. The naked wrist.

Clamp-on bracelets so veins, those incipient geysers, hide. The closed and vulnerable wrists flash like shoulder points under iodine-oil at the beach. In sand, sun, and waves, all flash and movement. Never take them off. What's underneath's taboo.

Wonder Woman and the Disrupted Body

Imagine Wonder Woman with one breast. Draw her costume.
Alter the top. Only one bracelet. Is it wider? The wooden boot.

Wonder Woman's Rules of the Road—1962

1. Watch your wrists. Cut, they're geysers: sexual, lethal.
   Decorate all death sites, pleasure points: earlobes, throat,
   labia, lips, elbows, wris . . . t(s) with scent.

2. Your inner arms, thin and veiny. Perfume daubs won't save
   you. Silver bands, wide at both wrists, may. They deflect your
   own gestures, others.

3. Flaunt your belly if it's flat, muscled. Abs are to die for.

4. Stretches every day; don't forget the shoulders. Bounce light
   from the chin, collarbone, especially in motion. Be in motion.
   Bounce _____ from the wrists.

5. Those headaches? Nothing but a slipped halo, a fillet binding
   your forehead, a princess crown.

6. Brunettes have more choices.

7. Learn the uses of tools: a whip, a lightning bolt: watch and learn.

8. Flaunt your legs. They work, don't they?

9. Boots, always.

10. Tampons don't show at the beach.

11. Your legs work, don't they?

Wonder Woman's Costume and Address

How come she gets to wear her swimsuit in the city? How come her boots don't wrinkle? How come her top and bottom don't match? How come she gets to wear earrings with her leotard? How come she doesn't have to wear glasses? How come red, white, and blue isn't tasteless? How come she doesn't have to wear stockings? How come her lipstick's Fire and Ice? How come she lives with girls on an island? Is there an island of girls? Show some respect!

Wonder Woman and Daughters

She didn't have one, but she could've.

Aaron at Work/ Rain

By the light box propped in the window,
bare chested, scars rosy in artificial sun,
he crouches over his workbench.
Dental tools in their holder at hand, silver discs,
his torch, the tiny saw. Light flares, breaks on
his earring as he turns his head,
frowns, dark eyebrows almost meeting.
He takes a watch from his jeans pocket,
rubs it absently over his beard, electricity.
The braid clinks its beads as his head
turns, reading something. Now he rises, goes
to the cupboard, mixes wallpaper paste with water.
The pile of miraculous papers, shot metal
threaded with linen, he sorts to start
a papier-mâché hypodermic needle he's building on the table,
matches to the real one he used this morning,

adds it as a detail to the mask to change the meaning:
a revolution: what he's about. Out the window the black car
beads up rain. He never drives it. An emblem, but of what?
A memory of pain, his slouching walk just home from hospital?
Where is the child whose shoes I bought? Where the bread
we kneaded? Where our kitchen? Our dead?

Sarah Returned to Me, Wearing the Poet's Gloves

Her capable hands hang down,
covered in cashmere, between her knees
like a man's, the gloves the only interruption
in the field under the seminar table where my students
argue the merits of poems and the visiting poet.

The gloves were black, loose at the wrists—an expensive style
made in a postcolonial factory—and smelled of Ma Griffe,
which she raised to her face to inhale now and then.
The flower skin of her cheeks shone in overhead light.

Along with the gloves, she was wearing
a peach jacket of silk, loose at the waist, loaned
by Elizabeth Taylor, a colloid ribbon from Adam's apple
to collarbone. Sarah had been changed.
Yet she was the same.

What will you do with your extensive surgery? I asked.
Who cares, she said, smoothing her hands over her chest,
fashionably flat. Her abs below kapok shoulder pads
inverted to a perfect triangle, like page 24, *Vogue*.
The cashmere gloves crackled on silk.

Where I had been wedged, between an Indonesian cushion,
tufted in triangles, and a feather pillow, space developed.
Light deepened to stone. My eyes failed. In my ears,
the cannon crack of trees exploding one after another.
Yet Sarah was with me, our hands clasped.
The cashmere gloves left by the poet warmed my palm,
kept Sarah safe from cold skin. We walked
through the residue of the world, hand in hand, calm.

Company/ 3 AM

The cold kitchen, the cat circling my feet for warmth,
nothing properly in place or tidy, surely you wouldn't
be sitting here with me—no fit place to entertain
your sprawl of words, to drape your scarf—yet
here you are. The Hubble telescope is newly fixed
and clicking its news. Your pen tracks it, opens
a space on the page for the contraption of stars,
those tall, membranous chambers we saw on the news.

You are welcome here, imagined in so much detail.
So I put up the kettle for our second cup of tea,
the chunky raw sugar cubes, the vat of honey.
And look, I say, the new life your daughter begins
spirals right out of the girl you've been,
down to his thready eyelashes, the new moon fingernails.
That girl you were who took her belly home
made clear to her folks the need for layette.
You stitched the gowns, shifts, chose diapers, the pins,
even the belly binder you never used.
The same spiral star nursery the Hubble showed
ties her to you and you to him, this new child forming.

And how glad I am to listen
to the kettle begin its rattle,
its billow, its sputter, its hot gush
from the spout as I sit here
writing with you in the kitchen, where else.
3 AM, a good time for birth, eh, friend?

The cat on my lap begins her rumble,
the overhead light caresses the crystal
brainhead paperweight, the refrigerator
cycles on, all pulses and frail light
from the door opening, and I'm feeling better,
my pen extending its line clearly enough
for me to follow, the sugar cube in the cup
dissolving the sour while out the window to the east
surely light is trembling at the edge of the horizon.

Now if I could believe my own heart clenched
as raw sugar and the caramel-freckle-brown
color I love, the news I carry scalding enough
to melt it . . .
            only a hot tub filling slowly as light breaks
over my knees, thighs (they opened for you, child,
you didn't need to ask!), my belly, my ribs,
steam climbing over my heart turned syrup . . .
then I could lift, embrace my daughter
as he is, changed, turned right around,
all expectations sloughed off, child,
you are risen, new again, from the sweet
bath of your mother's heart.

First, Thus

—The title refers to a designation used when pricing books: not the first time in print but the first in this particular edition.

Darkhead pushdown long, so small
tall otherman playing stardust melodies
fractured into waves so high apart
recombined into soothe and measure,
as in birdcry out the window, drowse
between every pain so pronounced
in one locus, only here he is,
as promised, love, love,
love out the window, see what
we've made come visit.

Elbows ache to hold, that's the plain truth,
so whatever else you've got to say, say this:
fingers were made to touch fingers. Open the light
up and tune up the corners, this lad's
jumping and another beside him. So grin!

Blessings in crackling thick
hair tied into clumps, dyed fluorescence who shaves
between or wraps string packages over waves
so harsh they jump the ears to crumbs get out
gotta get out recombine listen here, the idea
you've got is the idea's endtwist, mine twists
around both and Voila! here's visitors.
How long the stay?

One by one over land and sea, in air
they came, tied by thread together, o matter twisting
glistening red causation, no never mind the thrush

somewhere sings whether brown thrasher
or varied in that city oil ooze person to person
and the beast sits on our laps so long we crouch
down. Push, s/ he said and someone did. Welcome, son.

The Storehouse

For once we add to the measure
the storehouse keeps safe,
not come in the night
with burlap to probe the grain,
diminish the golden hills. For now I know
the phone pulse at two brings
news of a comet, look up.

Your garden voice deeper for sure
but you, for all we've been through,
are identical genetically to the daughter you were,
your locutions your steady fingers on the trowel.

Yaweh, eternal, forever at play in the universe,
jester, let me stay last in line as I am now.

Early Morning, Left-Handed

Lear's five *nevers* over,
the fool hanged, and Cordelia
and Lear dead at last, Edmund

reported and yes he was loved
by both evil sisters, so what.
I'm awake in the dawn. Cold
stone floors. The cat. His
father loved him too, I tell
my son on the phone, my
son just married. Let him
cleave to his wife. Let my
old flesh resume its boundaries,
let go. No divisions of the kingdom.
Will they write of my courage
killing the snake? We know
the dreamy answer to that one.
Honey tea swirls us sweet;
never fear the village fair,
lights stay on all night.
Tea bags bottomless coffee
cup. Ashes in the grate sweeten
the garden provender. Clay.
Ripeness is all. The fool lives on,
my left elbow's cartilage feather.

Visitation: Pink Foam Letter

Under the seat directly in front
a child's alphabet letter

Under my heavy briefcase
a new texture, sponge

On the wet tarmac waving
adult child, son.

Here thirty thousand feet straight up.

After four years trying, scars flat, waving
my son, a fine visit.

Now forever as I travel
the pink S my company.

The Funeral of X, Who Was Y's Mother

This woman who died last night in her daughter's arms
saying thank you, to whom? God for the easy death
called The Kiss, which the Rabbi tells us is God's blessing,
the touch of His lips to forehead that withdraws the divine
spark, life, from the body? Or thank you to her daughter,
most blessed by this witness, who wonders aloud which
meaning, a question in my ear as I bend down to her.
You deserve thanks, I say, either way. And we laugh
at the courtesy of her mother, who died during spring break
"so I shouldn't have to miss classes."

Shakkinah, the holy part of God that is Woman,
we are told, so a child the Rabbi says, leapt to his feet
at her footsteps in order to honor the divine spirit
within her. He grew to be honored, but this mother,
"her price was above precious gems."

She was one of six surviving children
of parents who had "left behind in Europe ten others,"
no reason given, but we know, counting the years
backward. Will it never leave us, this grief particular
as sand we are told to brush off after the whirlwind

abates? Each grain in the eye moves and scratches
as I search the bowl of sky horizon to horizon
for a sign of the lost. Each particular ash invisible

as she is within the daughter who remains with me,
in my arms, bent for news whispered with deep delight
that the final gift a parent gives, to die in a child's arms,
is enough. We laugh and cry at once, which is seemly,
while the Mother of us all cries out and laughs, One
part at best, and holds me as I bend to myself to discover
not what I can't hope to understand—that which
we are enjoined not to worry—fondle, turn over
and over—but some small way into the magnificence,
abundant and ever moving, of the breathing and continuing
    flesh.

All Odd and Splendid
(2008)

Everyone looked remarkable . . . so absolute and immutable down to the last button feather tassel or stripe. All odd and splendid as freaks and nobody able to see himself, all of us victims of the especial shape we come in.

—Diane Arbus

I

History
Everyone today looked remarkable

Vocation

Light comes in the window, must be seven AM,
time for breakfast, but the aroma traveling up the staircase
is roast turkey and now that you've opened your eyes on the window
light is dim, so it must be coming through the open door.
Crouched in the window, chiaroscuro, leaning back on the screen
a bent guy in a hat, his face lined with dark,
bends forward into the room and smiles. No, he's laughing
and then he whispers, "I've come for you, it's time."

And you decide—now that you're awake you know
you can do it—to negotiate, maybe not now,
you're only eight, but later when you're twelve,
no, thirty, so far off, and he nods,
he's amiable enough, affable
as you'd hoped he would be.
And then he is gone.

You get up—didn't you used to have pink sheets on your double bed—
same price as the twin and more flexible for the future, who said that?—
but they seem to be blue percale, royal blue with red and black stripes,
and while you're brushing your teeth in someone else's bathroom,
maybe the one in the Belgian pension where you celebrate your birthday,
you decide to go swim in the dark waves, no, maybe to the dining room
where you'll order puffy pancakes with apples, or strudel, or maybe

you should write a book someday,
shouldn't you write a book, shouldn't everyone
who has met death in the window and put him off
for a while write a book?

Diaspora

The gates were closing and the time was late
in spite of our efforts in the car
our suitcases packed, our coats tossed off
goodbyes said, or not to be said

in spite of our efforts in the car
the houses closed, the plants farmed out
goodbyes said, or not to be said
the neighbors told, the little ones in their beds

the houses closed, the plants farmed out
the station doors opening on uniform corridors
the neighbors told, the little ones in their beds
we fanned our faces, opened our books

the station doors opening on uniform corridors
then there was smoke, and damp, and sky
we fanned our faces, opened our books
we shut the windows, began to move

then there was smoke, and damp, and sky
our suitcases packed, our coats tossed off
we shut the windows, began to move
The gates were closing and the time was late

Childhood

She wove my hair in braids
before each day began.
I tore each plait apart
on the walk to school.

My clothes were always clean,
dresses each worn twice:
pinafores starched stiff
by hands not quite my own.

Daisy diagonals, white and gold,
marched up and down on blue.
Left to right, up and down,
the windows between in curtains.

The weight that bore us down
was air that could be fire.
Our uncles walked the roofs
binoculars to their eyes.

At night the shades were drawn.
Cannel coal filled the grates.
The winter cold meant ice
and blades to skim the pond.

Heel marks on linoleum
meant rubber for the war.
We crushed the cans quite hard
their labels first soaked off.

We filled white cardboard boxes
the size of small dolls' coffins
with brushes, paste, and cloths.
The red crosses on the lids
meant something we don't know.

Water Ceremonies

I

To pour. First, to lift the heavy pail.
Let us consider morning,
a child cross-legged on a tile floor
bent over the water garden. She
wears a flowered apron over shorts.
She half-fills emptiness to leave room
for the half measure of light
to fill up every iota of space,
replaces the lid carefully
to balance on the lip of the vessel.
Who is the beneficiary here?
We ask her but she doesn't say.

II

To lead and delegate. First, to name
the Club with code, initials only.
Then to find a mission:
all girls against all boys.
We vow to like all girls
no matter if they are mean or good,
to hate all boys
no matter if they are kind or bad.

You, Carlotta, are fearful and must not be.
If you will change, sign here.
If not, resign. Here is a line.
You, Veronica, will be first.
You will make decisions.
If you so choose, sign here.
If not, resign. Here is another line.
We ask you only for your pledge.
Here they drink.

III

To lift up. She takes one side,
I take the other. The heavy waves.
Together we catch the ocean.
If we are careful, we can carry back
what's salty to the berm of the wall
we've made, pour out the water
to make a moat. She takes one side,
I take the other. So our childhoods pass.

IV

To go on. Then I knew he was odd.
His arms too long. His hip thrust at a twist.
He balanced on the fountain, walked the brim.
Splashing to the center he could stand on one leg,
but his eye was cast. He was born with a caul.
What could I do? Already he was loved.
His voice in the morning fluted
a name. He knew who I was.
Others might cast him as ugly.
I gave him a halo, bent to praise.

All Odd and Splendid

The especial shape we come in
is insufficient, says the child
come slippery from the body
of another especial shape that comes in
the shape of its mother. Giving birth
is no treat, let me tell you, she says.
The nobody born will become somebody made
but the surgeon on duty just then
was entering tenth grade as the crisp nurse
sponged out the child's eyes. Splendid,
thinks the special shape called the mother
reaching out her arms. The child, unchanged,
begins to cry. Excellent, says the nurse
handing over the child. Nothing odd about it.

Wilt

When the phone rings
Aaron says *hello*
and I ask, what are you doing?
He says, *building orchid petals*
out of thin sheet silver.

Now I know something important
about the body
left behind in shards
which seem to have melted
into the body of my child.

Then my mother
from her temple of brain
says something to her daughter
about rain and rocks something
about the shape of earth
as night pulls a skullcap
over the mountains.
She seems to want me to notice sky
as a wave of salt and pepper hair
falling over an eye, something that winks.

Son

He is always saying and telling me
something urgent in the same tones
I use when I am telling him something
urgent but nobody is listening.
We are alike and unalike.
I like him I do.
He says he likes me
So what's the problem.

The problem is birth.
What an opera,
the lights, the dais,
the cast of characters wearing
the same gown.
We're both there
forever. I am.
Where is he?
He's left the building

Entered the stadium
where the team is getting ready
to tear each other and everyone apart.
Is he garbing up? He says no.
But I can see his pads in the backfield
still skin on the cow's back. Io,
I think and he laughs.

He Graduates from Clown School

"A lot of what I thought was magic
is habit," says Aaron,
chewing his nails. He wears
one red Chuck Taylor on his left foot
a black on his right. He reaches up
to adjust his wooden horns,
shrugs sequins straight on the vest
under his tux jacket then pulls on gloves.
Presto, his hands are red puffy leather.
Trots fast down the grassy knoll, drops
into a green pit where his teacher
bows, straightens, smiles, and calls out,
"Give me your best shot and hug me after."
The crowd around the rim cheers.

Aaron is ducking and weaving.
His dark face shines. He is walloping, punching,
crouches and POW! he uncoils, connects,
all his energy building and disbursing
until he seems to explode

twenty Goodwill china cups
on the floor of the garage.
I watch rage doing its work.
What girl wouldn't give
a good night's sleep
for the chance to break china
with her mother's blessing?

But that girl is this boy now
who wears boxing gloves
in a natural ring with his teacher
who is hitting him back, POW!

and nothing I can do—was there ever?—
will stop the fight
or these men from making
the hits land hard, head to head,
to prove something to themselves,
to the watching crowd, to us,
about men and their exclusions.

He/ She: The Bike

Aaron is leaving
or is he coming home?

One woman I am, or the girl,
hitches up her socks, clips
one corduroy pant leg close
and unlocks her bike. Soon
she'll be flying down the hill
we hiked up.

It's time to split
myself into two women,
or no, a woman and a girl.

Aaron has left the door open
behind his new backpack
hitched up on his shoulder
as he bends to enter the car.

I am pushing up the hill
what someone promised was wings
as he turned a wrench in the spokes
and bolted together new life.

Credo

I believe in the vision eight months
into your change
us side by side
you in your green pajamas
your brother's head bent
past my shoulder to the book.
I hold your small hot body
against my breast
as I mother of sons
Cornelia and her jewels
read on. My right arm is around you
the newest entry in our family
Bible. Your new name will be written. I will write it.

We read. Your small brother
is building a tent over us

where he lies
still as an accident
his bones knitting
until he is mended
a grown man. And you still not here yet.

In my vision I slept
you within me my knuckles
raw from worrying the tent flaps closed
next to your brother who was lifting them.
You were growing. I knew that my body
could hold you as long as necessary.

Spring Snowstorm

Each hour of day fills, excessive and pure,
with snowfall through the eyes of windows;
all color spills down the walls of each room.
The bird bath has a cap of twenty inches.
And still snow is coming and the light
grayer under the pines and spruces
out the east window. The swings
are quiet under a pile of ash white.

Under this snow, gathering itself
in ditches, in hollows of needle fists
where robins already have begun
to build, the earth must be inflamed.
Yet I can't see it, only the stasis
of the ground beneath the movement
of snow falling. This day is the first day of spring.

Snow falls through the hours
of the day long after the hours of the night
and we have been told snow will fall still
for another slice of time, up to the pickets
of the far yard and beyond.
This first day of spring
someone is five years old.
Someone else is seven.
And the one whose words
I have been reading all afternoon
the one whose flesh is falling from his bones
somewhere in Ohio, his voice is speaking.
The flakes are tiny now in the gathering cold.
The veils wind flings over the junipers
merge into a milky silk.

All day I have been sitting and reading
the words of students who themselves
are playing at soldiers in the drifts, ordering
their lives with snowmen and pizza, beer
and whatever touching they do. For a few hours
alive in this excessive and pure place
snow comes and comes, replacing the sight
of earth in spring with layers of wet. If I refuse
to breathe, I can hear the germination of wild carrot
in the ditches outside of town. If I refuse to breathe
all beauty will be cold and remade forever.

Dante's Words

What did he call her that day? A woman
who was only his mother, bound by time
as a semblance of a woman
who could be more, a woman
unbound, more manly than light
nature allowed women?
She didn't weep. She was a woman
born of Holocaust, cold
to what's transitory, cold
insults hurled by women
as he still was then, her lovely stone
child, a woman hard as stone.

Now he is a man, stone
muscles, the soft breasts of a woman
gone entirely, his refashioned chest, stone
musculature fashioned by hours stoned
on lifts, endorphins, an ever increasing time
at bodywork, focused, intent, his eyes the color of stone.
She is the mother. Her heart, a long-buried stone
under her breastbone, beats out the pace lightly
only for herself. He has become his own light,
his steps never faltering. The light
he sheds is a beacon, a luminous fire-stone,
son, a specific against season's cold,
oh warming child, a human son, running in the cold.

Or so I think in these long months of winter in my cold
garden asleep under its mulch. Wrapped by stone
fences, the bird bath is upended on the patio cold
against ten clay pots emptied of earth, cold
snow filling their mouths. The empty fountain, one woman
in stride, is emptied of her geraniums, her cold

belly filling with snow, the residue of dirt underneath a cold
scrim against her clay apron. When will time turn
to refill her body—this year with herbs, thyme
and rosemary—to make an apron of cold
leaves against the heat? Her fountain waters, all light
at play, overflowing a cascade, will be sunlight.

Nearly morning. Spring chill through the window. Light
begins to enter the room where I sit, cold
in my bathrobe, waiting for the light
to warm the room, to seep through the linen nightdress,
light to cover the body old as the library stones
just starting to gild on their plinths, the lions in sunlight
rosy at the horizon. In these hours, oh Light,
come as I sit writing, alone, a woman
fretting, fretting as a woman
does, about her son, his flight home, his living room light
clicked on this dark morning miles away as he packs to come
        home in time
for more life, more darkness, more sunrise, more time.

What is time
bound this morning with light
hinges? Time
that seeps through our bodies, time
that scatters, dissolves, washes cold
rivulets down the leather bindings, time
of restoration, spring, time
to gather the straps, the phylacteries, to number stones
on the graves, the grave markers, the heaps of stones,
each one brought by a mourner, in remembrance of times
spent heart to heart, the breathing ribs, the whispers of women
at work together, the making and undoing, the binding,
        the woman.

The gray woman
who planted her garden in stone,
this woman, her flesh cold
in this early morning cold,
still weaves her silks and linens. She stays still, early morning sunlight
crosshatching the loom, the pages, the garden, our sons, through time.

Sunday Morning, without Couplet

I am wanting to die. Therefore, I turn to
books. Someone will tell a story, start to finish
fear, hatred, weakness, then gain to begin
toward the end, conclusions and wisdom. I am
so hungry to live in the world of sunshine,
star patterns, veils of birth, nebulae from space!
Breathe, breathe, breathe, breathe, walk out
to the fence between neighbors: one died horribly.
The new people yell, scream obscenities I hear
above the voices of their children, who thrive.

Tyr

My children, the stories always say, One god with one hand, one god with one eye.

In this story, Odin is the god with one eye,
his eye traded for a drink from the well of wisdom,
the well of wisdom guarded by a frost giant.
"What will you take in exchange for a drink?" asked Odin.
"I'll take your eye," said the giant. And he did.

So Odin became the one-eyed, all-seeing, all-knowing god.
Everyone knows about Odin.
Tyr is his brother, the one you don't know yet.
The silent one. Our hero.

In the beginning, Tyr was the most important god,
the guardian of oaths. You'd swear by Tyr,
the god of keeping promises.
But the most famous thing Tyr did,
he told a lie. The lie he told saved the world.

Once a giant wolf called Fenrir was going to eat the world.
None of the gods could stop him. This wolf
was stronger than all the gods put together.
So the gods asked Odin, "What to do?"

Odin said, "Fly to the spirits of the earth, the gnomes
and the worms, the dwarves and the Norns,
and the gods of fate and ask them for this exactly:
a bond that can't be broken."

The spirits of the earth in reply made an oxymoron.
They took everything in the world that was impossible:
the breath of a bird
the beard of a woman

the sound of a cat's footstep.
And more you will remember for yourselves.
And they wove these things together
to make a fetter softer than silk and finer than thread.
And all the gods lined up and tried to break it.
Of course they couldn't, not even Thor, who was their strongest.
And the gods of the earth said, "This is a bond that cannot be broken."

Then, my children, the gods invited Fenrir
to Asgard, their home, for a gala party.
And they said to the guests, "Let's play a game."

Fenrir was the son of Loki, the god of tricks,
who hadn't been invited, of course,
since he wouldn't want his son to die.
And death was the outcome, don't you think?
A party game was the best they could do without Loki,
the only subtle one among the gods,
a kind of trickster, we would say, an entertainer.

To Fenrir the gods said, "Here is a bond that can't be broken.
We're strong. Let's all try to break it!"

Fenrir suspected a trick but he was very vain,
very strong and he wanted to eat the world.
So he picked up the bond and pulled on it
but nothing: it doesn't break.

The Norse gods may not have been very subtle
but they knew how to flatter. They said,
"With your fine body and strong muscles
you can break it, you're so much stronger than we are.
We'll wrap you up in the bond and you flex one time,
like the Hulk, it'll fall right off. We believe in you."

Now Fenrir isn't as smart as his dad,
but he knows a trick is somewhere at the heart of this story.
And he knows the gods really hate him.
And, my children, he hates them, too.
Besides, he doesn't want to eat the world before Thursday.
He says to the gods, "If I can't break this bond, will you let me go?"

And the gods looked at each other and they said, Yes,
having learned something from Loki.
"Promise?" says Fenrir, the wolf.
What do you think they said?

Now, my children, here is the crux of the story.
A lie is the foundation of civilization.
If you can't trust someone to keep their promise,
what can you trust? The ties that keep up the heavens?

Fenrir asks for proof. And the gods thunder,
"Are we not the gods? Is not our promise our bond?"

The wolf says, "Maybe. But one of you step up.
Put your sword hand right here, in my jaws.
You'll let me go if I can't break the bond!"

The air around grew quiet.
Once the wolf is bound, he is bound.

Tyr, the quiet one, stepped up.
He lay his hand down in the wolf's jaws.
Fenrir can feel Tyr's strength. He feels his fingers,
his entire sword hand in between his teeth.

Then Fenrir lets the bond that can't be broken
serve as a noose to tie him up.
And Fenrir feels his own strength.

But of course he can't break the noose
because it's not made of anything at all.

The gods walk slowly away down hill, have lunch, and play dice.

And that, my child, is why we have a planet to call home,
and why Loki, father of Fenrir, came to hate the gods,
and Tyr became the god of strength
since he learned what he had to do to save the world
and then he did it.

And Tyr is also the god of truth
who has only one hand, his left hand,
which he has learned to use well, as some of us do.

And the heavens? The vault of the sky still hangs
steady above us although we pierce it often
with our arrows and our mortars; clouds drift
at evening between us and the stars. Try to hear their stories.

II

The Transfer of Power
So absolute and immutable

Once

he made the decision, he packed up
the car, wrote notes of instruction
about the furnace, the extra filters,
the air conditioner, the location
of the humidifier. REMEMBER TO BRUSH
THE KIDS' TEETH, he wrote in soft lead pencil,
all caps, and turned to pull open the door.
Only then he remembered his razor. The others slept on.
This house was my house, he thought, the tiny sounds
of damp breathing, the early finch against the screen,
flame peonies he'd planted by the breezeway
letting go their ants. So he took a minute more to take up
the menthol lather, to his chin, then under, and then
the blade.
                              When she woke,
he was gone. She stretched, pointed her toes, rose
and slipped through the door. His side of the cabinet
was empty, everything gone as expected,
but in the creamy bowl, under curds of lather,
a rusty shine, his blood waiting for the sponge.

Storm

The harsh winds blew the snow into a froth,
the snow into a pile, a noose around the house
that bound the front door tightly closed.

The couple stayed indoors and slept a night,
a longish day they waited while the sight
of each ground out a fury. What to do?

They hated what they saw. The heated room,
the glowing stove, the bread dough rising
on the glassed-in shelf. He'd had his fill
of flesh, of winter's cheer at mid-day, gloom
at early dark. He wondered where they were,
familiar home, familiar two, their cat
he'd loved for roaming, home to lap
at milk that's warmer than bright ice. Now dark:
the wind, the troubled pair at table, silence
in and out of doors. They knew the month
was rounding somewhere else to mud and birdsong.

And then it broke, the weather warmed, a rush
of melting filled the pond, the window wells, the backyard
fountain, found the untiled chinks, moved bricks
that lined the paths, uncovered bulbs, made fingers ache,
and backs, then freed the driveway then the earth.

They rose up early, worked like men with men
to find that place renewed, in each. Then went.

The Transfer of Power

Let's say, they'd say
for years beginning a game.
Let's say the general's aide
decamped with the wife
of the general. Let's say
the stage director ran off
with her manager. Let's say
they said and began a genre.

So let's say you're getting to the point
where day has fewer hours, no, let's say
fewer sunny hours to play in the garden
with the soldiers, most of whom have lost
their heads. Let's say you've got to settle
down on the trip to Kansas behind the swings,
settle for the night at least, here's the fire pit
where we left it last winter, let's stay here.
The soldier's heads belong to the maidens
or the shoals of fish offshore, we saw them
swimming the Hellespont on Friday, after gym.

Pack up the boxes, boys, dinner's over.

Let's say I'm getting to the point where you've got
to take over. You've got to pick up the slack,
pay the bills, shovel the driveway. The doctor waits.
The borders are insecure. The flour in the tin, weevils.
Firewood is scarce and the mule's eaten. Open up
and get ready, let's say, for the next chapter, the curtain.

An Evening

In the church,
a concert hall for the evening,
a son sits shoulder to shoulder
with a microphone he's rigged
for this occasion, premiere of songs,
his music set to her words, two poems,
ten years between the writing.

A small metal square
set between prongs on a music stand, this recorder,
an emblem of their time together
so many years apart, so many days.
Sound waves break on the metal membrane.
Of course she cries. The audience applauds.
Her heart seems to open its fist.
Which words are set to his first bellow?
The voice of the mezzo soars over the beat
as wind outside whispers to the city streets
and rain freshens the pavement for its cabs.

Infant, in New York

Not quite brand new, four weeks
from birth you begin to grin, to coo
for your father who sings back your vowels
exactly in German nonsense as he swings you
easily in an ellipse around his sturdy body.
You flop. Or almost, but you're caught

in time. You frown. Fourteen days from now
at six weeks you'll laugh out loud. Your mother
in her milky daze catches your eye as you whiz by.
Her German diminutive, a word for shark, refers to
your meeting her body, which next you do. Our oh,
your liquid sounds at breast, stock-still, relaxed,
define you newly arrived after a three weeks' delay.

Your long starfish fingers wave outside a blanket
of purple microfiber that catches shine from light
to throw it back, on us. It's you who breaks our silence.
We're listening. We speak to you the first of many sentences.

Visit

Booboo is what they call her, baby round-face,
blue eyes squinting under straight red brows her daddy's
baby Booboo
nobody but a stranger.
Spiky red hair a halo.
All gums when she smiles.
She bounces and waves. She grunts to let you know
grunt back. Teaches you language.
Waits for your response. Grunts, Grins.
Fusses but doesn't often wail.
Is she smart as her parents? Who knows. Probably.
Seven months.
What was her daddy at seven months? Twice her size.

Which says nothing of her sister, Booboo's sister, clambering
onto the high seat of the swing on the hill. Letting loose.
Or traveling to the tree park to pick the bird's cherries.
Then afraid, climbing the splintery wooden slide
to the top, touches then holds tight the cold metal bar, over and over.
Climbs onto a lap for a story, someone in the lead she's following.
Other stories she sings to herself lying down on the coral tile in the
    livingroom,
everyone else in the kitchen. Or curled on the cold slate of the hall still
    singing.
We make a spoon necklace same as the kitten's in her book.
Mama is patient and cares for them all.
She herself is a big sister who says when we ask,
that at school she is Anna Link, almost reading.

Four/ Two

She's pulling my toes,
scraping my skin, opening
my blood, eating my fingers,
she says of her sister.
Great giggling. They're both
talking at once on the telephone
six hours away by direct flight.
They've been sick and we're recovering.
Ohh, says one into the phone, she's
trying to open my butt, she always
does that. Screams of laughter.

Eva Unwraps a Band-Aid

She's three and bleeding
From her thumb. She shows me
Where Lego Horse snagged Truck.
She asks, can we go to the cabinet?

I hold her up to reach the mirrored door,
Lift out the box from the shelf.
With one hand she opens the lid, retrieves

What's needed. I put her down.
She tears the side of the paper by the strip,
Opens the wrapper, pulls the tape.
I shape the gauze around the cut
And kiss her hair.
                          She never smiled.
Not once. Nor wept. Nor does she now.

War

Button, feather, tassel or stripe

Complaint

What about air fast   then static
or thick in the lungs of the infirm?
And concrete stairs designed by folks
without degrees, what about engineers?
Milk was sour in the hot coffee,
first specks then curdle and the last in the jug.
Brains spew facts then shrink or were supposed to
be gathering specifics for eons. What about heart?
Can be fixed oh yes or replaced
but pain   worry   recovery
down slow halls. What about it?

The perimeter of the new patio
all sand and also sand between bricks.
Jump and it disappears. Nothing but holes.
And then fall. Everything emptied   no standing pools
birdbaths turned over   pot saucers upside down
fountain turned off and dry. But rain's in the reservoir!
What about mosquitoes during a hot spell? What about breeding viruses?
The long kind and the short. What about them?
The pet has no food. And says so, again and again.

And what are YOU doing about it? What?
Watching birds? Magpies? A rusty colored wren
with flush at the breast? What kind of dove
you've never seen before? A hummingbird
with a rosy bib? All tiny body invisible wings
sucking up red sugar water from the feeders.
Oh. I get it. Diversion. Something heard from a burning bush. A hum.

Flight

The flight was fast through darkening clouds
building cell on cell. The air was cool
in the cabin. The movie, a musical,

quieted our alarms
with costumes, all fringe and jewels.
The flight was fast through darkening clouds

growing, towering, then blowsy
trailing wisps, settling flat on billows.
In the cabin the movie musical

went on; we sat rapt. At least I did,
twisting my rings. No longer the fool.
The flight was fast through darkening clouds.

And then the air outside was glowering
and the steward said by microphone *fast cooling.*
In the cabin the movie musical

stopped, then resumed. *Tighten your belts.* I did.
In the vents something howled.
The flight went fast through darkening clouds.
In the cabin, the movie musical.

The Public Baths

What passes for soap is marble here
where light is candles at night or by day
the piercings in walls. Steam. Flutes. Harps. Boys

singing or humming. The deep gutturals
of conversations. Tenor overtones.
Pubic curls and linen towels. The one
who limps leans on the one who whispers,
Apples, guava, smoke, salt. Parchment wilts
in the wet as the ink runs sand. Where
is a scribe when you need him? Sir,
take my hand. What happened? *The war*
was annals of transportation over mountains,
you could say we tried everything new
for the leader, or that a mother's curse
rebounded and he was born with a caul,
you could say that women are evil
or that the hem of one born of one can never
be whole. Look to your right. Such disaster
of flesh. And the brain a beacon. You
all here, sodden and bold in the heat, consider
this: if one shall be broken, the other increase.
Eat flesh and rejoice. The bounty of the fields is next.

Pets

The yard man is exactly the age of his dog,
six years, which is thirty-seven, he says
between lips chapped and swollen
from what he's been doing in the truck
with his helper. The dog waits,
the yard waits, filled with its pales
and spikes.
        The dog follows so closely
at his heels. Why? He must be afraid
of being left behind, which must have happened
a time or two in the years he's been cherished.

What is a pet? Some thing
breathing, that's one. Some thing
warm, that's another. Something
to curl over when the world shuts
down for the night, or is it the body
shuts up, so tired, so ready
to exchange air freezing for
the warmth of . . . whatever is
in the bed, that pet we're discussing
as we fall down the lines here?

Pet, have you been cared for
long enough? Maybe not,
cold weeks alone in the nest,
a bucket by the bed, that whimper
from you as the others romp
and roll belly up for the scratch.

Whoever we are, surely we deserve
the moment each day when our eyes clear
to see that the loved face is ugly,
the hips turned inward, the fur patchy,
the eyes protuberant and blind,
the gait unsteady, don't we?

And that other one, who turns his back
on the scene? He always shows up again,
so we know he loves with keen hunger
and would adopt, take home, and set out for us
a bowl filled with every kind of kibble made
from tallow and the leftover flesh of our kind.

September 11

My sneakers, having taken me through a bed of poison ivy
to the windows, now transfer their oils to the bathroom rug
and no wonder in this time of monstrous trouble
I have knocked five times on the glass, and you have come

to open the door, for which anyone would be grateful,
your bristly head bent to the knob, round glasses reflecting
light from the glass of water that tips as you brush by,
intent on my call, so the spill sprays over the teak

in much the same way as the physics of matter
determined today that marble and steel would vaporize
or turn rubble under such pressure. Meanwhile, I'm inside
the door, returned to our hearth where the fire

place holds ivy, the summer having just closed down
and the grate in the basement covered with dust
isn't ready to be hosed down, isn't ready to open her arms
to keep us far enough, but not too far from the blaze
that we ourselves have set, unwisely,
in a house made of twigs and straw.

Fire Should Be Measured by What Didn't Burn

—National Public Radio News

Passion is inferred by what isn't said.
Absence will be valued by the one who notices first.
Pleasure can be ranked by all other thoughts kept out.
Fatigue is always spoken in a narrow range of voice.

Wars are justified by the troops who didn't die.
Progress is best measured when sleep shuts out the rain.
Fidelity is most natural when the ear believes in pressure.
Hunger is most keen when the menu spreads like ice.
Will takes up its post when the mind is bent on territory.
Resolve will turn to weeping when the curtain falls at last.
Lapis cracks but slowly as pearls are ground to dust.
Medicine's no specific unless the alternative is rust.
Sacrifice can have no meaning if the witness turns away.
The field is only battle when the mess hall shuts its doors.
Wind brings down the enterprise, no matter our delight.
The crowd moves toward the exit when the puppet master speaks.
We put our shoes on standing if our dinner table's bleak.
A life's measured value is who didn't come to call.
Noise can best be noted by the silence afterward.
Death can have no meaning. That's what we learned in school.
Your going into silence is the thing we can't endure.
Whatever comes will come. Leaves are flying in the cold.
The flocks about their maps. The cord wood in the frame.
We've made the best we can of the absence and the void.
The furniture of living's exquisite. Believe it. Say no more.
Keep all the curtains open. In the window flies the snow.

Paper Strip

I mustn't spill over
margins. The desk
isn't mine to foul I'm
writing in ink. In fact
country mine white
slick one side rigid
boundaries nothing
organically loose to
grow in the body or
dirt. Formal rigor
for pen and brain.
Why have I come
to arbitrary limits?
Everything lovely
is discipline: borders
time, dedication. Okay,
why did the phone ring
& ring & ring in the emp
ty house? Where are you?
Fallen air from the slippy
surface of the reverse? Oh
page be my friend. I need you
to guide my thoughts on loss
exactly the opposite of absence
which I think may be death
this page filled up completely edge to

IV

Seeing the Changes

Arousal

—CN, d. 12/04

Seasons of lights   the usual round.
Where guns emit light darkness is.

We can lay the cloth for supper.
We can intuit the blessing.
We can light candles, multitudes,
ever again the sappy stars.

The heat comes on like flannel.
Our aches dissolve   a sucked water.
Out the window birds in some distress
flying or hitting the window.

Only earth retains her usual shape,
her cones leaking, her rounded places
flattening, her crust where the bulldozer digs
giving way for the coffin, this one.

We trust the body to soften   to flare
to moisten   to be changed under pressure.
Where you are writing we are waiting
for the ink to dry   for the stalk you are to rise.

Coma

By dying she comes closer to peace
or peach, the color of her skin,
a message from the future
when her eyes the color of the respirator
open on a mad world where she'll dwell a while.

We watch her settle slowly back into sense,
hear her unaided breath hitch and catch,
smell her slide into an animal self
test the air for scat
as she drags her piss bag
from bed to chair to door
complaining. She is unwilling
to rejoice as we do, finding her
here even as she fights
for pills for food for heat
caresses with eyes the faces
gathered around her bed
then turns away toward the wall
coughing. What means all this?

Nothing, says the red bird on the branch
darning winter out of the nest. Damn nothing.

A Friend

So little, her breath. When it stops
she falls. Her body all hinges. Bends
forward at the waist, sinks. Knees fold
out. The whole enterprise collapses.

Then rush to the pneumatic doors, Emergency,
the medical scurry. Needles, masks huffing,
and some kind of rescue without grace
or discernable plan. Not that they're paid
to care. No. Their real adrenalin is worry.

And you whom I love? Where are you? Where are you going?

Her account in the car. She feels as if she'll vomit and shit
at once. All the heat in her body rushes to her middle,
a wave of intense heat, and her fingers feel as if everything
essential is relinquishing them. She must be a writer leaving
her account of death behind. I'm listening and driving
at once, and we're both so calm. Two lively women,
in control. The young respiratory therapist has asthma.
She tells me I should have done better to bring her in
hours ago. We stay and watch but our listening is over.

Her Dream

Hyped on steroids for her lungs, she dreams:
the Commedia jester, my younger son,
transforms himself into the king;
alone, austere, his power evident
in his posture, conservative we might guess
from the cant of his shoulders under grape velvet.

He has chosen his counselors, these she spells out
as two, his nieces, tiny now but in the dream well grown.
They're warmly treated and received with love,
their parents in attendance, charming and respectful
to their king, their brother long denied, and to us both, old women.

She and I, she whispers, are there at court,
coifed blonde and brunette, laughs, too old to serve.
But we're draped in silks, sheer linens, fine wool
in winter in the shape of, she doesn't know the word
exactly, but tunic will do.

And we have, her voice lifts here, our choice
of dwelling: under a desert sun on stucco walls,
exquisite warmth on skull and hair. A benison.
Three good rooms for each. Everything we can use
we have at hand. We look just fine.

Our skin is older than it is now.
In our waking land, we're both in nightgowns talking on the phone,
she's seventy something and I'm some behind. But in her dream
our hawk's beaks are well defined. We have our choice
of jewels but no earrings grown too heavy for our lobes.

She talks for an hour then goes still.
As death turns the knob, she flings this fluency before him.

Objects When the Body Fails

I *Eggs*.
Hard boiled, cooled, dunked into teacups
Of cellophane colors dissolved in vinegar.
Six for each child. In the center of the table
A pile of markers—many colored, stuffed in a jug.
Stickers, and scissors with red and orange handles,
The wire egg rack in the center lets the colored ones drip.
Each kid has deep grids on their knees.
Four kneel over a table covered in oilcloth.

Red, yellow, blue sails luff over the edges.
An adult in the back bedroom reads a book about soul.
In his thuddy chest a daughter rises like a rainbow egg
Lifted from her cup of vinegar bath.

II *Pots with copper bottoms.*
One set for every house and one we suppose
For the nuns in their convent on the corner.
Pinky bottoms from lemon and salt
Or the chemical cleaner that fizzed dark
On the counter until washed off.
Peas steam in the pint with soda dissolved in water.
Better raw but not so digestible, served with butter.
Selma Levis used marge in the bag
We squished until the yellow blister popped
Under the thumb like bubblewrap, which came later.

III *That one object made of rubber.*
Glue color, the shape of a capital O
Squished into an oval if you pushed just right.
Lived in a white plastic lid clipped over
The bottom then clicked closed. All powdery.
Discovered in the bedside table drawer.
Someone's mom said it had nothing to do with us.

IV *"Particles," says Susan*
when I ask what she's afraid of.
A fluidy rattle is her body's constant ground.
This time she's brief on the phone
But I hear the workmen in the background
Grinding off plaster behind plastic sheets.
They use anchors to keep the plastic down:
A bottle of bleach, something called "All Solvent"
And six bricks wrapped in beige linen napkins
Around the perimeter of her dining room.

V *Water*.
When given a choice
Of water over air
We always picked water.
Maybe amnion was our model
Though we couldn't say why
Not even now, for the life of us.
I tried solving that riddle.
It's later, and we prefer air
Where we try to flourish
Like orchids on bark
Our invisible support wires swaying
On currents from the wall vents.
Probably she'd like a river of air.
I wish I could give it to her.

VI *Bed*.
We all travel from.
Where are we going?
Her bedclothes are torchy brights, flowers
Under cashmere throws all teal and chili.
Her gowns are feathers.
She sleeps well and her dreams . . .
If I'm lucky she tells me.
I report they're mostly the color
Of paprika on egg salad her mother fixed.

VII *Roadside Attractions*.
Good to soften the pain.
And movies, and soft foods
That sweeten as they go down.
Lotions, peppermint, visits
From friends, injections
Steroids or anesthetics.
Books on tape or disk. Some paper.

A library card someone else uses.
A hang tag with a blue chair
In the car, for transportation.

Beloved, 24

Get in   with a packed suitcase to ride
the prairie rain-pocked   sleet marks the wide meadows
where is his body?   traveling   under shine it comes
in a nest of pleated linen   we return
in the wrong direction   then turn
to the sleety roads   toward your body
we breathe to hold away
what holds you fast   has come for you
    watch over you this cold evening as we go

we refuse to take up your absent wonder
we stand by your body as time takes you over
we are ice in the mud under your fingers
we refuse your breath   we will never leave you

Funeral, then Flu

Not the gym   Not the notebook   Not the streets   Not the
    block   Not the verge
Not the skyline   Not the midnight lights.

Service, service, service   blood on the knuckles   slice, grate, cut open,
    pour   dish
and spoon up and into, over

Nurses   friends   saints who eat drink   nothing. The neighbor
    dying young of cancer
to whose porch he brought   Thanksgiving dinner last year   the
    slices of ham   sweet potato   cranberries   nuts in a zippered
    bag   hard shelled sweets   pecan pie.
To the partner of the one
dying young of cancer
who does not eat.

Fever in the night   coughs   shivers   spewing   misery   and once
    you loved them all.
In the coffin
the body silver
as the boards. Silence

no rise nor fall
of the chest
the worker's hands
nails with their dark halos
yesterday he worked for a living.
Now purest absence.
Weeping and the rending of cloth.

We who can do no other
serve the living who can do no other
Fluids   electrolytes   sugars   salts.
Stir and mop up.   Collect wash
measure dry fold turn
and the best of us do it cold, cold.

Into the nests of bedclothes at night,
water bottles tissues books tapes creams
we rise at night in the next room
when the beloved cries out tosses
the memory
of the journey just over
the beloved youngster
dead in his coffin   silver
as his broken chest
father and lover
The same ears
of the one who spews
and suffers his fever
rising day after day
in flesh radiant enough you'd think
he could raise the dead in his arms one might think so,
measuring fever against the cold
the dead other who must begin
to generate heat through his icy stasis
creatures working
even as the other begins
to mend under the indifferent
care of the one who used to
love them both who cares for
the quick and the dead
and can do no other
having made them
exactly with the body's instruction

who can do no other
but bend to the will
of the indifferent maker
who is said was said always
always to love them all.

Suite

I Aubade
Because rain fell all night
this morning the bird bath
in its ring of fragrant hostas
is filled to the brim. The rim barely
holds in the shining ring of water.
Part sun part shade is where
a half-dead apple tree leans;
light touches but barely
the tips of the branches
just at the edge of the garden.
Beyond the dapple
in full sun the old sandbox sits.
The upright swing next door
is just beginning to sound like calling
and the screen door closes and opens.

Suddenly after three aloof summers
the feral cat comes to sit on my lap
each morning at six, on white linen
where the bathrobe tie falls to my knees.
She brings her long claws and her sharp teeth
and the technology of her intermittent rumble.
Today she settles then turns to the window

where the wisteria drops its purple earrings
and they fall but not yet to the grass.

II Look at this amaryllis! Three weeks ago
in the rush of holiday change
I whacked it good with a chair
took down the stem
opened a three-inch tear
and mostly severed the bud.
Should I throw it out? Cut the broken stem
to force in water? But I'm too busy
to do more than replace dirt in the plastic pot
then shove it into sun. I went to the kitchen, put up stew.

Aaron was surprised the morning of his leaving.
"Mom, plants heal," he told me. I'd forgotten.
So here it is, ready to bloom:
Three fat buds each three inches long
and the tears healed. Straight stem.
Not exactly beautiful, not callas from the florist
but maybe one of those signs and wonders
we can use? I don't know exactly but figure you will.

    III *Early morning in June*
White linen robe
gift ten years ago
in the pocket
white linen square
bordered with lace
my grandmother made
half a century ago
transferred from her drawer
to my suitcase after death.
I reach in order
to blot my face.

The flax swaying in the fields,
The loom at its work,
The plant fiber transforming,
Those at work breathing,
Touching thread, the winding
Sheet and the binder
The moment beyond this breath

IV I've put up chili, or what looks like chili,
added eggplant diced and fresh rosemary
from the patio flat. The tomatoes mask
additions so we'll never know that coffee
makes the vegetables float. Already August.
Squirrels scurry acorns on the bricks into pots
of dying geraniums and whatever hurls itself
down makes the usual noise. Loud the cat
about her silvery mouse on the indoor tiles. Look
out the window at that sunshine. Still summer.
Who can know what's ending
over land where the uncut hair of graves
waits to be measured, plowed, then opened?

      V Her Ghazal
The season turns at last.
You ask me a question, why last?

The gingko accepts snow's burden.
No matter, limbs bow at last,

Or trees crack. Yesterday you made a visit.
After surgery, morphine, stitches out at last.

Silence is news. Meat in the sink, signs of sustenance.
Signs that ask, Does life transfer at the last?

Bodies in bed take such a small space.
Two sticks, we will be given away at last.

Or go fast alone. Some miracle. The sky is dark.
Now morning. What's left?
You alive, at last.

Again

> Friendship, like the immortality of the
> soul, is too good to be believed.
> —Ralph Waldo Emerson, "On Love and Friendship"

Do you suppose you could be wheeled to the garden?
Would you like to listen to Bach's cello concertos?
Do you think chilled grapes would make you happy?
Does your mother's voice call you to childhood naps?
Does sleep all afternoon invite your cotton counterpane?
Will voices reading to you compromise your journey?

Remember warmth stored in sand when you're lying by the ocean?
Imagine your first dress from childhood's celebrations!
Dust the toes of your first pair of patent leather slippers.
Look into the reflection in the birdbath on the porch railing.
Growl with the dog, who wants to taste your dinner.
Speak up when silence overtakes you. Enter silence like a lover.

We're angry when they leave. They're angry when you do.
Know that the ending of bereavement must always be reunion.

Can afternoon light find your pillow?
Who strokes your hair when your face is damp?

Palms rinsed with tepid water can sometimes return the favor.

Her Dying

You will die soon. We all die.
We all go out from our houses.
My house, for example, is Willow Grove.
Your house—you still have one—is Garland Place.
The roofs are yellow, a tile called Cyon Picaresque.
Hang on or
You'll slip or
You're falling
Into the run off.
The white rabbit
Your heart
Thuds blue, tart prickles, burnt
Towers in the far garden. Prairie overtakes your bed.

Now you're coming alive,
Scioto pears in your palms,
Your nightgown, your slippers, your hair-ribbon
Resolving into wet ash.
We've tried to
Reach you, stitch pain
Into bread for you.
Once we walked together in the garden
Our sons ahead and behind us . . .
Something soothes so smartly since sunup . . .
Look at that orchid
On your tongue it tastes like heaven
You reach for   pricked pull away.

You're becoming the polished boards of grief
collapsing into the house they
Now look! A soaring over the rooftops with legs

Flapping, warping air as it goes,
A zigzaggedy culvert of bird-Vs.
You go west from Garland, they go south.
We on Bread Street watch
You leave, hear your breathy messages lapse
Into mountains of sibilants hush hush.
Do not go without us
We call into your growing silence,
but you go, cease,
ceding yourself with your breath to us.

The Changes

Everything we promised you was so
is not. Wounds filled with your blood
leak out their bandages so your gown
is rosy wet. Your frail spouse
who begged for news, our promise
that he would not have to watch
or lift the gauze, was told good news.
We lied. Each day he tears the tape,
repacks what used to be your breast.

What we said to you was not is so:
pain's presence where you have no flesh,
numb where what is left is still intact.
No one who breathes can be your friend
least one, who lives and knows
and will not tell.

Where yesterday they bent to kiss
your breast today is gone, missed

every minute dissolved in sound
throat alters; breath is drowned
then rescued, lost again. We make of this
truth what we will. I cry now because I can.

A Body of Water

—after Donald Hall, for KN

Lake air   dusk
warm outside   cool in the house.
On the rock   table   residue
of redwood, hemlock, spruce.
High over the water   window
teak table   rubbed linseed   seventy years.
Everything round   lake   table
mats   water carafe   the pot
for sugar, crystal shot glass for salt,
silver spoons   their bowls tucked
into sweet and brine. Eyes red with both.

A slow wind   here the trumpet vine fallen
with its struts, there an azalea twelve feet around.
Two tin olive oil cans strung on cable
moving from the center of the window,
bisected wood, the eaves with their eight struts.
In twenty years the trees have risen.

Wind breathes
needles soften on their branches.
The house holds, houses do, the contour of ground,
clay holds the new fence at garden's edge where it was.

The light ripens late tomatoes   rhubarb
by the stable doors, Pickpocket gone, new wood.

Now the lake stirs, wind, diagonal ripples
laze and hit the old dock. Open gate
white against the color of wood chips
pine needles   the gazebo filled to the tenth log,
oh children children   and Squash the dog, Buttons the cat.

Not crystal the vase made by a child,
not daisy   an open geranium in blue pottery
cream drips the color of petals
the bud of the geranium   unopened green
center rose red   years ago daisy shading toward yellow
sky gray   then late sun on the dock, oh come out
come out.

Someone has died. She was a woman
who'd forgotten her name. The names of her children.
Her companion. Her life. Eggplant, rosemary, wind, blue.
But a restless roaming. Vernon, Dale, Ron, Merle.

Elegy for Two Poets

—S and R

The pet calls
but no, the silver bowl is full
and the woolen throw at the foot
of the bed is pulled askew.
On the roof
sliding ice into slow melt
makes water accumulate somewhere
beyond gutters' overflow.
At the junction
of star and sky a flash like electricity
arcs into fuse before fire rages.
Pilot, we call as we rush higher.

There is a great river called
what. Where will you cross
when you have put down your pots and pens,
whose maps to guide your powdered inks?

We cannot endure it, these deaths like paper
put to the flood, the breath all gone so decay sets in
at the juncture of breastbone and rib, the emptying
cavities where color freshens. Your words un-
braid like hair put to the match, fused. Underneath, not even a body
of water to tear into banks, no bridge to construct from spent matches.

And your children are dead, the boys who grew
in the purses of your bodies, now ash as the grate grows hot.
Not time enough to push and spin at once, not words and flesh
at once, not courage and porridge, not portage against the flood,
no help to pack or arrange for details, the sharpened knife,
    the static truck.

We who spit into the ink pot for you, we dip our braids
to make your route with the powders of your leaving,
trace the river bank, then get up to carry brick to keep
back the melt of ice from foundations, we breathe
as best we can from our drying lungs, to keep you
just a while longer, a month? May we have you
for a day, an hour, the minutes we use up in words
to remember the flash of your freshening minds
at play in the language, how warm your shoulders
holding us, saying hello, saying thank you, goodbye?

V

The Especial Shape

2 AM Migraine

Is this the blue hour, no.
But the cat in her six fur bodies
leads a way out of bed to the kitchen.
Absinthe of the middle years, the queen's kingdom.

The gold overhead light steadies under the switch.
I am not buried in oiled pearwood yet.
Night's veils will part.
A book's pages fly to my prints.

At the corners of my eyes
bright flashes signal the night jaguar pacing off her dark café.

Moving Pictures

—*The Maquettes of Robert Arneson*

With a wooden paddle
the size of a bat
he hits the clay head hard.
Feathery eyebrows
then his unglazed eye.
Who is this old man,
his dare, his frizz of hair,
his doctor's coat?

"Make comment on human fallacies without concession,
whistling the while," he says to the camera.

He's a little overweight
slightly paranoid
and arrogant, he says.
Why play it safe?
"Clay can't hurt you,
it's pretty informal."

Who was it developed the glaze
in his mainstream?
Maybe bladder cancer
made his face fall into
tile at pool's bottom
and just stay wet? His own neck's
jerked off every caryatid
Splat! on the hard piazza floor
and the head still laughing.

No decay possible
when everything's
fired. Such a huge kiln
to open on your own face!

Dark Haired, Dark Eyed, Fierce

When the photographer came
she asked him how to appear
in charge, the commander poised,
a female authority, and he said,
"Cross your arms over your chest
and raise your chin." She did
on every website hit for months
through four strong seasons and the fall.

Now in this ad she's wearing red,
arms and legs akimbo, her four-inch
left shoe's heel pushed into her kneecap,
the neck's fur scarf dripping past her lap
to crotch. The legs are open.
Her nails are bare, her eyes veiled
only by cropped hair in Theda Bara fringe,
in shadow, ringed with kohl.
                        What are we advancing here,
all four limbs bent in puppet disarray?
A female pliancy? The yoga's payoff?
Are we still fierce, in dyed red seal
that's edged with kid, Gianfranco Ferre,
suspended in your transparent vinyl egg?
My undershirt and briefs are net. The fur
beneath the fur is brown.

Professional Travel

Tomorrow we must pack.
Competition is the reason for this meeting. We're scared
silly to be flinging
linen and denim into a suitcase,
pushing the hard lid closed.

By evening all open minds will close.
Old friends in the lobby pack
each other's ears with greetings. Competition
is the order of the day, whose suitcase
is more costly, whose new contract scares
us silly with envy until we're flinging

praise around, or starting a fling
with the hot new painter, closing
out others whose silence, artist's block, is scary
or maybe contagious? Look! There's Horace Pack
alive at sixty, his leather suitcase
and jacket matching. This year he's no competition

for the Writer's Prize. But life's no competition
for him after near-death. For him a fling
is a metaphor for breathing. He's pushing a suitcase
on wheels, heavy with books, carefully closed
on his wife's artful packing.
Being here is no scare

for him, really, no scare
for us, either. Competition
rides our blood, arteries packing
danger into an adrenaline fling.
Earlier episodes cauterized are closed
in a title, "Ashes in a Suitcase,"
red tag attached to a black suit on the cover, in the suitcase.
Name and address flaunt our location, the world. We're not scared,
but filled with essential knowledge, closed
off from the company. Winning the near-death competition
one year is no guarantee—we know it—only a fling
with a new lover. We're not ready to go. But the suitcase is packed

or unpacked, whatever. Fear's unavailable for reuse in the competition.
Scared or not, we're here, maybe that's the point. Fling
that suitcase from the platform! Know that the damned lid is closed.

Alice

> What we call history is nothing more than a continuum—in reverse gear—of
> the present.
> —Alice Steinbach

I

Continual occupation and change
weaken one's sense of one's feelings
so looking forward to something
—a dinner at Orchid's for example—
can distract from impatience, the desire
to see you again, which may lead to
—which impression must I want to convey?—
boredom or disappointment since the future
might be considered a department store
of choices, luxury goods I want to own
and use up. A black Armani suit
for example, perfect for the lecture circuit
beginning in October, or the cocktail hour
I enter without you, or the art opening
where we go together in our jeans.
Surely I feel something, don't I,
a kind of ennui, impatience
at forgetting the location of the suitcase?

II

My feeling this afternoon—the blue hour, no?
is like yours, or Billie Holiday's as her eyes
roll up into that note we hear from the balcony
above the thump and below the machinery's
back-up beep. We feel something, surely,
on vacation from our continual preoccupation
with change. Don't we? The extra rich ice cream

melting? Peppermint panties? Ads for pain killers
plugging into our anxiety exactly as arteries slam shut?

III

You asked. Here are my impressions. Rushing forward
backward gets us nowhere. We're all alone
with these big possibilities. Talk is expensive
but we can pay the bill. Can't we? Our waiter is drugged.
This soup is delicious. Pale beets, imagine.
These earrings of gold seeds and calcedony are lovely.

IV

At four when I wake the door is still open
to the balcony. Police helicopter? No lights.
Fire? Someone is missing? A wind.
My heart is occupied to the tune
of the blades—thwup, thwup. A mystery.
Thanks, Nancy Drew, but I'm sick
of preoccupations, appointments to deconstruct
the story shuffling through the SONY PSYC.
I can, you know, so well trained
nothing narrative escapes analysis. Am I correct?
Am I cold? How much do you charge to cuddle?
No wonder we like the feral cat who stays
only long enough to drool before fear takes over.

V

You're here but you're furniture,
a leather sofa that springs open into a bed.
You could be anyone so long as you hold up the nightclothes.
We've had a chat over excellent veal
pounded sliver thin. Yes, we're both against war,
big business, wind power, and material goods from China
if they're shoddy and poor design. We agree
it's best to say thin. Gandhi said eating meat

incites lust, didn't he? You've got mud on your boots.
In my house you'd have to go around or take them off.
Yes, I see they're a fine design, leather gloves
for feet, durable and not synthetic.
I'm tired. Where did you say you're going?
Shall we share a cab?

VI

> Her "storytelling voice is just as strong as her drawing grammar."
> —Alice

Subtract one and you've got, what?
Half a talent? Half a couple,
one of whom shoots the dogs?
I promise to stay put if you do
but how? Something about big
machinery, a helicopter doing our work
on a tiny laptop connected to wind, your weather blog?
Talk to me! Oh, I forgot our subject, three restaurants:
"a table is an altar," says the Talmud. Twice a week we worship.
I'm sad to be throwing out my storytelling voice
over pizza and beer, hoping you'll deploy
your drawing grammar in a way I recognize.

VII

Once a time lapse is enough,
isn't it? My favorite suitcase is red,
a portmanteau into which stuff goes,
the necessities for a good visit.
Seven days' purge through the portals of the ear
means a stream rushing on down the mountain
below this balcony. Still sitting here
this morning, thank God for the ascent
made by the cable car fifteen times already.

What are you doing? Thinking about me?
Alice goes to her room.
Travel without the beloved is travel in letters
on the page. Is that it? Never, never, never,
never, never said Lear over the body of his daughter.

VIII

Did you have a good trip? she asks
as she hands out soap, hard currency for gifts
to distribute generously. Here the mountain air is chilly.
Are you surprised? I sit reading on the balcony
overlooking three mountains merged, like cleavage.
Late in the day we might drink champagne. It's fall,
another end or a beginning. We've brought clothes
we've never worn, pack up piece by piece through hours.
Alice is traveling in Provence, alone or with a learned guide.
Soon we'll decide now is exactly the right time to go home.

VI

All Odd and Splendid

Terza Rima

Where to begin this morning, Sunday eve?
With death? He did, she did, I will
or no. Be blunt. The kitchen knife.

The rope in the garage. The window sill's
shards of broken glass. The hot rail
in the middle of the subway. Pills.

Against all I wedge a plastic pail
filled up with sea, my cousins tugging
at the handle, hot sand absorbing water.

Then the sunrise. Dependable plug
for despair, for fear, for other indignities
that keep us shivering under covers.

Like you? Like him? Like one
who does the shopping, buys the flowers
in their simple pots, lifts the roast into the pan?

God! We rise, put on the coffee pot, shower
and dry this body, lift up the window to smell snow.
Where can we find spice in this, or power?

On coasts of air, in shoals of coral, with winds that blow
the fog away so landing lights make out the runways
as we land tomorrow? Dear Lady to all this saying no

I beg indulgence, forgiveness, insurance, and the blight
that leaves no scar on those we love, but only on my shoulders
rounding as they take on weight, the trip I'll make

By air, this time. The lift-off shocking,
the plane turning its back on sun, traveling
west in early morning, racing somewhere.

Sunrise, bird breath visible in cold, the children's chant,
earth turning, the Pleiades, the goddesses and their dogs,
the mind at work, the body's song, the water in the pail,
    the warming sand.

Now

It's Fourth of July
again where shall we go
up the high crest of the hill
to watch or onto the driveway
where kids crouch to light
God knows what special effects
in the dark mosquito hum?

This year the velvet quiet
drops like too much cover
too hot when you want
to stretch out but can't.
Something alive nuzzles
your side keeping company
with the old body until you love
too warm. The silence stays put.
If you lie still and breathe
soon the small chill of midnight
will find your pillow.

Tenor Part

The thistle in the border
behind the tree peony
whistles a riff on the subject
of succor: expect none from me,
he says as light folds down
over the flap of the patio.
I who sit waiting for fear to stop
attend to the spikes
and the bud brush
not yet ready.

Learn, croons the garden
from its fringe of weeds, Lamia
stretched over the brick walks,
the Periwinkle vine mat
strangling Lilies-of-the-valley.
Late in the afternoon, as it is,
the wind makes cream
from the seeding Dandelions
and in Italian pots the expensive
Geraniums push forward their lavenders
and neons to reach for the sun's last rays.

Splendid

Now she's sick, cut.
He almost died but didn't.

Is my baby ugly? he whispers.
I answer here. No.

His arms are short. Her neck wobbles.
What's the matter? Everything.

For twelve days and nights the wisteria
grows tricolored lamps on twisted branches
that cast no light to read by.
Each year we sit on a bench reading.
We sit still.

If he lies on the floor and hums
If she builds towers and bridges with her fingers
If gray light bleeds lavender onto the pages
What can be said to be missing? What else can matter?

Love This

early morning light, the chant of the cat,
coffee hot with milk, chenille royal purple
heat against cold, the dying dead,
children safe & far away, the children's children

coffee hot with milk, chenille royal purple
evergreen sprigs in the bittersweet wreath
children safe but far away, the children's children
safe in their beds where I can't see

coffee black, chenille rags of royal purple
children safe but far away, the children's children
evergreen sprig in the bittersweet wreath
seasons change but I'm still alive

children safe but far away, the children's children
the clock ticks out, clicks time over
seasons change and I still alive
have bags to pack, worlds to write.

The clock rolls over but still some time
heat against cold, the dying dead
bags to pack, words to write
early morning light, the chant of the cat.

Thank You Very Much

Never, never, never, never, never
—King Lear

indeed for the mush giant Hosta become with frost,
for mighty fine women up from their beds to put on coffee,
for chores reduced by cold, for cold nights lengthened at the hem.

Thank you very much for undertaking this audition,
for entertainment unraveling five rows back and center,
for free tickets' admission to the big ones, birth and passion,
for novels uncut; for heads unencumbered, as yet ungarlanded,

for the unanswered phone, the instruments in the band not warming up.

Thank you too for the filled freezer,
the fur parka, the dead animals on the verge big ones this season,
for sweaters at discount, stores filled with designer clothing,
for thousand-dollar vacuum cleaners, for used cars with not much mileage,
for unnecessary telephone poles in subdivisions,
for cell phones that vibrate, for leather upholstery,
for toothbrushes and green toothpaste from Maine, for undeclared wars,
for braces on limbs and teeth, for surgery, for sutures,
for stents and staples, for health insurance,
for generation, for shoelaces, for tap dancing
for love for love for love for love, for love.

List & Story

(2020)

This book is for Dale Nordyke, companion and ringleader.

Here, hands full of sand, letting it sift through
in the wind, I look in and say take this, this is
what I have saved, take this, hurry.
—from "Prayer" by Jorie Graham

We are afloat
On our dreams as on a barge made of ice,
Shot through with questions and fissures of starlight
That keep us awake, thinking about the dreams
As they are happening. Some occurrence. You said it.
—from "My Erotic Double" by John Ashbery

Autobiography

I've stolen a chair for you, sawed off the arms.
For breakfast stirred up plovers' eggs. Once
I flew to the moon in order to press your hands to her face.

I strung a magic key around my neck for my roller skates.
On my feet they clanked and threw sparks on the sidewalk.
My mom wore an apron when she wasn't wearing gloves.
I wore silk to the dance midnight blue with a keyhole neckline, a soft bow.

I married for the childbed and didn't die.
I walked out the door on my own two feet.

Alaska wove color through the sky.
The dog sled team at a full run shat frozen turds that missed me.

Up again at night I learned hot milk beats tea every time.
The walls all color wore well and framed up paintings I accumulate.

My house has a bedroom.
Much of my life is over.
Pleasing others is my greatest sin.
When my ribs knit I swore never again to surrender. I lied.

My knee healed with a scar.
Four husbands vanished on horseback but the crops didn't fail.
Winter is a season like any other.
Now spring is all. Spring moving into summer.
Sleep in wind in voices.

What's under pressure breaks out in cactus flowers.
Ants abound in the arroyos and coyotes.
Some of what I couldn't stand to lose I lost.
In every room a pencil.

The Spa of the Three Widows

I *The Spa of the Three Widows*

At lunch this year as anyone can see
or I do draped in a black shawl
that these friends have lost on the grief diet
the weight of one healthy adult man
the one missing from each of their sides
of the patio table where we're sitting.

They bend together over their burgers
—chopped beef or vegetable—and salad
no wine this time to discuss the past year
when their husbands have taken by the hand
Death and been dispatched by his tools:
disease for one, collapse for another,
and for the third a fall from a cliff.

Behind my shawl I speculate
about the sulfur tubs in the meadow
beyond the patio where we dine
a specific said the brochure for a bad back.
Too much to carry I think listening to the widows.

II *The Widows Call Me Butch*

They have deposited the insurance checks, signed the forms,
spent tens of thousands to settle the estate, pay hospice,
hospital, doctors' bills, equipment rental fees, the nurses.
Their lawyers are cleaning up. His children have split the spoils.
Soon they will carpet the den, move his desk to the basement.
Their brooms have swept salt from the floors of their bedrooms.

Now it's time for them to work on me, still innocent. By butch
they mean *not feminine*—my posture, clothes, my presentation.
They can help me look better even at my age. They hold up

turquoise T-shirts and pale pinks to check for color
a bronze lipstick and nail polish. At their direction
I buy everything and add a sea-foam fleece jacket
cut close to my curves, warm and inexpensive.
Each night my red phone hums as I call my husband.

III *The Widows Shop for Makeup at Sephora*

They wear shorts and sweatshirts with the name of our beach
embroidered on their pockets   two navy, one sea-blue.
They turn up their shiny faces to the salesgirls
for the application of color to their eyelids.

They are absolutely still
seated on cretonne stools so the scarlet,
zinced purples, buff and tan can be applied close to their lashes.
Their eyes are transformed, all green and blue iris, as they open
to the fluorescent light. They buy brushes thin as a fingernail
in a kit for travel and blush compacts set with gold filigree.
Then they blot the sore places under their eyes with Kleenex.

IV *A Widow Weeps*

Ophelia wears Mephisto sandals that rub her foot sore over a vein
a big pain that seems to erode her calm.
Later in the car while the others go into the drug store for bandages to
    cover
I loosen the strap on her shoe by a notch.

From the backseat she says, Don't speak!
Then wails. I am stone silent as instructed.
But when her small hand pushes between the seats
I take it and hold on. Her pain shudders between us.
What will I do? I say all the fragments of the prayers
I know to beg for the edges to dull.
                        Artemisia returns with a bag.

Clio unpeels the tape   positions the gauze and presses.
Silence. Then we go on to the beach.

V *The Widows Dance*

The waves have been flat all afternoon
the sky a dulled mirror. We have lain
in the light for hours protected by hats

and towels and shirts. We have slept
and talked and now we are walking
and looking down to find stones in the shapes
of hearts, or those wishing stones with halos
stretched front to back or up and down
or the flat ones for skipping on water.
I pick up the ones most resembling fudge
with stripes of coconut that we buy in the shops
sweet to hold under the tongue.

We have walked along the wet sand
until the white cliff in the distance is just above us
and the tide pool has filled with muscle, a swirl
that pulls us back hard. We hold on and push back.

In the distance one widow is dancing. The sun
has come out and makes of this vista a dazzle
but we can see her flirting with the waves.
Maybe he is there under the surface.
Maybe she can see him. Or maybe she is alone.
We reach to hold hands and run to join her.

VI *For Heaven's Sake*

Okay, we're sitting by the window   wind a blow
through our hair   when what should we hear
but the sound of blade-chop through air   go figure
so we decide to swim   but another interruption

children's screams on the grass below   go figure
then we decide on lunch   who has the coupons?
we'll wait   and we find them   but what happened to the key

missing   go figure   did we put down our bundles on the counter
or did we   what did we do last night after gin & tonics?
Imagine our subjects of conversation include sex   and abuse
but never the deaths of husbands or their defections.

VII *First Days Back*

I come home from the beach
to my spouse who is alive and vigorous.
Thereafter two days of antibiotics.
The spring comes on.

Each day arrives in a shower of pollen.
The birdbath water is covered. The Norfolk pines
put out for the season are packed at the forks with yellow.

Everywhere, birds: robins, cardinals (one flew
at the windshield as I turned into our driveway,
a streak of flame), and here should follow the list. Omissions.

All night thunder, lightning, dreams and hard rain.
My wedding bands look so simple worn down.
Should I put back the bright stone beside them?

My morning horoscope counsels patience.
I'm sitting at the keyboard in my black shawl
a nightdress of cotton and nothing more. Black
shoes with orthopedic arches. Three rings.

VIII *Another Year*

> We are here . . . and we were never here.
> —Ann Patchett, *State of Wonder*

Turquoise beads and a golden chain to celebrate
Another year of grief work, an amulet to hold
In the hand. Water rushes downward
Outside our balcony. Green predominates
On the mountain. Those few dead pines
Stand still in wind roiling the ski runs
Now tucked up in color.

Last night's clap and sear
Left three rides on the mountain
Broken. Such a storm!

Because they don't ask
They buy everything decorative.

Their bodies are thin also
Lines on the face where lines hadn't been.

The one who bends over by the roadside
wears a size two special order.
The one who drives now
Has her fist closed around the amulet.
The other rests, smiles and sings along
In the back seat of the rental, a Cadillac—
Why not?—as the ocher and cerise and magenta
Shopping bags shift in the trunk's shadow
And they navigate the mountain's curves.

Transportation

My father bought a wagon to deliver
groceries, then the shoe store's leathers,
the mercantile's piles of rugs and towels
or anything else those neighbors needed
carried from one place to another.

Then he got a truck, more trucks, and a terminal building,
a phone and typewriter and billing pads,
and put his mother to work in the front office with
an adding machine, a gas pump and a motto:
"We move everything but the world."

He bought a Packard, broke his back
doing some fool thing in the alley,
married Dolly, pretty but helpless
and over years moved the family from
Harvard Street, behind the skating rink,
to Highland Heights, in spite of covenants
against Negroes, Italians, and Jews.
Nobody ever stopped him.

Somehow money piled up, enough
to keep his widow and child for many years,
until the fleet of trucks and buildings
with his name and motto in rolled gold
stopped, were shuttered, sold.

Where is he now, a sliver of bone
and serge dug into a closed cemetery's dirt?
Or reborn as some ambitious boy
in Agra, with a taxi, ready to transport
tourists and their stuff

wherever they tell him to go
or wherever he wants them to go.
And here's a survivor carrying stories
from one life to another, yours, readers.

Home

Well,
I tried and tried for years
but the wallpaper wouldn't stick
the hanging lights were ugly
kitchen and bathroom tile
turned yellow in light.
That house wouldn't have me.

I opened many windows
moved myself from stale room to room
threw back chintz curtains then sheers
sat in my mother's princess armchair
trailing wisps of Joy perfume
stolen from her dressing table
my thumb in a book. Papa's
leather club chair dragged to a place
on the carpet nobody could see.

They were so glad to see me go.
They bought me a plane ticket
and a trunk they helped
fill with clothes I chose unwisely
and they got me to the airport.

Ten months later
my English teacher
husband unlocked
our apartment door.

Go

The year I was eighteen
twelve months of love
magic in leaves I stretched for
reaching upward
to pause
in early dusk
on Boylston Street
walking to Charlesgate East
the year I turned eighteen
"alive" in Hebrew numerology
as my father died.

How leaves that autumn
brightened their yellows and reds
to color light overhead
each day on my walk home.
I carried the future with me
damp luminous sticky redolent.
Still my father died.

What could I know of solitude
of stillness that season?
The sprint of life.
The pain of arriving.

Late September

At the screen door the fat squirrel watches me.
The year turns day by night by day
cold in the early morning, hot at noon, warmer as night comes on.

We watch the TV screen flicker. Action and reaction. Drama.
Always a corpse. Always the rush of attraction. Always the bumbling detective.
We love each other. One of us moves badly.
Is this old age? Let us grow older.

Somewhere in the world our genes replicate.
No voices here echo ours.
Ristras fill the autumn markets.
The broiler releases the scent of ripe peppers roasting.
Heavenly this place we've come to this season.
Grouse warble under the brush pile.
Are they paying attention to the hawk?
He pays attention.

You ask for four small pears, ripe.
And tomatoes, heirlooms, their shoulders cracked with burgeoning, ripe, ripe.
Fresh corn, last of the season.
Basil-infused olive oil, baskets of purple garlic heads, wreaths of dried herbs.

Well, another autumn aesthetic.

As a young bride I wandered the markets in a coastal city:
barrels of fish, barrels of mussels. Blood on the pavement
near butchers where I bought some of our provender.
Apples my friend gave away to beggars on the overpass, sometimes a flat
    of strawberries.
Our fingers were sticky from tasting, try this
and this. We tried everything offered.

Photograph

The grassy hill descended from the brick garage
down steps to the back door of the kitchen.
Shrubs bordered the foundation.
The two girls wore jeans over filmy underpants
lace cream satin bras under their T-shirts.
They were going to a wedding, one the bride
the other her attendant. But not just yet.

They walked down arm in arm, one's head
nodding to the other's shoulder, air a pressure
on their limbs. One of them had to marry.

The morning air was chilly, the garbage can
they picked up, one each side, was heavy
in their hands and balance hard to keep
going down, the clanging as they walked.

Here we go alone, and like it better so

> Here we go alone, and like it better so
> —Virginia Woolf

This life is said to be
in order to cultivate the desert
educate the inhabitants,
work together by day
and by night to sport.

So the term comes to an end.
The end of the conglomerate
of bodies all with deep pockets

all ready or perhaps
not ready to fill them with
the making up of shapes
and the casting of them down.

The season of drabs begins.
And oh we are grateful
for light when it comes
the slow unfolding of
the elongated sheen
of the amaryllis bud in the window
turning his head so discretely
to Zeus—is that his name?
The one necessary for the inevitable unfolding
in the pocket
the vernix licked off by the rub
on some texture at the bottom of the bombazine;
is that fabric used any more for lining suits
the enfoldings at seams, the outpouching at wrist
or waist?

Nevertheless the sky
is discovered to be different
in the morning or at evening
when walking toward the horizon
at the base of the hill, the bottom
of the street, the verge of the playground,
alone at last, and just now on the curb
the residue of the last car speeding
toward the garage, the snow packed down
by the car and the solitary dog's paws
as he rushes to his bowl by the fire.

Flowers of Immortality, Eau de Parfum
by Kilian, $235 for 50 ml

> Shivers of flank and shoulder
> already drawing absence nearer
> —Linda Bierds, "Simulacra"

We think they are delicious, these traces of freesia and peach,
evoking an utopia where people like us live apart from the world
of supermarkets and beachballs, waking at dawn
to rediscover the moon gone pale from wandering
sinking now into the mountains by our house.

On the porch is a daybed covered in chintz
where you're welcome to sleep all night
below the blazing spectacle, no gas or electric stink
to disturb stars in their patterns, striding widelegged,
waists belted, or mounted, or rocking away the end
of a journey we've been making so many years in the dark.

Or you may decide to doze away the morning, or
early afternoon, after you've smelled then devoured
a white peach martini, one of a set of three on a fan of flowers,
blossoms on the clay plate left out for you on the railing.

Or late afternoon, your hiking boots unlaced,
poles resting against the rose crystal lampshade
on the wicker table, the left one slowly settling
to the floorboards, the scent of white musk seeping
into your head as you sink ever closer to bouquets,
freesia in jars set by your body, bundles of organic
carrots to feed you in the coming company
of shade and philanthropy, pure loveliness, vanilla traces,
black currant, even the Tonka Bean, a live iris outlined in paint,
yourself gone forever, if ever hospitable,
the angels

II

Women and Poetry

Among all my desires at the time . . . one of the strongest was to put my full
trust in someone; in some man.
—Sigrid Nunez, *The Friend*

They want to be told what's what by a man,
women at the north end of the table nodding together,
one so newly married she writes as if the poem
is her writing hand, lonely for the ring.

I wanted to be told what's lovely by a man
as I was by my famous teacher who taught women,
especially the beauty seated on his right, to incite riot.
Her pain seemed an Ars Poetica,
her poems all naked body, enticingly sensual,
flushed in sun and shower, come from the pool in stanza one
to become in stanza two an erect and threatening penis
in a changing room shared by a man and a girl.
Was she the child? we wondered. What difference to the poem?

In my class, we sat together in a darkening room, late afternoon.
I am trying to love poetry as a stay against confusion,
flesh for now a stay against death, as lightning, incipient storm
with its causal gods, breaks closer to morning.

And now I write alone in the kitchen with only that growl to push me.
No man's voice here, no transformation, only poetry.

Women's Lib

Women turned their loyalties from their father's clothes, huge discarded shirts.
They had been missing.

All night dreaming the map of the future their subject had been the artist at
    work
in a room under the stable.

It is vital to pull yourself up by your own roots.

We were making love in the weeds, slamming the daisies flat.
Milkweed swollen then bursting. Outside birds.

Mostly the television is on, but we didn't notice.

We went to the movies.
Someone in the back row touched my arm,
"Let them eat cake." And then I got angry.

Feathery trees embroidered on batiste:
old clothes in a poetic mode passed out of fashion.

Blessed be the womb put to use or not. Now dance.

Collaboration

This one writes, steps up, steps back.
The other holds the pad still, a blank.
The fear of pencils is one's contribution. I can't.
Shut up, says the other curtseying. I can.

They do, these two. Look here's their book.
I can read, says one. I can talk, says the other.
To celebrate, one wraps fingers around a glass.
The other waits for steak.

One pushes the other, picks up a knife, hungry.
The other plays with salad.
One holds an apple very still.
Good job, says the other, fingers the handle.

The apple peel falls into a lovely spiral.
Already the other is pushing it towards disposal.

Women and the Global Imagination

> Her weight compares to no universe.
> —Valerie Martinez

I am thinking, looking in the mirror at the women behind me
coming and going, what do they say? What do they wear?
Robes, or I see rolled-up khaki shorts at the south end of the room.
Do we speak a common language?

"I tattooed my eyelashes on, I'm older and my eyes stream with allergies."
Another woman reaches out her hand to interlace fingers.
She took the drivers' test at 35, passed at 40 after someone fired the driver.
Another woman never took a test, borrowed the truck.

"My daughter's engagement gift was a high-end cell phone.
She had a diamond, one caret plus some points."
And insurance.
And she got an MD degree. Or law.

We took out the garbage. Lived with our aunties.
We farmed, gardened, strapped on infants, plastic water jugs. Pumped.
Got a loom, or better, a sewing machine.
Hemmed tarps and bedding like grandmother did. All Local Products.
The summer was scorching. The winter froze.
He entered me on the fourth day. Why did he wait?

Computer programming is one way to succeed. Computer parts another.
Weave for the tourist markets.
Fewer couples marry, procreate.
The news is told on TV by a blonde woman in a sweater set.
She wears pearls on Mondays, carries a pink .22 in her pack.
Jets crash, someone kicks an eight-year-old to death, another drives four
    children into the sea.

Really, we're screaming.
Drought again after hail the size of baseballs.
Lean in. Yup, me and my sister, the girls, always the source of trouble.
Relocate us. We'll boil water on the grates we find under houses.

Houses. Yours is different from mine. We don't have one.
Borderlands and coyotes.
"Once our stories were round / but the wolves made them square as
    houses," wrote Diane Glancy.
Let's go, get out. Yurts. The grass is always greener on the other side,
    unless it's sand.
Vitamins and coconut water.

Six decades later, see what we've got. Me, too. Borders. Walls.
Let's collaborate against powder.
Mascara. Tattoos. The medical establishment. Drugs. Additives. Allergies
    and opioids.

All messages
as we march,
fight for relief.

The Burnt Journals

Each thing has come back to answer for itself.
—Hélène Cixous, translated by Beverley Bie Brahic, *The Day I Wasn't There*

Here, the burnt journals.

"She made, at her father's house,
a bird, red felt body, pipe cleaner legs,
green petal feet, and underneath, freestanding,
a tiny piebald baby in a nest."
This bird, without its baby, stands on a shelf
in a cold room next to the remains.

"He stormed around breaking glasses;
the children dropped glue on the table.
My lover arrived late for dinner.
My sons followed after him, small shadows."

. . . an ornament, "fifty hours of frustrating work,"
in the shape of a guitar. He hung it on the tree.
The real guitar is hidden in the closet for the child to find
among his overcoats, so he won't forget the maker (he never forgets).

"The great houses lit from within,
all the elaborate paraphernalia (a bride's goods) of life . . .
today, gifts set in high relief against peace—
all gifts, treasure raised from salt, debris.

"I lean on rituals of the house.
Is it possible to live forever in silence—children
drawing new fish in the aquarium and singing, waiting to go out?

"I want to know how women sound inside their heads,
not what they speak to themselves in silence, but what they could say aloud."

An account of two weeks with a lover.
In black crayon, top right, his handwriting.

"One more hour . . . twenty minutes, no more time. I am here."
He waits for me, dressed to kill. Guns in the house.
He will negotiate the contract. He will sign much paper.

Night dream: she has given birth, is nursing. Many details.

"She sits in the rocking chair. From the shut closet, a cry.
In the closet, wrapped in a snowsuit, under the zipper, one of the twins
she gave birth to, this child in her arms. One twin died, she remembers,
but this one is alive and mewing, a swollen belly, a perfect little head, a face.
She'd forgotten him.

"No. I can fix everything. She can nurse this one, too.
The rest of the dream is his little face turning away.
We must tell someone, take him to hospital, tubes into his belly, he can be
    saved."

Awake now. The sun is loud. Morning.

April, decades later. He burned the journals. I am long gone.

That human phrases or even a word carry doses of malevolence is well established . . .
The poison circulates via points of resemblance or coincidence between all animated
beings and more particularly by the word I which is in every mouth.
    —Hélène Cixous

Dear Sky

I'm here to say I'm sorry,
A little tune from off Broadway
And 142nd Street where
We walked together to the subway
Years ago. I thought we could
Hold hands. Then you were gone.

Most of the time we lived
Together in the backyard.
Once we made love
Under the lilacs behind the house.

Afterwards I drove around a lot
From here to there, worked hard
To avoid looking up. All night
Every night you were gone. No surprise.
In the middle dark I'd sneak to the garage
Release the hand brake on the Buick
Roll down the driveway to the street.
Who could see? Who'd care?
You were there across town I knew it
Somewhere behind clouds
Your eyes like lights.
I'd drive to the park, look up.
How much I miss you.

Now that I've moved away you're still with me.
I'm not afraid anymore.
How heavy you were on my body.
How burnt I was from exposure.

April

Pale blooms on trees poets sheltered among
to become floral on their book jackets. We girls too
stooped among lilacs for the camera, to show we were Nature.

Photos of cousins among peach blossoms in the backyard
were caught in a silver frame. Next, here we are too,
posed among branches of magnolia, a nest.

Did we forgive ourselves later, our skirts filled with scent
as we crouched over the incense burner to get ready?
Flower cups blooming on cactus as red as we were at center.

I never said I'd live among blooms for long, did I?
In *Blade Runner* he said, "Time to die" as he did,
that beautiful automaton.

One Toe, Crooked

Let me tell you how it is with me:
a bad back, spine like a snakeskin
shed in the shadow of a pinelet,
weakened innards, a liver fit for soup,
and a brain the size of a lentil. The worst
is the one toe, crooked like a staff
carried too long by shepherds.

One day, a fine mid-autumn
with sun's eye full open against air's chill,
I took to the woods to find my dinner.
What with one thing and another

I swayed and shimmered my way along
the path, gravel stuck to my knees from a fall,
my felt shoes catching stones.
But still, I got to the gate where geese cross
coming home from the pond.

What would do me that night?
I was one only, with an oven fit
for a child with money, my prize.
Each night I lit it with a fagot
of willow and some wormwood leaves.
It had an iron basket suspended over the fire,
good for roasting corn and potatoes.
Tonight I was hungry against the chill coming.
No ice yet, that was full winter
but now a clutch of eggs to boil in the kettle?

Truly then I saw a girl
lovely as a stalk of silver grain
come around a corner that an oak made
with my barn wall. She carried a bundle
squirming like a peck of tadpoles,
and clutched to her chest a stack of books
bound with a strap. She saw me
as a wraith and ran. Was I a wraith?
My toe hurt like hell itself gaped open.
But Ectoplasm I wasn't. Plain flesh.
Still, she was afraid. Then I could see her babe's
mouth open, its cries louder with each bounce,
the flannel it was bound with coming loose.

As I watched, standing bent over my toe,
she dropped the books. The belt around them opened.
Pages fanned out on the ground
like parchment put to flame.

What did all this mean in the daylight?
The girl, her babe, the lost books cascading
and over everything pain ascending,
covering our light, all that hope,
the future somehow gone dark as a cavern.

I bent over the mess, began to gather it up.

List and Story

I

First we must go for flowers
To the nursery. Spring is here.
My heart speaks, an utterance
Packed with many meanings,
As the begonias have petals
Some one color, some another
And all blending into that plant
You choose for the hanging basket.

My brother at fifteen went to war.
He was an infantryman, a photographer.
He opened the camps with his fellows.
Then he came home. He lived at home.
He lived in his bedroom. He studied.
He graduated. He married and . . .
You know that story. Sons.
At forty he took a gun
Into his mouth and pulled the trigger.
He was in the woods where the bears go.
He drove the old car. He didn't leave a note.

He was gainfully employed. His sons . . .
That utterance. And then peace.

The red petals have fallen. The flushed
Petals remain. Leaves like steak knives,
Serrated, fleshy, the darkest green.
We go to the garden with our children.
We have graduated. We have married.
The garden is our pleasure and utterance.
Marriage, that pleasure. The making of food,
The making of the yolk and white of one egg.
The whirling of the mobile under which we
Make our children. Such pleasure moves.

Let us tear the garden into ribbons.
Let us transplant the white daffodils
With their bonnets that bend backward.
Let us move the magnolia corms.
Let us divide the bulbs and the peonies.
Who will take the children. I will, I will.

II

Who let the monster into the house?
Who cooks the food for him, shops,
Plays the flute, drives the tumbrels?
Who folds into the hay blankets, drinks
The red wine, wears the jewels? Who
Hangs the blade over the fireplace
With its jeweled hilt, braided scabbard?
Who watches the savaging of the children?
Utterance. One child. Where were you
To say no, leave a note, take up the gun?

The body of the flowers in the hanging basket
Is multiple, blue stars and anise, pansies
And feverfew, the hanging vines of sweet potato.
Its utterance is heavy moving in wind, creaks.
The children play in the garden, on the swings,
In the sandbox. One carries a greasy bag in his fist,
Bologna and chips, a slippery bottle of pop.
They lock the door. They cavort on the rug.
And it was evening. The monster reigns.

Utterance: spring. Summer, fall. Winter
Silence and the smell of balsam. Pastries
That you roll out on the floor, shape into log,
Apply frosting, display. Bow. Décolletage.
And it was morning. The children under the tree.
Gifts and more gifts. The timbrels and bells.
Bach and the great Germans. Some candles
Some fire. Who let the monster into the house
With his axe, his dragged tree, sticky sap?

III

I slid down the shut door, locked it.
I hit the floor, stopped. I wept.
She thanked me, that child with blood
On her cheek. She thanked me with her bruised tongue.
She thanked me with her utterance and disappeared.
Never again. Never again. Never again. And so forth.

And it was morning and it was evening of the fourth day.
The basket was hanging on the porch in the heat of the day.
In the night, in the cool garage with its lowered door,
A moat between night and the house, lurking . . .
That utterance. A gun, that utterance. Disbelief,

That utterance. And in the house the children . . .

And now the story is over. Silence. Penance.
Utterance, the page and the oranges. Pears and wafers.
Forty years in the desert of the sandbox where cats dig.

Six Objects in a Gold Foil Box

—Barton James Raz, 1927–1966

I

"That amethyst geode is like a drugstore urinal."
Does she mean Duchamp?

To me, the skin is spotted like an outlandish zebra.
(Spots on a hide ought to be striped white and black.
An inert zebra is too heavy to turn over. I might be mistaken.)
The heart is purple when we pry it apart.

II

His mother's best brooch this one isn't.
But we all like it whorled on the bosom of her house dress.
All pattern, swirls of cream and brown where her breast
—is that the right word?—would jiggle but doesn't.
What is it catches light from the window?

III

Pumice? The caldera of a volcano?
What ought to be good feels bad, all scratchy.
The pillow is supposed to fit spots behind knees, on rough elbows.
Scrubbed hard red stripes interrupt skin.

The cat spends hours reaching into the plant pots for something
worm-eaten, dropped from the pin oak in autumn before the pots come back in.
So heavy the pots, so light the acorns she tosses up onto the tile floor
where they skitter. In summer, when pots go back out, what's left will begin to sprout.

IV

A faint chime, ruffled by fingers stirring scarves in the drawer.
Look. Among the silk welter:
a tiny top hat, a filigree bridge, a sailboat with a moving jib,
a bust of Lincoln fingernail size, and a lamb.
Scooped out of the silk, circling your wrist,
a jingle as she fusses with your hair.

V

Oh, empty bowl on the piano shawl,
etched crystal chrysanthemum,
the cold blue multiplies diamonds on plush curtains,
a plum scrim between what's present what's merely absent this season.

In a square state, let's say Highball,
folks come down to the river to drink.
They bring cups to ring on stones on the bank.
Something crashes. Something wearing purple falls in.
She used to be pretty. Now she is a zebra
with spots, nothing human at all.

Mirror hung sideways, how does your light quicken?
Your prisms absorb all heat in the room!
So pretty the glow we can't see by.
Whose idea, big boy? Not mine.
I admire you from below, listen for your shatter
as the silk cord lets go.

VI

Can Eeyore be a cheetah, please? I ask Nurse,
but she doesn't answer. The answer is no,

no matter how much I want it.
My jaws are firecrackers in a wooden crate stamped 1,000 LBS. on the lid.
If we wait long enough, I whisper under the coverlet. If only I can grow up.

VII

Put everything back in the box right now, under the foil lid.
I'm Pandora, ready to slam down the top.
Inside are virtues and vices, who cares which?

I do, says the tin soldier with the red plush heart.
I'm not a pin cushion. I'm a defender.
Help me up! Let me out, Queen Bee!

The zebra with spots has a jeweled heart, all glitter and roil.
The broach, neon headlights for eyes,
blinks on the highway verge,
all loopy possibilities,
all mammal, all explorer, all body.

Wait! I'll be his brain I promise him,
my pen writing a house for him.
He's all gone.
But I'm conjuring broad fields from the charm bracelet, loofa, mirror,
the rotten acorns, the empty bowl, the glittery brooch, the geode, his flensed skin.
I promised him. I promise him.

War

Graceful but badly armed
soldiers hit the field
to be slaughtered of course
like vets who die later
guns in their mouths.

Beloveds have been made ash.
Family settles down
to the facts of property.
Drapes blow at windows.
Probity.
Winter driveways
shoveled by hired men.
And the shelves papered
with oilcloth flowers.
Sickened by meats
some have new clothes
to cover their bones.

News is stories
of victims and survivors
faces we know.
Caps on their heads.

Let us take up the veil.
Wail to waste hours.
Breath is soul some say
so if body falls soul falls.

Who wants the wars we make?
Who wants not to leave the field?
Who wants to live with heroes?

I want to live in fields with beetles
who scurry under counters
oblivious that their lives are saved
by sending away the exterminator.
What good is care for the world?

A Covey of Scaled Quail

The bedroom shade is half drawn.
Snow interrupts the field
Cliffs of sand held together
Intermittent shrub and rock.

We wait by the window
Frame of a white falling
A rush of cold against which
Our breath moves.

Now dark interrupts the snow.

Under the juniper slowly
The odd bird scurrying
Then two, then a group
That vacates in ranks the dark under
And goes into fog. Covey. Many.

Where has this covey come from?

Dry air sucks up snow then leaves
What falls to stay a while as we do
Inhabitants of another intermittence.
Footprints to discover at dawn
As cold drops over the mountain
And we wake to watch another day.

Another Story

First he was coming out the door.
Then he was on the path, his hand outstretched.
Smiling.

High summer.
Then six months, start to finish.

Now she identifies him prior to burning.
Then she goes home to flowers, the funeral meats.
Imagine the sight of the city beyond the windows.
Imagine his harpsichord in the music room.
Their several flutes on the shelf.
Imagine the sunset in those windows.
Day two, day three, day four.

The widow slept with their daughter two nights, holding hands.
Death seemed to burn away her life.

But she would revive, like a foot asleep under the weight of a body.

III

The Impossibility of Stasis

1. Stone under the tongue.

2. A scarf of sparks to set the house afire.

3. Breath exhaled then held and held.

4. Breath inhaled, a gasp, paroxysm.

5. The infant crowns, a last spasm.

6. Peppermint dissolving.

7. Spray, the apex of a wave.

8. Notes in the air of a chilly hall.

9. Body suspended en pointe.

10. Thuds onto the floor of the stage.

Now moving toward the audience, flying.

The Past and the Future

Once I wore a dress of iridescent icy peau de soie;
The sleeves were shirred, short on my dark arms.
After a season, salt rotted the silk into pure blue.

Yesterday on Skype I talked to you for an hour.
You looked like a Whitman sampler lid,
All color-blocks, modern art and candy,
A grid. You stayed together through shifts of pixels,
You abroad, me at home.

Last night, great flashes and percussion in our sky.

If I should lose the accompaniment, I would stop.
No rest but cymbals then silence.

Watching Bulls/ Falling in Love with the Dead

"Stormy Wing sure can ride!" shouts the TV.
Beethoven is playing in the next room so the bulls
seem almost tender as they put their feet down hard
either side the head of this cowboy they've just bucked off.

Outside finches on the feeder chirp in the shadow
of a Cooper's Hawk over quail chicks' chirr and chuckle
as their papa shakes his topknot, fusses to call them under the brush.

Oh but now I remember them all, a parade of lovers shaking their butts,
lifting hats at the last minute! Sweet ones.
I sit still to remember my part in this bucking and charging:
What a ruckus at the best tables, me dressed in silver peau de soie,
feather buckles on velvet shoes tapping the hems
of tablecloths falling onto the plush carpets.
Or running alleys at midnight, chasing coins of moonlight,
always restless, wearing out the season's sandals
cinched around my skinny ankles, feet tanned and calloused,
hitting the still hot pavement hard.

On TV, "Chicken on a String," the bull with the fawn belly,
twists under the strap Cowboy Bill adjusts so carefully
before the ride, his broken hand taped,
the moistened rope laid carefully between fingers and thumb
before the gates open. "Let's get 'er done," they yell
to each other, switching rides just like the boys did, or I did
once a year or more, sometimes a month or a weekend.

They were easy to forget, that's the truth,
riders dead to me as I ran on through pasture gates,
bulls distant on the horizon, cowboys sitting on fences.

Uh oh. One falls off, rolls under the gate, and out.
Clowns divert the bull. It was close to the end he tucked his palm under,
smiled and spun from the core what looked like a flexible, perfect ride.
But that centrifugal force pulls you to the side every time
and
      almost
            always
                  off.

A Conversation about Text

> To start a harvest my mind is clearer now on how to proceed. I look forward
> to the second half of what might be a year's project.
> —Michael James

Or a life's. To finish a project
suggests the rest of breath.

To envision this story properly
you need at least three veils
draped over holes of rust.
To open up a doorway
first wood then a splintering.
Through the opening
at the point of what now we'll call a window
we see a garden or a painting of a garden
—ekphrastic this text—
through which the miniature magnolia called stellata

opens its stars to be stilled
spilling light.

"I am energized about this project
more so tonight than at any time before.
My mind is clearer now on how to proceed.
Time has become a big issue with me
as each day passes. I don't think
I don't think I've ever felt it
so strongly as I do now
since adopting this new life."

Time is stilled.
The background figure through the window
has turned her back on the foreground
where a huge man squats
his weight entirely static.
He's a balance for her absence
though he thinks her nape is exquisite
individual hairs ascending into a mass of dark silk.

Imagine our surprise for then we hear the rusty hinge or maybe two
on this side of the opening to the garden
or the picture of the garden on which might be hung
we can't know exactly how
the veils.

"And I wonder too if it isn't just age
and the increasing sense there's less time left
each second must be maximized.

But then the impulse just to find a hidden place
and camp out for days or weeks—what a dream!"

The woman stirs

the silken hairs at the nape of her neck stir.
(How can they be seen moving through the veils?)
They do and the bark of the dogs in the garden
is barely heard by the figures on the porch
farther back at the glass tables eating lunch
fresh greens and a quiche
drinking water
nodding toward the water below
barely seen in the distance but seen. The talk.

"So I mention this in appreciation of YOUR time,
which to you is no doubt worth its weight in gold,
as it is to me. I am energized about this project
more so tonight than at any time previous.
And I resent that duties call me away from my studio
just when I feel I could pull something forward.
Well, I'll work on it nevertheless, in absentia."

The man in the picture is rising is moving to the window
behind the woman or the picture of the garden or
toward what we now see is a fireplace mantel
over which is hanging something metal gilt.
His bulk moves past the back of the woman's head.
Then his arms rise to unfasten a sheen.

I ask you is this horizontal balance
a necessary counterweight of rust
to the presence of the vertical veils
through which we see his fingers
individual then all ten working together
to detach gold from the dim hooks and take up the sword?

—for Michael James

Emma, fabric, wool and lace, 1970

Soft sculpture by Dorothea Tanning

> What would Molly Bloom think of Emma Bovary?
> —Dorothea Tanning

I

After the huge Oldenburg oilcloth light-switch
that sags on the wall of the museum
we turn the corner to find Emma,
tiny pink cloth belly without a head, in a nest of lace.
The belly button is stitched in. Here's the signage etched on a plaque:

". . . the semi-abstract sculpture with its rounded breast, abdomen with navel and
limb-like extrusion suggests a disassembled and reconfigured female form. Femi-
ninity is accented by the addition of a lace garment that encircles the form. This
bizarre distorted and somewhat monstrous body can only have been born from the
realm of the unconscious. Emma [is] 'sur' real—above and outside the real world
as we know it."

Where is the breast? I don't see it. Yes, now.
The single bust defined by a row of stitching.
We're in the Nelson-Atkins Art Gallery.
The new Bloch wing is carved from light.

II

This wing of the museum displays the work of masters
whose breath mingled with our own for a while
in an age we shared: later contemporary art.
A Rothko from his dark period, a year of his life
before his suicide, 1963. And here, around the corner is
this little recumbent cushion on a tall plinth called Emma.

I think it's a memento of months carrying a child, pregnant,
the headless whole no larger than a pin cushion
someone brought as a gift after the birth. A tomato or a strawberry.
I had become fruit, vegetative, immanent for months
and now delivered of a masterpiece. No lace.
Dorothea Tanning found the lace quite useful as a nest.
I have been a nest.

III

In the shops:

to celebrate long life, a birthday,
a green white and red quilt made in the nineteenth century
in a pattern called "Gizzards and Hearts"

is charming, two faint and large rusty stains
at either end to celebrate the life of the body,
mind busy reclaiming and naming mementoes.

IV

The fires rage in the hills above Santa Barbara
where a room is reserved, a flight booked
through flaming air—all to cancel, of course.
The hotel clerk says he is leaving to join the firemen.
The hotel is filled with evacuees.

I will not be an evacuee.

V

I will not be an evacuee, not yet.
Did Dorothea Tanning think of Emma as evacuated?
Is her lace pubic hair part of a lace cushion? Emma is tiny
in the company of huge paintings, gigantic sculpture.
She is displayed on a plinth. She is surreal. An abortion?
Surely not. The birth of the self?

VI

She was 101 when she died, her maker,
Dorothea Tanning. Her website flashes
pictures of her work. Two books
of poems published in her lifetime,
which also is mine. She stayed alive
until the last minute. As she died
I gazed at Emma, said yes out loud.

IV

Nick Spencer, Two Days Dead

"He took himself," Richard says
at dinner—a shrimp boil, andouille sausage,
steamed corn and new potatoes, high summer.

Moon flowers stud the bushes each side of the front door,
moist blossoms seeming too heavy to open.

To the left, on entering, and above your head,
tiny white flowers—are they moon flowers, too,
a variant, full-open? So when Richard says later,
over pear ices, "next life is different," he means
next human life, doesn't he?

In the backyard, from the dining room window,
bittersweet climbs both male and female,
established enough to go on bearing, as Richard says,
through generations of us.

On the table, platters of clay hold shrimp
in mounds, pink, & golden corn cobs broken into servings,
and pale browns, the potatoes, like nipples.

So many subjectivities, shifting portals
made of layers, like silk, and Nick caught and broken
through to the next layer—like petals like berries.

And we here together talking, swaying forward
to try to bring ourselves home.

The da Vinci Moon

The da Vinci moon is rising by Saturn, its pierced mate.
They are lovely, a slipper moon as mother would say
thin as the edge of a mercury dime.

Tonight she is smiling her sliver or slipper at the bottom of her face.

Beloved paces in and out of rooms looking from the windows
at the sky west where the sun is making a rosy stripe at the horizon
then east at our lady moon smiling over the arroyo.

Soon when dark comes, rooms with their furniture will disappear.
Out the windows the perimeter of the moon shows a chipped halo
or something else I can't say.

A Meditation on Respect

Whatever else you think, think this: death comes soon.
There. I've said it.
                              And on this morning, sun spilt
gold on gray pebbles under our back window.
Yesterday three Bobcats, mama and two kits,
came there and slept the morning away. I swear!
They came panting with matted fur, skinny, fell
in the shadow our house made, a shade not
much wider than they were, stretched toe to tail.

There. I've finished the first stanza, Rispello.
Eight line blocks, each one eleven syllables.
Some hours later the Bobcats woke, went off,
their backs turned to us watching from the porch,
kits no longer skinny but still small, wind-fluffed

by breath come up to move clouds along the sky.
Below, we tiptoed fast around corners looking
to find them up on the hill. But no, they'd gone.

Here's one example of someone alive, afraid,
counting life up against death with her fingers.
Hear me: that's Bobcats where we live. Coyotes
we track by listening, rarely see. And crows
as big as hawks. And hawks and eagles. Rabbits.
More. Jackrabbits, twice as big as dogs. And birds.
I could make a catalogue, hummers we feed
with sweets, bright finches, yet why bother? *Death's face*

obscures. Yet now chamisa is in bloom
all over the arroyo. See what I mean? Yellow.
The world is fractals, numbers. Still the world rots.
But is not lost. Enough. Look out. Where cats were,
now on the wall a lizard waits in sun for lunch.
My love is melting sugar in red water
For migrating hummingbirds. Pet in atrium,
Sleeping in sunshine, calico coat aflame.

Remember Joseph wore one, a gift, in fear
of his brothers? He was right. Death's robe, no color,
covered him then he was gone—to Egypt, lost.
His jealous brothers and their father also grieved.
A gift of death turned into exile is good?
Do I think I've made an argument for life?
Not here. Not now. Though we are old, many others
die as babes in arms, in gowns, or rags, wrapped close.

Just as Bobcats, so cared for by each other
sleep wove them into one body. Then they go.

As I will, that's the truth, the rub, the whitewash
no one buys. (They favor light enamel crème
that covers better.)
                    Reader, will you sing out
a theme from Bach to comfort us listeners
sore from hospital, sickness, stitches, bloody
wounds, recovery sure or not? Bless us.

Meditation

I can't I can't I can't I can't I can't
Who's talking? Shut up, compassion.

Put on socks and shoes meditation

Walking meditation
          Once around the desert
          no dog, nobody

Counting heart stones meditation
          in the basket, on the ground

Walking the dog meditation
          out loud, out loud: listen dog. Metta

May i/ she be safe may she/ i be happy may she be/ feel well may she live/
     die lightly

Gratitude meditation: each day a white stone
          picked up by the front door   by the back garden
          put down on the ground   white stones to a make a mouth:

If my mouth were as wide as the seven seas
it would not be enough to praise Thee

Be quiet.   Make lunch.   Notice the thumb, the work of the
  thumb.   Notice the edge of the   knife blade

Wash the dishes meditation. Metta

may our friend be safe may she be happy may she be well may she live/ die lightly

I can't sit still   death death death death.   I can't i can't i can't i
  Who?
        May she walk in the shadow of death and fear no evil thy arroyo
          rock and thy cottonwood staff   comfort

Breathe breathe/ breathe breathe

Rausch means soul means breath is breath is soul
        breathe breathe/ breathe
        until the body/ stone
        fractures
        to release

The Mandala of Now

I could get in the car, drive the spring streets to the Lux Art Gallery
Buy sculpture made of books sanded into stones by that one artist.
Or go to the popcorn and ice cream store.

I can sit all afternoon in the long room on a cushion, cat on my lap
To read in the scent of magnolia cut from the lowest branches
Of the old tree by the front door. Or sit and breathe, mind emptied.

How lucky I am in this air-filled body at rest, my mind taking nibbles
As a robin hops down the hill, flies up to the birdbath
Or the thrill of the dove, wide open as she heads for the window
And misses, lifts and flares out.

A Symposium on Love

"Damn the word," said Justine once, "I would like to spell it backwards as
you say the Elizabethans did God. Call it evol and make it a part of "evolu-
tion" or "revolt."

—*Justine*, Lawrence Durrell

Age is an evolution—or devolution—of lust.
To be lost in revolt, as one must be growing up,
invites erotics into the palace of the family.
Air spiked with ecstasy. We all know it.
Then voluble in bed might signify lust
or politics, depending on whether
you live in a hovel where the velocity
of wildlife, certainly a mouse, about its vital business
shadows the movements of governments,

or a hotel, hovering over the chasm
between mountains where we stopped.
Olives. Lupine. The sound of violins
through the balcony window resinous
heard through steam: treatments for the liver.
Into the porches of our ears pours music
reverberating through marble spaces. "That old man
wants to live," whispers a medic
mopping up. His vulpine mask a blur

through silk curtains as he bends over
to lave bodies slippery with oil. He cares for us.

Here in the mountains where we feel free
olives are served in gin straight from the freezer.
The menu reports that olev is an alternative
a citrus fruit found in the garden below.
A solo viola with piano plays at a wedding on the patio.

Is olev a word in another language
an oval fruit used in a harvest ritual
a kind of citron   a renewal   a stand-in for love?

Maybe instead you wrote, "Nearby some wedding party is tuning up.
It's hard to hear their voices. We've enough lunacy on this balcony
overlooking the ceremony to interpret youth and age. Drink up!"
She whispers, "I've loved you for half my life."

To reprise: voluble in bed can signify
the exhaustion of lust and the birth of politics
depending on where you live, a hovel
or next summer's hotel on a coast where olives are eaten
crushed with oil and tomatoes on pasta. Viols can be heard
from a balcony overlooking the river.

In a hotel notebook become a diary you can signify a place
where you stayed one summer, the air an oven
you entered to make love or sleep.
Your bed linens were streaked with damp.
Remember oval windows above his elbow
trimmed with red and yellow light? I don't.

A mirror in the corner showed us at the moment
we became another person tiny and contorted
for a few beats who might change

into grotesque statuary or
a violinist of genius but peculiar, hard to reach
until the world called out to him and he went.
He appears tonight on the program.

Let us return to the moment, please.
Your new partner is to be found at the next table
voluble thank God after months of silence.
What's he onto now? Oh, the volume of trade
on the stock exchange. I'm interested. Are you?

Here in the mountains after sunburnt children with their dogs
are put to bed conversation veers toward the intimate.
Of course the subject is money. A plunging market.
What's to be done? Be patient. The people will speak.
Vox Popular in November. The new red may be black.
Be patient. "I grew up in a Victorian melodrama," overheard
might seem to change the stakes. For me, at least.

In a corner of the room under satin swags that frame the mountains
three women lean toward the axis of their table and whisper.
You can hear their hisses over the swipe of VISA through the bar machine.
If you . . . you'll disappear . . . Escape?
But how? Where do they think they'll go?

Meanwhile the elderly are falling in love.
You can. Erotic is the reverse of deathly.
Dour Mr. Thanatos rents out accordions
at base camp if you've a mind to dance.

And while we're speculating here,
if you have a comrade with a mind so rigid
you can hear the crack on the page as you read
his work, what can you do at 8,000 feet?

Maybe you can write some evolved and looser squiggles
to depict the guy on the plane en route in the next seat
depressed because no one will talk to him
so his head droops onto his chest
seemingly ready to be released into a basket.
Wasn't that the French Revolution?
That guy only wanted to convert us, not seduce.

Nearby some wedding party is tuning up.
It's hard to hear over his voice what they're saying.
Certainly we've enough lunacy on this balcony
overlooking the pool. Drink up!
A bridesmaid hands over a hanky. The best man is her.
Their fathers link arms. Their mothers smile.
By now we're sobbing into tissues and taking pictures.

Surely next comes midlife revolt. What do you think?
Oh look. A moose lopes over the top of the mountain.
The bell for dinner sounds. I've a mind to bolt
this place. Echoes reverberate on the balconies.

You know, I've loved him for half my life.
At the end, it seems the rest of the relatives died.

Pristine

I am sick with worry when you call.
You tell me a story about ears
How the doctor asked about your earaches
Peered in and pronounced "Pristine.
Clean as a whistle." And you were cured.

Because I am a maker of poems
And you are a maker of music
You tell me the word pristine was perfect.
It was the cure.

Yesterday I went to the hospital
To hear my heart beat in her various chambers.
I knew the sounds:
The *Fly Bird* from the right ventricle
The *Go Go* from the left
The *Here I am* from under the rib.

The Sisters

Once there were twelve sisters who lived together.
They were old now, within a decade of beyond old,
but still they were alive.

They slept in a room they'd shared as children.
Each had a life remembered: a beloved, pets,
their own children who were cousins,
who'd summered together at the beach each year
with their papas, their mamas, their aunts.

Now the sisters were old. In the mornings, they'd arise, put on cotton
   robes,
pull cushions from under their beds to sit on.
Each faced a window.
Each had a bureau just big enough to hold treasures.
Every morning they sat.

One morning the sisters awoke with sore feet. "Ouch," each complained.
Nothing to be done. They looked for their shoes, found tatters.
All day they went barefoot in the garden, in the kitchen, under stars.
When they sat down on their beds before sleep, tired, each found new
   shoes
sparkled with sequins, sewn felt. Treasures. Each sister lay down and
   slept.

Next morning they awoke again with sore feet, their sparkly slippers again
   tatters.
All day again they went barefoot in the garden, in the kitchen, under stars.
Then, time for bed. Surprise, each found sparkly slippers made of felt, some
   green,
some gold, some purple or opal, and many other colors.
They smiled at each other, lay down and slept.

Years passed. The old sisters grew older, their feet knurled and blistered,
piles of old shoes thrown out their windows into the backyard loam
like mementoes of lives extinguished. Dogs came to sniff and dig.
One dog, a noble beast, carried around a string of tatters in his mouth.
He seemed to dig when nobody watched him. Most of the time
he was invisible. The sisters slept more and more, in light as well as
   darkness.
In the air, a swirl of soft bells, the sounds of trumpet, rubab and drum.

One midnight, the eldest sister opened her eyes. Surprise. Around her
a whirl of sisters. And the noble dog followed along behind

dragging his tatters. Each sister had a partner, a clattering bone bag,
slender of wrist and ankle, waist and neck, who held her at wrist and
   waist.
They swung as the dog leapt and wove himself into lacy ropes and
   shadows.
Were you there? I was. I saw the sisters dance, the dog jump, the bones
   begin to flower.

Talking to each other

Whatever you say next
is an achoo, or an echo
of a voice you've not heard
in a decade, someone gone

or lost or dead, ho, ho, no
matter, the sound is welcome
so long absent and whether
it's saying something in human

speech or not, maybe the chirps
of lazy birds settling down,
you haven't heard anything
like it since you were a body

sloughed off, every cell replaced,
so long soi soi soi shhh air
in your ear or at your temple
so long so long
so long
ago.

First Light

Must we give up desire, ambition, goals,
the invulnerable body, the lack of pain—
pray for it, pray for it—in order to empty mind

learn control of breath, blood life
continues through plants and beasts, snow
melts, sun rises and sets day in, day out, birds
wing against sun, the sway of the feeders cold
                                    the single sun drop

caught at the corner of the feeders, pink
snared by mountains at sunset
go sit just where I can see pink highlight
coming the crags of dark
oh coming?

Seasons

Spring then winter then spring
all month. We plant flower pots.
We scrape sand from the floor of the garage.
We eat less then more then less again.
Each day birds hit the sun singing.
Rabbits leap around arroyo corners.
Rocks shrink in big winds, big rains.
Is that snow on the mountain?
All the while boundaries lower. Dharma.
The new cat settles in. We merge.

New women pregnant are out walking.
Old women suffer for their friends.
Children grow and leave spring in their blood.
I bow to the light within you.
I bow to the light within you.
I bow to the light within you.

Letters from a Lost Language

> An alphabet's molecules / tasting of honey, iron, and salt / cannot be
> counted—
> —Jane Hirshfield

"Our life in minerals," wrote the poet
to call up the patient sea.
He stands on sand called shore. Salt mustache.
The letters come, are caught, arranged, erase.

Here then is my life in letters. A great weight.
A metal alphabet meaning nothing one can decipher.
(Patience, calls out the poet from the margins.)
One letter like a chair flexes toes. One is a psi.

I have tried all my life
to carry weight from the margins to the center
one letter then another until the click
of the box says stop.

See the hasp of the lock on the transparent door?
See the shadows? Is one a belt buckle?
A woman swimming? One arm
of a scissors. A chair. A man waving.

A clown in a backbend. Dog
behind a bolt.

zzzz says the guard in the box
as he bows his pregnant belly behind Kokopelli
to make an urn.

Shadows move to ease light
from the museum windows.
Soon we will find the metal key.

Again, the poet brushes salt into glowing shapes.
Soon the fires will light
and we will return to mineral.

Published and Uncollected Poems

(1975–2019)

Writing Big

This is a note scratched in a corner.
Write big, says my mother.
This is a note cracked in a mirror
saying **mend**, saying **good**,
saying, **you bastard sounding off
in the loud voice of morning.**

Under the tree whose branches hide
the bird house you yoo-hoo to me
across the distance. I'm here.
Don't shout, dancing around like
some maniac rubbing the ground
with his feet. The night-light's on
on the porch portal. I'm
here.

Mother used to tell me
**find a daisy field and lie
down in it.** I did. Now
you're there in the distance
calling and calling. **Look,
take these cuttings,** she said,
and plant them. I did and
they flower and flower.

You're in on it. Downtown
where you keep your office
you posture to the secretary
and dictate. She fills the
vases again and again
daisy, daisy and this orchid.

   (1975)

Fiction

Okay, I confess:
I made it up, the big house
the children, everything.
At night you sleep beside me.
No. I made it up. Out back
is the real shed where you live
with your wife and children, your
cats running wild over seed bags
spilling in snow, rats gnawing the burlap.
See there are no curtains at the window!
The light pouring over everything!

I live in the big house with my husband
and See how happy everyone is behind our
curtains? See, the snow falls straight
down, fountains of birdseed in the feeders,
tracks snow sieves into in the moonlight.
Moonlight, every night!

No, I confess it's different.
We live together in the wild
woods. The stream in the distance
bends in the distance towards us,
towards the tent we made from pages
of magazines, recycled rags,
the plywood platforms of mousetraps.
I always wear my hair loose and your birds
steal it from among the pine needles at the base
of a big tree we will cut for wood this winter.
When Christmas comes, we leave out my hair
for your birds and they weave it into cloth
for a tree wreath. Our parkas are fur
from friendly animals and our children
sleep in my pockets equipped with nipples

courtesy of the Sierra Club to which we
have always belonged and *National
Geographic*. How beautiful it all is!

Really, I live alone beside this quiet pool
in an Alpine Meadow. The money gathers
interest down below in a Swiss bank while
I bathe daily in the nude, always delicate
and white in the weak sunlight, in the
middle distance. You are nowhere in sight
today but once a week you bring supplies,
books, cigarettes, chocolate and cheese,
and best of all, a supply of fresh bread
to crumble. Cheers! We have our ritual.
We are ecstatically happy without children
or pets but when the deer come up from the lower
meadow we are glad to see them, or I am
in your absence. My tears occasionally flow,
salt for the few weak fish, the salt grass
that in winter turns, yellow? no, sallow
like my other skin. Your ruddy face glows.

   (1975)

Long Night

Somehow, across the street in the yard
of the cloistered nuns,
the sun has made radiant again leaves
of the tree in the yard. They flame
in this early morning before winter.

   (1981)

2 AM, after Dental Surgery

> All night I listened to grown men cry and call for their mothers.
> —war vet on TV

—For John

Infected,
his head is swollen
into all the spaces
of its stretched skin

Now my son's lips slightly open
to tell his deep memory:
how a child after heart surgery
he woke up in the nursery
recovery room feeling in his chest
"no pain, but as if a cartoon
elephant or other animal
had fallen from a great height on it.
I knew I must not move."
In the same voice he says,
his voice a whisper (I bend closer)
how the dentist's patter
was absurd, the drill meanwhile
cutting through the bone
and what he fancied was a laser
slipped away the flesh above his jaw
"like cartoons where legs
are run over by a lawnmower
but you know it hasn't trimmed
them off or even hurt them."

After he vomits and returns,
a pale, sweating, rigid gray,

I sponge his face and hands (I say,
"The way my mother taught me,")
and he sleeps.

O God of parents
who sit beside their hurting boys to listen,
what possible use is this suffocating passion?

(1985)

Graffiti

In the macro-political world
I wonder what's happening.
Folks stacked in crates
their fingers like Hansel's
wriggling, stick-thin.
Everywhere on streets
where streets are
women flail and everywhere ululate
their voices only sirens.

Some teacher asks his third grade class
to watch the jade plant fail
deprived of water.
Their documenting pages
—one each hour—
catch in their fibers
a slick edge of ink.
An organism dying.

Really I don't care, says the thin kid after school,
her ponytail tied off with thread, *a whit*
not a snit, not really. She lights up.
When no one's left in the booth
she picks up pen, writes down the bar's graffiti.
At her ankle, the slosh of beer wind;
at her breast, the rush of vodka sucking.
She writes it down, nano-seconds of alveoli bending
over each perfect breath she shapes her lips on
as she writes. She writes it all down.

    (1995)

Every Way

In agony again
in the kitchen again
sun fills the clear feeder
on the window my chickadee
flies to, flies from her old barn siding
house made by a poet.
How can
I stand more
transformations? Poet
myself, transformed by the mind of my child's will
into seeing at the instant of revulsion
—O rose thou art sick—
the miraculous change Mad
no less than Lear raving
on the moor without his fool.
My flat backyard
radiant with sunshine
lift up that bird.
Lord, help me to it.

Spring Again, Rural Nebraska

The history teacher is going to Russia
he tells me in the library
where I'm looking for an atlas to discover
what's become of Moscow. He comes back
to explain differences among Evangelical Orthodox,
Protestant, and Catholic church services:
in one liturgy the focus, and icons.
In another, the sermon. In the third,
communion, which is the Mass. I say I understand.
He explains to a Jew the uses of icons:
along with the text of liturgy they are holy
and evoke holiness in all humankind.
Icon and liturgy in Greek. Picture and word.
The library is cool and smells of yeast rising,
cinnamon rolls Cook is baking for lunch.

A teacher comes in for the video camera.
The eighth graders are making a film,
The Life of Our High School,
for seventh graders coming to register here next month.
The teacher explains to me, the film will be their map.

Florescent tubes hum. I'm in a Christian community,
the gym teacher tells me at lunch. He is an Adventist
he says, when I ask why he too doesn't eat the ham.

My teacher has trouble with his wife. She tells me in the hall
they've had a tough winter, but the kids are ready to go now
if he wants to move to a larger school. She's small, carries
a football under her arm. As she turns, I pat the shoulder
of her powder-blue parka. She turns to pat me back.

Today is Friday. We eat fish. I've vacated the basement apartment
of the principal and his wife this fourth time I've stayed. Vacuumed.

Flannel sheets from the bed, the towel and washcloth bunched
into the used pillowcase in the laundry room. After class
I drive out through hazy dust, air thick with pollen, home
in time for dinner with friends. We sign our tax forms,
mail them, drink a little, and hope we've got it right.

Why do I love this life? This year the small birds are migrating.
No snow geese and whooping cranes. Too late.
But I'm back on the central flyway.

Masses of dark birds in air last night, grackles?
Wind high, sky clear but no,
farther into the country, beyond the tracks,
standing still in a field, I saw robins and meadowlark,
finch and red-winged blackbirds,
juncos and cardinals,
then a dun one barred at eye and throat
I've never seen before,
great waves hitting the twilight.
The air thick with their singing.

    (2002)

Lost Glasses

—with a line from Madeline DeFrees

The blue boy with spoon-shaped fingers is cold,
he is shivering. The new blood in his body isn't working.
He gets up to ask the teacher can he go home.
His birthday poem about a bike won't be finished,
I'm wind blowing down a high hill.
Here, he hunches his shoulders against something
no sense of mine can enter,
frowns and looks bewildered. His lips draw back. He is shivering.

Now something about touching my neck in its open collar,
fingers on faces, warm blood flowing
dependably, the strong, mingled smells of fluids
leaving the healthy body, the neck pulsing
in its sheath of rosy skin.

I lost my glasses on the beach but here
the trick is to keep speaking, to keep looking
though the world is blurred, the tiny shrimp moving
in their salty basin only words to soothe this moment
of confusion, the sharp, unavoidable desire
to enfold a sick child and cover his ten fingers
with my brown ones, to make a pocket
of my sun-warmed body around
what's shivering, what's cold,
what's barely moving.

Everything that moves, loves and is afraid.

(2002)

Anna Bites Her Friend Emma at Preschool

Baby Eva barks in the night
we get up in our pajamas
go to the hospital on the train.
A hot room bigger than our kitchen
wet light, more kids than the park
Look, are those faucets in the walls?
Drips and where's peppermint?

Someone screams, someone littler
than I am and also someone bigger.
Everyone not crying has a mask
tied with elastic over their face
I can see in. They shiver and
one kid breathes hard like that dog.

Eva barks, then someone takes her away
with Mama, maybe to a faucet and a mask?
I sit very still. Papa holds my hand.
Light hurts and where's the air
for Eva who cries and makes noise
in the corner where I can't see?

Papa reads me a book then says
we have to go home on the train.
I've been very good but Mama
and Eva will stay. Papa carries me.
He is warm and tall. Then nothing.

(2004)

Round/ Square

If you're born round, you won't die square.
—Boxing announcer on TV

Born round? Cut ties and roam.
Borne heavy? Breathe out.
Boon to none? Boon to self.
Burst or swell? Broken;
That's the ticket into the thicket.

Be as you are. Be hungry.
Enter, sit down. Fall into the page.
Be right here. Grey and gray.
Gravy at the corner? Mop it up. Turn on the faucet.

Wrists hurt, knees stick? Brain's aloft. Lofty.
Lifted to the window? Clouds. Cloudy.
Hungry? Breathe it.
Jettison history? What comes next is nexus.
Never mind silence. Something's always the end.

(2004)

Dwell/ April

Revelation is not a process that stops.

I can tell you what happened but not why it happened.
—Alicia Ostriker

If the car stopped in front of the shop,
opened, and a group of six got in
and you are a witness to this event,
what does it mean?

If the woman with the red rasta braids
carries a cup of coffee between
her mittens and the steam obscures
her face as she belts up in the front seat,
who is she?

If your partner stands at the door to the shop
to watch, face unchanged and their posture,
and you sit still to see and frown,
what is the end of this story?

You can decide to remove your hat
so snow wets your hair at the back,
or cover your fingers with the flannel pockets
of your parka; but you can't change the story
about to happen, or happening, or happened,
no matter how hard you try.

These options are yours: peel a potato;
wash out the laundry, sit by the bed
of your friend in the hospital; drink chocolate
as hot as you can stand; buy railroad tickets,
or bus; begin to read a new novel;

open your head to the light
that is always swarming.

This story is the start of spring
unfolding in the heart a flurry of snow.

   (2006)

Fragments

> The characteristic thing of the twentieth century was the idea of production
> in a series, that one thing should be like every other thing, and that it should
> be alike and quantities of them.
> —Gertrude Stein, *Paris France*

Whether the shine through double doors
opened to wind's silver sleeves comforts her
looking back into the hot room, heat softening the oils
of a dining room table, only a hard crystal glare is
visible in noon light; is it crystal or more silver?
She rises, reenters the house restless as always,
lucid as always, as always hungry and ashamed.

Having been sick for a year,
having been weakened
in the body, having been
ready for death, having
watched the children
sleeping, themselves sick,
having lost or been lost
to Eden, having revived,
having watched them revive,
now she is ready for the ocean.

Or, she thinks, alone at night,
for a little peace. A tromp through the world.
Under robes she sees a beggar's bowl extend,
reed soles dissolve in the mush of the world's roads.
And over all the wracked heavens.

Now I am free and what whorls
and bumps, what declivities
and delicious inclines
attend me?

Yin and Yang, tiger and dragon, wet and dry,
and the lewd mysteries of death . . .
The eleven-headed quanyin at the foot of the throne
bends his several knees to the emperor,
begs a brush and turns out the silk
of his manifold pockets, and ink.
The sublime calligraphy, poetry, unfolds
in double dimensions as color leaps
to the edge: Three perfections,
"the most refined of artistic endeavors."
Northern Song Dynasty, China,
to practice *fu gu*, a reverence for the past.

The refrigerator door opens on
plastic wrap over chicken parts,
Styrofoam trays filled with slush,
dinner, and her part to follow after
having learned to make food enough
for nine people with grace, elegance.

"Throughout its history, China's emperors
and officials, sages, and scholars, poets and painters
looked back to earlier times for authority,
inspiration, and guidance."

An authority said, "double the pad
dipped in silver polish for the round
belly of the tureen on the table.
Any toothbrush abandoned by
a visitor will do nicely for lid
embellishments, the finial's deep
ridge. Do it." And she did,
gelled her hair and began to sing.

   (2010)

Birthday, Red-Tailed Hawk

When I came toward the house and looked up
to watch a bronze wing become the whole bird,
flash a red tail, the raptor's beak's gold,
and circling, the requisite small bird making a fuss,
surely the universe was saying Happy Birthday.

Not so the silence that followed. Nor my heart folded shut
against this spring day. A few more years, maybe,
and then the grave quiet.

   (2010)

Blackberries

—After Francis Ponge, for Beverley Bie Brahic

Certain fruits are composed on the page,
not edible, only ink, all juicy potential.

The soft-fleshed are easy, the berries a challenge;
So many alike. "An agglomeration of spheres."
A single silhouette on the table as one rolls to the edge.

Crunched in the teeth, sweetness if ripe.
On the branch, a rogue family birds pick at
Then release—from beak to anus.

Ripeness is all, says Edgar the son, to his father.
Men must endure their going hence, even as their coming hither.
Ripeness is all we have. Or the beige berries fall.

(2010)

Up All Night

On the balcony early sun.
Water hurrying below in the ditch.
Water rush, grass meadow, hedgerow.
Birdsong.
What else can you call
to call back?

In June snow on the low mountain,
green what's its name?
Truchas Peak.

Below little fists of daisies
a few open handed.
Rock of granite gray and cream.

Suspended a branch grows slowly
through the hole it made in a rusty can.
Logs propped over the ditch.

In the far field a horse is blurred
by the wings of the mountain jay so close
I can see only bright flicker and swoosh.

Don't stop, beetle on the porch floor,
don't stop. Don't stop. Don't stop.

   (2016)

Abecedarian II

Abby said, "I'm packing
Because the ticket date
Comes Thursday. I'm
Definitely ready to go, whatever
Effort's required:
Fill the yellow thermos, please. I'll fill the striped carry-on."
"Good Luck!" she waves out the car window.
Huffy me, left behind, she sulks
In their room, sniffles.
Just my luck, she whimpers.
Knowing at the same time her drama is as fake as her tears.
Lump it, her
Mom might have said,
Never seeming to have felt

Overwhelmed as she felt now.
Past time to move out, she thinks,
Quiet for a change, no fuss no
Recriminations. Nothing left in the closet.
She'll feel better soon
Turning over in the pool
Under the waterfall;
Visions of dinner later
Wake up her body's
Extra appetite for pleasure as
Youngsters all over the globe,
Zealous for life, for more, move into new rooms.

   (2016)

A Story from Mah-Jongg Club

The first time she used her key
it was the ex-wife Rosie cruising
for her things, to take them back.
The next time she broke the lock.
Then she projected herself as a girl,
protoplasm, so they tripped over her,
the ex-husband, his new wife, their baby
just now crawling on the carpet.

The new doors had locks.
The windows were secure.
The old house, used to ghosts,
settled around Rose still roaming
with one silk stocking in her hand.

The baby never saw her but the new wife did
her belly rounding on the second child.
The husband? He'd forgotten all their names and scents.
They all made porridge as his mother had.

(2016)

The City of Suffering

is made of cork, variegated
levels that collapse one into another.
One cut piercing the top floor,
three on the second, five on the third,
an arch for a door. Pink over-glow
with a rough stripe of charcoal.

It fits neatly under the glass
of the wheeled table that holds up flowers:
lily of the Incas, purple phlox
and a golden globe with spikes.

How did I come to stand here, looking up?

(2017)

Another Story

Or, was it so awful to be a disloyal daughter
the cygnets wondered aloud to themselves
twice at least a day. They were a clutch
of females wondering where their daddy
went on his days off. He'd told them
to stop with the pestering, preening
his chest feathers with his beak
where the shafts were broken off.
He smelled funny. And his song rasped.

Later, when they were fledged, they circled
around him. Time for truth. Where
do you go? Swans were notorious
for silence and their dad, no different.

Did you guess there's a human girl, Leda,
two counties away past the big apple tree,
so succulent even the tips of her fingers
dripped nectar? Her nape was reddened
her belly rounding. Grain grew in her
footsteps as she came running to the pond
where their father landed for the weekend.

Were they disloyal? No, they grew up
scanning the ripples of their own pond,
looking for a way to grow their plumage
into regal garments, feather underwear
to attract the attention of a human God,
ready to lay the egg of Helen of Troy,
ready to cover her calcite housing
with their warmth, until she hatched.

(2019)

New Poems

(2020)

Dear God,

You make green our desert, the jackrabbit to leap there;
The mechanisms of birth and of death, that shrivel;
Mucus to heal and the shine of secretions, okra and cactus.
Mold that devours the stem avoids the flower for a day.
Even the eaten lobes pour forth their buds.
You are the author of stars and their long light.

You made us to bear children out of great pleasure.
You provided the starch in the collar of our womb.
So also you opened it.
Let our children who are grown prevail.
Let them have what they will, your earth. Let them go forth.
And let those who pay authors with substance choose them.

Tomorrow is my birthday. You made my mother, Devorah,
Give birth when she was said to be barren. In a storm,
You gave her strength enough to hold up the lamp
Over the kitchen table for the doctor who saved her infant son;
Who then became a man who studied stars; who died young;
Who left behind two daughters who now study stars.

I am withering in my age.
Yet you have made a door outside of which
Rattlesnake, primrose, the miraculous spider the size of my palm
Flower amidst the sand.

You who are beyond names gave us names to praise
So we will name until the ends of our days.

Let our children also praise as they go forth to deliver.
Let your creation be a model:
Your healing shine, your connections. Tarantula.

Arms/ Belief

Arms will be wings. Arms are sacks of pain.
Arms lifted the child, rinsed the pot,
planted flowers, strong arms
their engines stripped, shut off.

Where do I wander in all the sleep
that overtakes me?
Sounds of words keep the anchor
in sand. Anchored and caught, I mean.

Everything drifts or else I do, as Orestes
did after his mother did-in his father
who did-in their daughter
to catch wind. The sails bellied.

Even our stories are spare and violent, like pain
whose profile is unfixed
and can blow away, sand.

Once upon a time a monk who
was then a scientist became a monk.
So much wisdom
needed to embrace pain, teach us to sit still.

Atrium walls enclose benches
flowerpots newly filled with geraniums,
phlox, sweet potato vine,
so many on the sale table
without names. In the walled
garden they thrive.

Beloveds

The thin air is laced with fear
and tenderness. Girls playing,
years accumulating. Objects
lost or discarded, new plans.

Listen to tambourines,
planes in the skies. Yoo-hoo,
calls Mother down the stairs.
Prickles of irritation. The dead
discarded like tangerine skins.

Time to order the disorder. Still
in this huge mountain's nest, again
we unwind together, shedding options
or I do, unpacking, washing fruit,
(the body and its cut-out clothes)

making breakfast. Remember
paper dolls? Blunt scissors
for the left-handed so tabs
tore off and dresses fluttered.

I'm tired. Residue of tending
and minding. One of us
brought photos from Scotland,
storks in their nest, three or four
standing in a hat of woven sticks.

We are balanced like that
in the mountains.

Clothes

The wedding dress, white lawn
starched firm, the bodice two points
like tulips, organdy overskirt and
linen embroidery over a bell-shaped
skirt, also in points, white linen
shoes with heels so high they sank
into the grass of the backyard where
the usual vows were said. Two straps
of silk over skinny shoulders.
The veil.

The sight of Lisa, a skull balanced
easily on bones, dying and still
upright, chatting, joking, her full
head of hair not yet gray. How
can she die? But she did.

And the navy silk with the pure
white collar, six inches wide and
bias cut to surround shoulders
yet low for show as needed.
Buttons of glittery up the front.
Worn with black velvet kitten heels
with small glitter at the instep.

When she died, what then?
The crowds of her friends?
The well-wishers?
The flowers?

Echo

Something is happening to my body
—Elliott Carter

Something is happening to my body
I tell my son on the telephone.
He knows about my new hip,
has seen the incision.
He cared for me like an infant.

My body is walking, happening
I tell the physical therapist
as he stretches out hips.
A thin line on skin,
all that's left.

Happening body is really something,
I tell my companion
as we climb the hill's hip.
The decision to mend wasn't mine.
My body cares for me, as it has.

Is to my body as breath, this hip.
These arms that rise.
The wind tries
to blow me over but what
happens is balance.

Something happened to my body.
Something mends an echo in air.

Formal

I *was made to be someone else's mother.*
She says so and believes what she says.
What she says is impossible, four misses.

In this desert new to me we are happy.
I say so and believe what I say.
Everything old is left behind, in graves.

Moved to a better state, she finds a job.
They say so and believe what they say.
White walls in their house, at last a view.

They fight like crazy over nothing but the heat.
They say so but neither is listening.
Too late the season turns. They've filed.

Each one waits in line for authorization.
They say yes and believe what they say.
The clerks call the manager but no proof, no receipts.

You've been dead for several months, gone for years.
I say so and believe what I say.
You weren't missed for a minute, not until now.

The smell of his shoulder while dancing wasn't pleasant.
Believe me. I've never said so until now.
Yet we married. Our bed was delicious, but I left him.

In the middle of the night, a breeze then a wind.
The coyotes yip then howl, believe what they say.
At noon the sun scalds even the cottontail under a juniper.

You are hiding.
I say so and believe what I say.
Your sons carry on without you, racing cars, buying houses.

What is pain? he asked me over lunch, his eyes filling.
He asked me and believed what I said.
I answered his question, absence.

Seasonal

Undershirts and flannel
lined jeans and hot gin
and fires and hot coffee and fires
and lost votes and cash and
who is buying a car now?

Gifts and who has the boxes
saved from recycling to mail?
Moths in our sweaters and so
we buy a fleece, not like Jason,
and candles and coins wrapped

in gold and where are the birds?
Not at the feeders and where is
the cat? Not by the fire. It's cold
and we find pack rats on the patio
and bobcats hunting them

and it's time for holiday books and
gatherings and the moon in its
usual quarter behind clouds and
where are the stars? Where is
your family and mine and his

brother, her nieces and the paper
with its seasonal news in sections
behind scandal, the specials on TV
and to stream? Nothing seems
exactly right but I'm walking

the frozen road again today and
tomorrow and yesterday and
the birdbath is all ice, the cholla
upright and crisp trees don't thrive
here who can blame them?

Let's sing, light fires against plague
and never blow out the candles again
against custom and we're worrying
about the fires and how are you
doing? We're fine and snug.

Looking out the Window, Accordion Polka Accompaniment

Hour by hour, minute by minute, toes and fingers alert
and jiggling, second by second life runs down and out.

Somehow from daily filaments memory braids past lives.
A glimpse, the beach, the salt ocean, someone's hands holding under and up.

And then night again with its stars and stories.
Soup he made with onions and cut rosemary.

Gardens make the best metaphor
discounting loss and the scholarship of grief.

We're in a season of drought, which is better than flooding.
How can she get on without his ashes in the front hall closet?

On the top of the refrigerator in the clean kitchen, warm kuchen.
Aunt Jane cuts her a piece after school, with milk.

The sisters sit on the front steps, sob into each other's shoulders.
Who's dead now? He was dancing on their uncle's shoes last week.

Everything past reconnects from flash to flash.
Everything future is blank—even next, this second.

Picked up in the Garden, with a Line from Mary Oliver

I thought it was fragile, not buff and muscular
but now I see lacy fronds
(they smell like grass)
and the branch is young, from this season,
germinated in sand by rain and left alone to grow
tough and pale green, perfect on top but torn at the roots
by my fingers now holding a pencil by the throat.

In air from the fan it wiggles slightly
laid on a table, root
fragment blowing free.
Now a top leaf begins to move,
a coolness, and the adjacent white tissue.

I'm as still as a gong unstruck.

What moves now inside, the opening and closing
of filaments, tiny doors that keep it alive

as the frond begins to wilt
into its gray-green
and pea color
attached to roots, acrid, all moving
in fan air
like bodies contracting and twisting loose
from tension,
the tree-like tilt dropping head first,
roots lifting, rising.

Oh, why does everything ascend at last and too soon?

Eva Sings

She takes my hand
pulls me into the kitchen.
She's a tiny child. We sit at her table.
I overlap the chair. She fills hers up.

She's eating the last piece of cake
surrounded by cookie cutters.
Alphabet letters, shapes.
Christmas is soon.

Now it's time to make cookies, she says
out of the cake:
stars, and cookies that connect,
like this. She shows me on the tabletop.

Nana, now it's time
for the cookies to bake.
I'm hungry, nibbling crumbs
trying to see the cold kettle on the stove.

Now it's time to make more things.
I get some Play-Doh, roll it out, not very much.
She rolls a snake, coils it up.
A bowl for the salad, not very big.

Now we soften the bowl. She shows me how.
Just as good as new but we still can eat it.
As her tiny fingers move, she sings.
Did you hear that song on the radio?

It's just a song I made up.
Not today, but tomorrow,
we will get by, you never know.

Risk

—after Rick Jackson

My father's hands are broad and scarred,
index finger's nail replaced by a whorl of hard tissue.

He is prying open a stuck window.

By the ocean children are broaching high waves, mounting and falling,
    mounting and falling like foam.

Father, why don't you raise your head, see the putty in the old frame begin
    to powder, the glass begin to shatter?

Child, he says, what matter the tendons in the arm when the whole body is
    made of salt and water?

After the Memoir, Revelations

So you're here? Still dizzy from another dodge, close shave, reprieve? . . . Listen, how your heart pounds inside of me.
—Wislawa Szymborska

Here on the screen of a computer
thin as a chip
is the peeling back
of transparent layers of intelligence.

Now do you feel yourself less?

Surely more than a tulip bulb
more than the cat
more than a computer
in some ways?

And now feel cooler air in the house
smell coffee falling through filters in the kitchen
taste grief in our throats—oh children, children—
hear the laughter from last night
reading to the Beloved
who turns away listening to another computer
and listening said, and speaking back says something.

Did we hope for these misunderstandings when we wrote what we did?

This morning, someone dizzy for the second consecutive morning—no
    surprise—
finds on the kitchen table a stale fortune:

Success doesn't take much, it takes everything.

"Nobody Teaches Life Anything"

—Gabriel García Márquez

Are you Nobody, too? Dickinson asked.
I didn't want to be Nobody, but I was.
Put to bed at a certain time for ages, then
sent to bed by myself. I ate what they did.
A lazy student I sucked up escape
in storybooks. Nobody taught me
except how to read and swim.

I'm somebody now but not available
to teach life anything. Sorry.
What do I know? The fragments that flash?
Papa casting his fishing weights in an arc
over the yellow rings at Cobb's Hill Pond?
To stand and push hard on the pedals of my bike to fly?
My brother's big hand in my little one.
Mother's green brooch. The white silk sheath dress
I wore under graduation robes. Don't tell.

Shortly before my being banished
the shower moved in an arc down. My hip broke.
Thereafter followed many months of limping.
Life didn't stop. Did you think it would?
I'm a good teacher but as that famous writer said,
nobody teaches life anything.
Life keeps moving, an infinity pool
falling invisibly over some edges.

While I'm waiting for an edge,
summer unfolds her largess.
Today a golden skink wriggled
his body over the welcome mat.

Walking a gravel road with a cane
I saw a rabbit race one side to the other.
He was just born, that tiny.
Are these chapter lessons from life?
I'd like to teach life how to stop Job's brain cancer.

But that's the point, isn't it?
Life knows everything and doesn't care or can't stop.
As we're learning to see edges,
life keeps flowing and going and racing and pulsing
and best to do is to keep eyes and ears open
for hints of what's coming.

Or maybe the point is Spring's plenitude,
which includes sugar ants and roaches
and—well, you get it. An infinite dump-puzzle.
Life knows everything from birth to war,
to building a wall that comes down and
goes up, comes down, and goes up again.

Maybe I'm moseying around time's pool in my coral swimsuit
watching for Death to put his booted foot over the lip of
no, not the pool but my bedroom window,
coming in without asking when I was six.
I talked him out of taking me then.
He promised to come back later.
Not wait forever.

—for John

Policy Discussion

What he needs isn't any new strategy.
We weren't intent on killing each other.
But how we approached the problem was disorganized.
His handling of the carnage was . . . make your own
flip analogy.
Each piece of the puzzle paints a picture.
Remember, we're not using pliers.
Remember the absolute benchmark isn't achievable.
They couldn't in fact come up with much.
But we are very attentive to an uncharacteristically
benign strategy.
At worst, you can encourage positive change.

A Life

The season is summer, as usual.

What happened began as always, with shoes.
Sneaks. Red with white laces, grubby.
Then navy shorts, white T-shirt, navy and white neck bandana;
and equipment, badminton rackets wrapped with sticky tape unraveling,
the raggedy feathers of the shuttlecock (oh, lovely!) wound with thread.
In the backyard a net, sagging. No cousins yet. The ping, ping, practicing.

What happened that afternoon, or another, or the rest of that summer?
She was restless and felt unhinged, young, awkward,
unlooked for by the others in the family, certainly unloved. (That's how I felt!)

But here they come, rounding the corner of the two-story house
with the screened-in sleeping porch over the scrubby backyard.

Poplar leaves noisy through the windy nights they slept up there.
Let's play now, get it over, and then it's time for lunch.

There was some laughing at the cousins' house, in the hall
outside the bathroom where they practiced with equipment necessary
for their age. Secrets they exchanged with grown-ups.
Aunt Phyllis usually stopped by the deli to pick up dinner,
dumped it into servers and set the table before Uncle Mor came home.
Did he think we girls had spent the day cooking?
Really we all went to the beach every day, Aunt Phyllis driving.

And where was Mother? In our house, dressed up in stockings
in the heat. Sitting still in her turquoise wingback
reading. She was home, she had to be home, she didn't drive
and Daddy took the car each morning. (Why didn't I notice?)

This girl hated it, except reading from the library
which she did as much as she could, Dr. Doolittle,
The Five Little Peppers, Anne of Green Gables.

She could tie her shoes, not in a bunny ears knot
but the right way, loop and around and tuck and pull.
And sleep-over camp was great, the brim-down sailor's cap
she wore for weeks, the kids, the tents, the mac and cheese,
the drinking fountain where they washed hair in cold water.
Hunting the snape.
Always laughing. Then after weeks away, time to go back home.
They'd cleared out her room, brought in new furniture
and drapes she'd never seen before, thrown out her school papers.

She survived even if not all the family did.
Papa died of brain cancer. She saw him fall.
And so did Uncle Herman, young, leaving
Aunt Jane to work at Sears. And then
Daddy, too, and she wanted to follow, but went
instead to college where the summer choice was home

to her mother in an empty house, a job in the café—
or married to her teacher, who had a fellowship
and an apartment and asked her with a ring.

And then they had a babe
to watch and a move to make, not just upstate
but across the country to another life, another chapter.

Sentences

Shoes are flying at the suitcase.
I haven't heard from you in ages.
Tickets dissolve in moisture.
Also, live long enough, piles of paper topple.
Turn your attention from the screen to the window.
Look out at the bluebirds now.
Your new shoes and shirts are electric.
Your new kitchen faucet divine.
Seckel pears, delicious if you know how to spell them.
Stir me lightly, please.
Enough about cooking, geese are skybound they say.
Let's put your laces through the grommets.
Whatever you may be saying sotto voce, your heart is pounding off-rhythm.
Speaking of cakes, the recipe felt like some kind of dark secret.
It'll have to wait because I'm checking out of this hotel.
My favorite had a house on the balcony.
We made love and ate soufflé.
A day in the kitchen roasting vegetables is the perfect anecdote.
I replace half the flour with almond meal and take the sugar down by a cup.
I don't regret a thing, no matter how late the plane.

The Truth

Since I can't see now
at least until the surgery is over
you'll have to wait for my messages
on paper. These electronic screens
aren't worth the bytes they embody.

Please consider me striding next to you
as you walk to your garden in the next block.
And at the grocery store when you pick up
artichokes, two for you, one for me.

The cat doesn't know the difference
between me seeing and me not seeing.
She doesn't care, so long as I open
the screen door to the atrium
where she sleeps under a ladder
of basil and Italian thyme.

Everything looks bright outside.
Lizards are doing push-ups, as usual,
and the rabbits are tiny and indiscreet.
We have a finch nest on the trumpet vine
and a mama who flies off when we look.
Here the air is hot at four,
cool at ten through the sleeping night.

Since I can't see, I can't name
what thumps against the glass door
to the room where I'm typing.
Outside is green now, and taupe,
and the tree's leaves are saw-toothed
in the blur. Not so bad, really,
knowing what's coming.

Let me remind you to be kind
and watch out for what you're running into.
Your new glasses are chic, you're a good person.
Don't forget to have a good dinner.
I love you. Good night.

A Wedding

Her son is best man.
At the reception he puts out his arm, asks to dance.
They do, a two-step alone on the vast floor of the ballroom.
She tells him, "I can't do these steps."
He laughs, says, "Yes you can. You taught me."
Then she remembers the rug rolled up in the white room
Whirling around and around, his sister clapping and dancing.
They circle fast around the floor under the light ball,
Her son dipping and raising his shoulders,
His patent leather shoes covered with light dots.
She hangs onto his shoulder, the cloth of his gray tuxedo.
He whispers, "This is the first time I've worn a boutonnière."

Everything whirls and she forgets
Where to spot to keep from getting dizzy.
But her spine is more relaxed than before.
She remembers when he was born.
She breathed into her body's cavities, hour after hour.
So where he leads her in the dance, she follows.

The music rests. "A break," he says.
At the last chord he spins her out, brings her back,
A flash bulb pops, they bow, he smiles, offers his arm,
And they promenade off the floor to applause.
Two-stepping all the way.

Credo 23

I believe in . . . the grace of animals / in my keeping, the thrust to go on.
—Maxine Kumin

The cat sleeps on the ledge,
sunlight a warm patch on her back.
When she wakes, a cloud of fur
announces her arch. She thumps
and yes, it's grace that she carries
to me sitting under the fan.

I'm thirsty, it's lunch time.
She finds water by poking her paw
carefully into her glass on my lap.
I move to the kitchen where she is.
I'm hardly limping in sandals,
the miracle of a new hip.
Her tail warps around my ankle.

High summer again; I am in its keeping.
Monsoon rains washed out our road.
The rabbits' number escalates, more
and more each morning as we walk.
Through my dark glasses the world
continues its flicker. Aware, I'm here.

Failure

One shoe. The other gone.
Found later in a nest of lint. In the bushes.

Blind from migraine. What's that raw noise?
Only small dials on the radio, all six slippery knobs.

Out to lunch. Friends talk. Her daddy's in despair.
I try for words. What luck! A father alive and she's fifty.

Early morning sounds. Someone's sick?
I flee to the kitchen. You're making coffee, fine.

A door is open. I look in. They're all gone.
A student says, you look so tired. I go home alone.

So much work! How about a road trip?
Of course I'll go, read in the car, bad companion.

Cold outdoors. Heavy clothes, all cotton.
Lighter near the window. Indoors, we shiver.

Chairs for sale. On the committee
friends gather, all peers: Old sitters, new seats.

Fort Pond

The lake between its wetlands steams.
Layers of wisp ascend over the water
rolling on a tangent to the dock.

In the hemlocks across the pines
a calling of birds, a flock
is difficult to see—small birds,
a flash of red—red-winged blackbirds—
but in the aggregate, dark.
The flock wheels and turns.
I follow with binoculars
until it rises with a hiss, loud,
and turns toward the far shore and goes.

I adjust the focus,
turn until I find the bird still sitting on her raft
where she was last night.
She is small but her breast glows red.
Is she the morning light itself—
or a Holboell's grebe—reddish neck,
white chin and cheek?
I'm so glad to see her on her raft, still in the moving mist.

The Great Blue Heron
we saw yesterday is gone from his cove.
His entrance is covered with water lilies,
bright flowers rising above the pads.
The geese who have landed, ten I can see,
swim quietly in pairs on the water.

Victory Garden, Grass Skirt

We had one but not the other
when I was very little.
Mornings before the heat set in
I picked up my yellow trowel
exited through the back door
evading, as usual, my mother.

The tomatoes were usually red
by the time of the highest heat
at noon. I had no intention of picking
one and eating it, hot juice
running down my chin, the smell,
the crisp taste of first bites pricking.
But you know that always I did,
first one, then another.
And no one seemed to notice.
I grazed vegetable gardens
all up and down the neighbors' hills.

In junior high, SueEllen Smith
brought from Hawaii the skirt,
a sample of vacation ecstasy.
She modeled it—we all did,

one after another and wiggled.
The skirt wiggled too. Hips.
Who knew? I wanted jiggly
breasts but no, it never happened.

My mother's favorite flower
was gladiolus in a tall vase.
Home from the grocery with a bunch,
niveous and gold ones in my arms,

I take down her heavy vase from the closet.
After my cutting and trimming, propped in circle
here they are, the only sign of reconciliation
in the room. Twelve ripe tomatoes in a bowl
about to reach perfection in the kitchen.

What happened? I don't know.
I didn't like that woman and she
didn't like me. I was a cruel child.
Verbs escape my memory
but our victory garden and
SueEllen's skirt retain their fragrance.
And I, too, love gladiolus spears
(fourteen buds on most stalks)
and the sight of my mother's hands
arranging and changing them
in the window of my childhood
as war raged in Europe
and on all fronts.

ACKNOWLEDGMENTS

Thanks to Kwame Dawes who thought up this book and to John Kinsella for his long interest in my work and to Donna Shear who said yes.

Thanks to Joeth Zucco and to Courtney Ochsner, talented guides through the process.

Thanks to Aaron Raz Link who did the initial gathering of new and previously printed poems, long scattered. And to Daire Elliott, his partner and my friend.

Thanks to John Link whose music and scholarship are my inspiration. And to Maria Schoenhammer whose kindness, energy, and focus are exemplary.

Thank you to Anna and Eva Link, always.

Gratitude to family and friends who support my life and writing. Many of your names are in this book. All of you live in the silence of this making.

And to Dale Nordyke, who entered our lives in order to improve them, love and more.

*

What Happens. Lincoln: University of Nebraska Press, 2009. Used with permission by the Board of Regents of the University of Nebraska, © 2009. (Book manuscript selected by the editor Grove Press Poetry Series, 1986.)

What Is Good. Chicago: Thorntree Press, 1988

The Bone Dish. New York: State Street Press Chapbooks, 1989

Divine Honors. Hanover N H: Wesleyan University Press, 1997

Truly Bone. Poems by Hilda Raz, prints by Karen Kunc. Lincoln N E: Blue Heron Press, 1999

Trans. Middleton CT: Wesleyan University Press, 2001

All Odd and Splendid. Middletown CT: Wesleyan University Press, 2008

List & Story. Nacogdoches TX: Stephen F. Austin University Press, 2020. Used with permission.

What Happens / What Is Good

Acknowledgment is given to the following for the first publication of some of these poems: *North American Review, Denver Quarterly, Poetry Miscellany, The Pennsylvania Review, Plainsongs, Earth's Daughters, Whole Notes,* and the anthologies *Alternatives: An American Poetry Anthology; All My Grandmothers Could Sing;* and *Forty Nebraska Poets.*

The Bone Dish

All My Grandmothers Could Sing, Poems by Nebraska Women (Free Rein Press): "Diction," "What Happens"
Alternatives: An American Poetry Anthology (Best Cellar Press): "Accident"
Denver Quarterly: "My Dream, Your Dream"
Earth's Daughters: "Restraint" (originally "Late March")
Pennsylvania Review: My Daughter Home from College Tells Me about the Gods"
Plainsongs: "Town/ County"
Whole Notes: September: Getting Married Again," "That's Something" (originally "Something")

Divine Honors

Thanks to the following magazines and books in which these poems appeared:
The Bread Loaf Anthology of Contemporary Nature Poetry, edited by Robert Pack and Jay Parini (Hanover: University Press of New England, 1993): "Teaching, Hurt," "For Barbara, Who Brings Me a Green Stone in the Shape of a Triangle"
Cancer through the Eyes of Ten Women, edited by Patricia Duncker and Vicky Wilson (London and San Francisco: Pandora, an imprint of HarperCollins, 1996): "Riverroad, Meandering Root," a sequence of twelve poems: "Repair," "Let's Consider the Consequences," "Weathering/Boundaries/What is Good," "Mu," "Breast/Fever," "Petting the Scar," "Fish-Belly-Mound," "For Barbara, Who Brings a Green Stone in the Shape of a Triangle," "Mapping/Bleating," "Bernini's Ribbon," "Nuts," "Who Does She Think She Is"
The Colorado Review: "Cobb's Hill Pond," "I Hear the Name of the Moon and Am Afraid," "Sarah among Animals," "Sarah's Response"
Judaism: "Isaac Stern's Performance," "Insomnia Again," "Vowels"
Laurel Review: "Opening/ Working/ Walking"
Literature and Medicine: "Weathering/ boundaries/ what is good," "Riddle"

Nebraska English Journal: "Graffiti," "Bernini's Ribbon"

Ploughshares: "Breast/ fever," "Service"

Southern Review: "Balance," "Petting the Scar," "From Your Mouth to God's Ear"

The Women's Review of Books: "Day-old Bargain," "Daylight Savings," "Chigger Socks," "For Barbara," "Trope," "Axe-earrings, abalone shell"

Trans

Thanks to the following magazine and books in which these poems first appeared, sometimes in slightly different form.

Atlanta Review: "She"

Connecticut Review: "First, Thus," "John and Maria's Wedding," "Historical Documents," "Prelude," "Early Morning, Left Handed"

The Extraordinary Tide: New Poems by American Women, edited by Erin Belieu and Susan Aizenberg (New York: Columbia University Press, 2001): "Volunteers," "Before John and Maria's Wedding," "Fast Car on Nebraska I-80: Visiting Teacher"

Kunapipi: "Insomnia III," "Trans," "Aaron at Work/ Rain," "Every Way," "Anna Maria Is Coming, or Maybe Thomas Barton, or Max!"

Nebraska Review: "Fast Car on Nebraska I-80: Visiting Teacher," "Avoidance"

The Plains Sense of Things: Eight Poets. Edited by Mark Sanders (Grand Island NE: Sandhills Press): "Drought: Benedict, Nebraska," "Fast Car on Nebraska I-80: Visiting Teacher"

Pleiades: "Women & Men"

Poetryetc2 and Catalyst 2: "First, Thus," "Aaron at Work/ Rain"

Rattle: "Sick"

Sundog: The Southeast Review: "Heart Transplant"

All Odd and Splendid

Contemporary Poetry by Nebraskans, edited by Mary K. Stillwell, Denise Banker, and Greg Kosmicki (Omaha: Backwaters Press, 2008): "Pets"

Blue Mesa Review: "Arousal" and "Beloved, 24"

The Cincinnati Review: "Complaint"

Crazed by the Sun: Poems of Ecstasy: "Spring Snowstorm" and "Tenor Part"

Margie: "Splendid"

Mid-American Review: "Spring Snowstorm" and "Paper Strip"

New Millennium Writings, 2006–07: "Elegy for Two Poets"

Nightsun 25, edited by Alicia Ostriker: "September 11" and "Diaspora"

Paterson Literary Review 36: "Vocation," "He Graduates from Clown School," and "Son"

Paterson Literary Review 35: "All Odd and Splendid," "Dante's Words," "Funeral, then Flu," and "Terza Rima"

Paterson Literary Review 31: "Once"

PoetryMagazine.com: "Thank You Very Much," " Son," "Alice" (published as "Negotiations"), and "Vocation" (published as "Knowing")

Pleiades: "Sunday Morning, without Couplet"

SALT Magazine: "Water Ceremonies," "Wilt," "He/ She: The Bike," and "Son"

SALT Magazine; reprinted in The Sorrow Psalms, edited by Lynn Strongin (Iowa City: University of Iowa Press, 2008): "A Body of Water"

The Women's Review of Books, 2008: "Her Dream" and "Coma"

List & Story

ABQ InPrint: "Another Story" and "The Sisters"

Askew Poetry Journal: "Late September"

Numero Cinq Magazine 7, no. 12 (December 3, 2016): "A Symposium on Love," "Autobiography," "Meditation," and "One Toe, Crooked"

Salt 17, no. 1 (2003): "A Conversation about Text" (published as "The Bigger Issue of Time")

Solo Novo: "A Symposium on Love"

Hyacinth Girl Press, for "Women and Poetry," in Women Write Resistance: Poets Resist Gender Violence. Thanks to the editor, Laura Madeline Wiseman.

Literary House Press (Chestertown MD: Literary House Press, Washington College, 2014) for "Flowers of Immortality," in The Book of Scented Things, and "Letters from a Lost Language," in Still Life with Poem. Thanks to the editors, Jehanne Dubrow and Lindsay Lusby.

Lost Horse Press, for "Women's Lib," in Nasty Women Poets: An Unapologetic Anthology of Subversive Verse. Thanks to the editors, Grace Bauer and Julie Kane.

Published and Uncollected

ABQ InPrint (Fall 2019): "Another Story"

ABQ InPrint, (Fall 2017): "The City of Suffering"

ABQ InPrint, (Fall 2016): "A Story from Mah-Jongg Club"

ABQ InPrint, (Fall 2016): "Abecedarian II"

ABQ InPrint, (Fall 2016): "Up All Night"

Margie 8 (February 2010): "Blackberries"

Margie 8 (February 2010): "Birthday, Red-Tailed Hawk":

Grist: The Journal for Writers (February 2010): "Fragments"

Patterson Literary Review, no. 35 (Fall 2006): "Dwell/ April"

Puerto del Sol, vol. 39, no. 2 (Summer/Fall 2004): "Round/ Square"

Pleiades (Fall 2004): "Anna Bites Her Friend Emma at Preschool"

Alaska Review 19, nos. 3 and 4 (Spring/Summer 2002) and in *Paterson Literary Review*, no. 31 (2002): "Lost Glasses"

Paterson Literary Review, no. 31 (2002): "Spring Again, Rural Nebraska"

Kunapipi 20, no. 3, special issue, edited by John Kinsella, Churchill College: "Every Way"

"Contemporary Nebraska Writers: A Miscellany," in *Nebraska English Journal* 40, no. 2 (Fall 1995): "Graffiti"

All My Grandmothers Could Sing, edited by Judith Sornberger (Lincoln NE: Free Rein Press, 1985): "2 AM, after Dental Surgery"

Forty Nebraska Poets, published as a special issue of the poetry magazine *Pebble* 21, edited by Greg Kuzma (Lincoln NE: The Best Cellar Press, 1981): "Long Night"

Nebraska Poets, published as a special issue of the poetry magazine *Pebble* 13, edited by Greg Kuzma (Lincoln NE: The Best Cellar Press, 1975): "Fiction"

Nebraska Poets, published as a special issue of the poetry magazine *Pebble* 13, edited by Greg Kuzma (Lincoln NE: The Best Cellar Press, 1975): "Writing Big"

NOTES

What Happens

Thank you to Robert Pack, Judith Kitchen, Eloise Fink, Ladette Randolph, and Tom Swanson for their support of this book.

What Is Good

Thanks to Carolyn Kizer for help with "Cradle," Susan Strayer Deal and Georgia Robertson. "Plate xii" is for Burke Casari; "Life Outside the Self" is for James Raz and John Link; "Dishes" is for Vera S. Cohen.

Trans

Warm thanks to Jonathan Holden, Robin Becker, Aaron Link, Constance Merritt, Suzanna Tamminen, and Marge Saiser for close readings and advice about this book, to Dika Eckersley for design and friendship in all my projects, and to LeAnn Messing as always for manuscript and personal support. Dawn Elliott and Dale Nordyke have been with Aaron and me through these changes. They are our family, which also includes Jeff Raz, Sherry Sherman, Micah Sherman Raz, Joshua Sherman Raz, Amelie and Abigail Raz, Jennifer Lenway, John Link, Maria Schoenhammer, Vera Spohr Cohen, and Jennifer Susan Stiller. We remember Jonathan Alan Raz (1955–2000) with love. Aaron Link chose the order of the poems.
"The Funeral of X, Who Was Y's Mother" was written in memory of Tilly Dann Geffen (1910–1995).

All Odd and Splendid

Many voices in these poems: Aaron Raz Link told me "Tyr." He is everywhere here. Anna and Eva Schoenhammer Link speak in their own voices or through their papa, John Link. "An Evening" is for John Link. All transcriptions and additions are mine, faults and infelicities too.

To brilliant companions and collaborators, all thanks. Grace Bauer, Steve Behrendt, Burke and Laura Rhodes Casari, Vera Spohr Cohen, Pat Emile, Lisa Linsalata, Wanda Freeman, John Kinsella, Eric Levy, Anna Link, Eva Link, Chad Nordyke, Carole Simmons Oles, Susan Atefat Peckham, JoAn Rittenhouse, Susan Rosowski, Maria Schoenhammer, Suzanna Tamminen, and Reetika Vasarini are in these pages. Jonis Agee and Sharon Oard Warner provide their warm support to many writers, including me. Janet Burroway and Floyd Skloot made this book possible. Dale, John, and Aaron are the matrix. This book is for them and for all our family and friends.

List & Story

Each book brings its own challenges. This one grew over many miles and years, from Nebraska to New Mexico.

Thanks to Aaron Raz Link and Lynn C. Miller, first and last readers and collaborators, the former over much of his lifetime, the latter over a decade.

Thanks to JoAn Rittenhouse, Ruth Rudner, and Sue Hallgarth for their writing, reading, and friendship. Elise McHugh is a friend to all writers through the University of New Mexico Press where we have been colleagues on the Mary Burritt Christiansen poetry series. Lynda Miller, brilliant artist and editor, enriches my life as she does the lives of all her friends. Thanks to Kwame Dawes, poet, critic, professor and editor of *Prairie Schooner* for his ongoing support.

Thanks to John Link, whose music is the ground. Anna Maria Schoenhammer Link and Eva Maria Schoenhammer Link extend the field. Thanks to Maria Schoenhammer for her generosity and to Daire Elliott for his place in my life.

Without friends, silence. Thanks to Carole Simmons Oles, Mary Ellen Capek, Phyllis and Arthur Skoy, Pamela and Kelly Yesner, Pat Emile, Lisa Linsalata, Carol Musrey, Elizabeth Hadas, Em Hall, Helene Stilman and many others whose names are notes through these pages.

Kimberly Verhines as director of Stephen F. Austin State University Press brought enthusiasm and vigor to the publishing of *List & Story*. Thank you.

Thank you to friend, colleague, and collaborator, the artist Karen Kunc for permission to use her color woodcut, *Written Word*, as the cover of this book.

"The Spa of the Three Widows" is for Pat Emile and Lisa Linsalata.

"Late September" remembers Vera Spohr Cohen.

"Flowers of Immortality" is for Jehanne Dubrow.

In "Women and Poetry," "a stay against confusion" is from Robert Frost.

"The Past and the Future" and "Pristine" are for John Link.

"A Conversation about Text" quotes the quilter Michael James as part of our collaboration, quilt and poem.

"Meditation" is in memory of Lisa Lenard-Cook. The song in stanza eight is a Jewish prayer.

"A Symposium on Love" refers to T. S. Eliot's "in the mountains, there you feel free . . ."

"Letters from a Lost Language" is for Aaron Raz Link and is part of our commissioned collaboration based on his assemblage of found forms in cast metal and label text, arranged on clear shelves in a transparent box.

"The corrections of prose, because it has no fixed laws, is endless. A poem comes right with a click like a closing box," W. B. Yeats wrote in a letter.

Thanks to Rodger Kamenetz and Michael Hafftka for *To Die Next to You*.

Lightning Source UK Ltd.
Milton Keynes UK
UKHW010708250321
380963UK00002B/84